SARSFIELD
AND THE
JACOBITES

KEVIN HADDICK-FLYNN

MERCIER PRESS

MERCIER PRESS
Douglas Village, Cork
www.mercierpress.ie

Trade enquiries to COLUMBA MERCIER DISTRIBUTION,
55a Spruce Avenue, Stillorgan Industrial Park, Blackrock, Dublin

© Kevin Haddick-Flynn, 2003

1 85635 408 3

10 9 8 7 6 5 4 3 2 1

TO THE MEMORY OF COL J. E. NELSON AND CAPT. E. C. SCOTT,
STALWARDS OF THE MILITARY HISTORY SOCIETY OF IRELAND AND THE IRISH CLUB,
EATON SQUARE, LONDON SW1

ACKNOWLEDGMENTS
The author and publisher would like to thank Eilish Ryan for her maps. Every effort
has been made to establish sources for the illustrations. In instances where this has not
been possible we undertake to make due acknowledgement at the earliest opportunity.

Printed in Ireland by Colour Books Ltd

CONTENTS

Patrick Sarsfield (c.1654–1693): Earl of Lucan, Viscount Tully and Baron of Rosberry

PREFACE

Patrick Sarsfield is one of the great figures in Irish history and has always caught the public imagination. He was a giant among men. Not only did he dominate them physically, standing head and shoulders above the common throng, but he possessed in an exceptional degree qualities of character which set him apart. Courage, perseverance and steadfast loyalty – these were the characteristics stamping his particular genius. Although never in overall command of an army he was the most outstanding Irish soldier of the Williamite war (1688–1691) and became a Marshal of France shortly before his death in 1693 fighting the forces of his great adversary, King William III, Prince of Orange.

This book does not purport to be an intimate biography. It is doubtful if such a thing is possible given the paucity of information about Sarsfield's youth, education and personal life. Sir Charles Petrie, the eminent modern historian of Jacobitism, spent a lifetime studying the Jacobite Movement and sought at various times to write such a biography, only to give up in frustration at the scarcity of circumstantial material. I have therefore set myself the more modest task of attempting a synthesis of our existing knowledge of Sarsfield's military career and of providing an account of the origins and development of Jacobitism – the cause for which he so fearlessly fought. Even so, it must be said, that in some chapters Sarsfield's appearance is brief; in others he is notably offstage. It may be said, therefore, that the man disappears in the smoke and tumult of battle and that his personality remains obscure. This is not in fact so, for the main outlines of his character are discernible – however indistinctly – at all times. But were it so, it would be a fate not specific to Sarsfield; it holds for almost every seventeenth century soldier of similar rank.

As the text will show I have a particular interest in the Revolution of 1688. Until recent times the unchallenged view of historians and lay people alike held that this event was, as Edmund Burke proclaimed, 'great and glorious'. It was presented, very simply, as an heroic effort on the part of noble-minded patriots to resist the crimes and errors of a tyrant and brought about the final adjustment of the English constitution which then became so near perfect as to serve as a model for the rest of the world.

The losing side was, as usual, not only beaten, but silenced and misrepresented. The winners were garlanded with the praises of those who reaped the fruits of their success. Whiggish writers found glowing themes for their pens when relating the courageous resistance and heroic deeds of stalwarts who saved our forefathers from 'brass money and wooden shoes'. To them, it was a stirring chronicle. James II was a fool, a tyrant and a bigot; he attempted, clumsily, illegally and with gross cruelty to overturn the established order. He sought to undermine the Anglican Church in favour of a despotic Roman Catholicism and to introduce into the Three Kingdoms Jesuit-inspired policies which would undo the gains of the Reformation.

The story, thus told, had an epic outline. It was reinforced by rolling narratives on the ardours of war resulting from Louis XIV's perfidious support of the ex-king, and by the treacherous actions of mindless Roman Catholics in Ireland, which led to the virtual devastation of that country. In the end, the righteous, naturally, prevailed. The defeat of James' Irish adherents and the ruin of French military and naval power ushered in the gratifying and undeniable splendours of the Augustan Age.

The day was to dawn, however, when this morality tale failed to drive scholarly pens and when other views, long unheard, found voice. Then we were shown the reverse of the medal and discovered that a keen defence was available for what seemed indefensible. James II, it was learned, far from being a tyrant or a bigot, was a man with the interests of all his subjects at heart and passionately sought religious toleration in his realms. Foully betrayed by the machinations of men who did not appreciate his lofty idealism, James was undermined by the sly intrigues of his son-in-law and lost his throne through the crimes of others and because of his fidelity to a hereditary Faith.

This latter view, with the concept of the Divine Right of Kings, constituted the Jacobite case and was held, we must believe, in undiluted form by Sarsfield. To give coherence and meaning to his career it is necessary to sympathetically indulge it. But one cannot be blind to the fact that those historians who have pressed it, have been no more scrupulous in emphasising the points in *their* favour than the Whiggish writers whose partiality they so vigorously denounced. Thus, half-truths, suppressed evidence, personal invective – and more – have abounded in the writings of zealots on both sides of the question.

There are, of course, excellent academic histories written by hands which have no axe to grind. But these, perversely, have the faults of their virtues: while impartial and unprejudiced, they tend to be anaemic and to repeat disinterestedly arguments and judgements without commitment or enthusiasm. They smell of the 'scientific' historian faintly bored with dead politics.

Sarsfield and the Jacobites will, doubtless, fall into one of these categories. Which one, readers should have little difficulty in discerning. If they conclude that I have a certain admiration for my subject they will have guessed the substance which a direct statement would have contained.

Finally, I should like to record my thanks to the many people who helped me to write this book, particularly to those historians and scholars whose books, articles and pamphlets I have plundered. I hope that I have acknowledged my debt to them all in the chapter notes and bibliography. My grateful thanks are also due to Mercier Press for their support and efficiency and for giving me the opportunity to explore the subject. I am also indebted to my wife, Una, and my daughter, Alexandra.Without Alexandra's help the book could not have been written. She typed the manuscript and, with Una, put up with my bouts of (I hope uncharacteristic) grumpiness as I struggled through the controversial period covered. Responsibility for errors and other deficiencies, unfortunately, lies with me.

KEVIN HADDICK-FLYNN
LONDON, 2003

PRINCIPAL CHARACTERS

Charles II (1630–1685): King of England, Scotland and Ireland. Ruled 1660–1685 (twenty-five years). Eldest son of King Charles I. Successfully opposed Exclusion Bill which would have debarred James II from the throne. Converted to Catholicism on his deathbed.

Copper, Ashley Anthony (1621–1683): Otherwise first Earl of Shaftesbury. First party political leader in English history and founder of the 'Whigs'. Taking advantage of the Popish Plot tried to debar James II from the succession by introducing an Exclusion Bill, but failed.

De Ginkel, Godard van Reede (1630–1703): Otherwise Earl of Athlone and Baron of Aughrim. One of the most able Williamite generals during the 1688–1691 war. Born in Holland, he commanded a cavalry regiment at the Battle of the Boyne and was given supreme command of the Williamite forces in Ireland following the return of William to England in September 1690. Commanded at Athlone, Aughrim and Limerick. Signed the Treaty of Limerick with Sarsfield in October 1691. As a reward for his services he was granted a forfeited Irish estate and received his titles. Died in Utrecht 1703.

Galmoy, Lord: Otherwise Pierce Butler. A member of the Catholic branch of the powerful Ormond family. His forces were charged with holding the north-western passes to Ulster in 1688. Came off second best in the struggle for Crom Castle on the Upper Erne (1689). One of the Jacobite signatories to the Treaty of Limerick, he left Ireland with Sarsfield in 1691. Died in Paris, 1740.

Hamilton, Gustave (1639–1717): Dismissed from the Irish army of James II by Tyrconnell. Became governor of Enniskillen and organised the regiments of horse and foot known as the 'Enniskilleners'. Defeated Lord Galmoy at Crom Castle on the Upper Erne and General Justin MacCarthy at the Battle of Newtownbutler (1689). Later became first Viscount Boyne.

Hamilton, Richard: Jacobite commander who overran Protestant strongholds in Ulster in 1688. Won 'Battle of the Fords' against Robert Lundy and put Derry under siege. Fought staunchly at the Battle of the Boyne but was captured and taken prisoner. Later retired abroad. It should be noted that the Hamilton family – the Abercorns – fought on both sides during the Williamite war. At the time the main branch of the family was Catholic.

James II (1633–1701): King of England, Scotland and Ireland. Ruled 1685–1689. Younger brother of Charles II and son of Charles I. He was the father of Mary II, wife of William III, Prince of Orange. Only Catholic monarch to rule Britain since the Reformation. The term 'Jacobite' is derived from his name (Latin: 'Jacobus'). Fled to France after the Battle of the Boyne. Never renounced his right to the throne.

James, Duke of Berwick (1670–1734): Natural son of James II and Arabella

11

Churchill. *Arrived in Ireland with his father in March 1689; participated in the Siege of Derry and the Battle of the Boyne. Given command of Jacobite forces in Ireland when Tyrconnell left for France (September 1690). Aided Sarsfield in foiling Williamite attempts to cross the Shannon during winter 1690–91. Left Ireland February 1691. Later became marshal of France and one of the greatest soldiers of the age. Fell in battle at Philipsbourg in the Rhineland in 1734.*

Lloyd, Thomas: *A young Co. Roscommon Protestant, he became known as 'Little Cromwell' for his prowess as a guerrilla leader. Was Sarsfield's most formidable opponent during the skirmishes on the Lower Erne (1689). Resourceful leader of the 'Enniskilleners'.*

Marlborough, Duke of (1650–1722): *Otherwise John Churchill, brother of King James' mistress Arabella, and uncle of the Duke of Berwick. Helped to defeat Monmouth at Sedgemoor, but changed sides at Salisbury in 1688. Took Cork and Kinsale for the Williamites in swift campaign in 1690. Commonly seen as one of England's greatest generals.*

Mary of Modena (1658–1718): *Second wife of James II. Gave birth in June 1688 to James Frances Edward ('The warming-pan baby') who became the 'Old Pretender'; escaped six months later to France. Was a more resolute 'Jacobite' than her husband.*

MacCarthy, Justin: (c.1643–1694) *Created Viscount Mountcashel in 1689. Served with British and Irish regiments in Flanders. Aided Tyrconnell in Catholicisation of the Irish army. Suppressed Protestant revolts in Munster. Captured following his defeat at Newtownbutler. Was commander of the first contingent of the 'Wild Geese' to go to France. Later commanded Irish brigade of the French army in Italy, Spain and on the Rhine.*

Monmouth, Duke of (1649–1685): *Claimant to the throne, was illegitimate son of Charles II and Lucy Walter. Pardoned for his part in the Rye House Plot and banished to Holland. Invaded England in 1685 in hope of wresting the crown from James II, but defeated at Sedgemoor. Related to Sarsfield through marriage. Executed 1686.*

O'More, Rory (c.1602–1652): *Grandfather of Patrick Sarsfield. Principal plotter and leader of the Insurrection of 1641. Descended from old Gaelic aristocracy; married into leading 'Pale' family of Sir Patrick Barnwall. Prominent member of the Confederation of Kilkenny. At the end of the Confederate war was last seen, escaping in disguise, on Bofin Island, off Galway coast.*

Sarsfield, Patrick (c.1654–1693): *Otherwise Earl of Lucan, Viscount Tully and Baron of Rosberry. Brought up at Tully Castle near Kildare town. Fought under Monmouth, his patron, in Flanders (c.1675–1677). Sided with royal army during Monmouth rebellion and fought at Sedgemoor. Rose rapidly in Jacobite army and accompanied James II to Ireland in 1689. Captured Connaught from the Williamites in October 1689. Fought at the Boyne, and his daring exploit at Ballyneety consolidated an already considerable*

12

reputation. Played a minor part at Battle of Aughrim, but undertook supreme command of Jacobite forces in defence of Limerick, 1691. Negotiated and signed the famous treaty. Later became marshal of France and fought at Steenkirk (1692); fell at Landen (1693).

Sarsfield, William (c.1644–1675): *Elder brother of Patrick Sarsfield. Married Mary Walter, daughter of a mistress of King Charles II. The first of his family to inherit Lucan Manor following the Restoration. Died of smallpox, 1675.*

Schomberg, Duke of (1615–1690): *Otherwise Freidrich Armand Herman. General in the service of William III. A soldier-of-fortune who became a marshal of France in 1675 but quit French service following the Revocation of Nantes (1685). Became commander of Williamite forces in Ireland in 1688. Did not distinguish himself during Irish campaign. Fell at the Battle of the Boyne (1690). Buried in St Patrick's cathedral in Dublin.*

St Ruth (d.1691): *Otherwise Charles Chalmont, Marquis de. French general sent to Ireland by Louis XIV in May 1691 to command Jacobite army. Had a reputation as a bitter enemy of the Huguenots; his incompetence led to the fall of Athlone in 1691. Against the advice of Sarsfield he decided to fight a pitch battle against the Williamite army at Aughrim in July 1691. His death by a cannon ball during the action is believed to have deprived the Jacobites of victory. Buried locally.*

William III, Prince of Orange (1650–1702), *King of England and Scotland (1689–1702) and Ireland (1691–1702). Posthumous son of William II, Prince of Orange, and Mary, daughter of Charles I of England. His power in the Netherlands was constrained by the States General until appointed 'statholder' in 1672 in the face of French aggression. Led expedition to England in December 1688 to oust James II. His motives are disputed: he was certainly anxious to secure British help against the French. Married his cousin Mary (Mary II), daughter of James, Duke of York, (later James II). His arrival in Britain sparked the 'Glorious Revolution'. His campaign in Ireland in 1690 was mixed: he was victorious at the Boyne, but lost at Limerick during the first Siege. Died in 1702 as a result of a riding accident.*

1

A Tangled Inheritance

THE FIRST SARSFIELDS

The surname Sarsfield first appeared in Ireland in 1172 when Thomas de Sarsfield stepped ashore with Henry II. He was described as one of the king's 'standard bearers' and nothing further is known about him, save that his descendants put down roots among the Anglo-Norman gentry of the Pale. During the reign of John (1199–1216) the family settled in Co. Meath, but after several generations moved nearer to Dublin and became known as 'The Sarsfields of Lucan'. In 1296 they fought under Edward I[1] against Wallace at Falkirk and in 1335 assisted Edward II in his attempt to put Edward Baliol on the throne of Scotland. They were, however, primarily associated with Dublin and provided mayors for the city in 1531, 1554, and 1556. One of these, William Sarsfield, was a close associate of the lord deputy, Sir Henry Sidney, and accompanied him on his forays into Ulster in 1556 against the forces of Shane O'Neill.

In the reign of James I there were two branches of the family. One had as its head Dominick Sarsfield who became a firm favourite of the king's. The nature of this relationship has not been established,[2] but it had its compensations for the Irishman: he secured large tracts of sequestered land, which were declared exempt from tithes and taxes. In 1627 a further measure of royal approval saw him created Viscount Kinsale, but the title was changed in the following reign as the De Courceys, the barons of Kinsale, had insisted that they had the prior claim.[3] Dominick then became Lord Kilmallock and one of his descendants – another Lord Kilmallock – married a kinswoman, Anne, the sister of Patrick Sarsfield.

The senior branch remained at Lucan, but Patrick Sarsfield's direct family was not established there. His father – who to avoid confusion, must be called Sarsfield Snr – had his seat at Tully Castle near Kildare town,[4] where Patrick was brought up. Both branches were Catholic, and had few qualms about serving the Protestant crown, provided their rights were respected. But life for such families was undermined following the Tudor plantations when a new element was introduced which was uniformly Protestant. The resulting alignments did not favour the 'Old English' whose position was seen to be out of joint with the new establishment. Over the centuries they had practically fused with the indigenous Irish and in the view of the newcomers had become degenerate. Despite their traditional loyalty they were perceived as part of a Catholic threat and their predicament was compounded by not always loving their Irish allies. Yet in the face of Protestant supremacy both

15

Catholic groupings were drawn inexorably together.

REBELLION

In Ulster, the plantations that followed the O'Neill Rebellion of 1603 were never accepted. The dispossessed lived in the woods and mountains and waited for an opportunity to rise and drive out the settlers. In 1641, the dispute in England between Charles I and parliament led to civil war and provided the Irish with a favourable moment to act.

A group led by some of the old Gaelic aristocracy, planned to capture Dublin Castle and instigate a series of uprisings to overrun the planters. To execute the enterprise the utmost secrecy was required but Owen O'Connolly in his cups, inadvertently spilt the beans. Dublin was saved, but on the night of 23 October the homesteads of the settlers in Ulster were assailed. Those who lived in the plantation forts and fortified towns held out, but many in the countryside succumbed. Hundreds were killed and others fled. Untold numbers died of hunger, disease and exposure.

On the day of the outbreak the lord justices in Dublin proclaimed a state of emergency and issued notices which caused alarm. Blame for the rebellion was imputed to 'evilly-affected Papists' without distinction. The justices found themselves, however, powerless to aid the settlers. Their forces were small and had to be deployed in defending Dublin. Encouraged, the rebels moved down to Leinster and were joined by insurgents from Longford and Wicklow.

The 'Old English' were faced with a hard choice. Should they side with the government whom they knew distrusted them because they were Catholic or should they join with the Irish, who were their fellow Catholics? Their leaders – essentially 'lords of the Pale'– were invited to attend discussions at Dublin Castle, but became fearful for their safety. Instead, they gathered on Crofty Hill near Drogheda to review their options. Among them were the most prominent Catholic peers: Fingal, Dunsany, Slane, Louth and Timbleston. As they consulted armed horsemen were seen to approach. At their head were some of the leaders among the Gaelic Irish including Rory O'More. The lords rode towards them and someone shouted: 'Why do you come armed into the Pale?' O'More replied that they wished to protect their freedom and 'to maintain his majesty's prerogatives, which, we fear, are gravely threatened'. At this, the lords, to an acclamation from both sides, replied, 'seeing these are your ends, we will join with you'. This was one of the most momentous conjunctions in Irish history. The descendants of the old medieval colonists had allied themselves with the Gaelic Irish on the common ground of Catholicism, against the newer Protestant Irish. The resulting bi-polarisation of Irish society has endured to this day.

The rebellion was to leave a dreadful legacy of distrust and bitterness. There is no doubt that terrible barbarities were perpetrated. Individual atrocities – like the drowning of dozens of Protestants in the river Bann at Portadown – have never been forgotten. But as soon as news of the outrages reached London, the number of Protestants slain was wildly exaggerated. A picture was painted of a depraved Catholic people consumed with a lust for Protestant blood.

THE O'MORE CONNECTION

For a family like the Sarsfields these events were traumatic. Although they were of the English speaking Pale and members of its elite, they had always lived on easy terms with the native Irish. They sported and played with members of the Gaelic aristocracy and found their hospitable ways preferable to the arrogant deportment of the 'upstart' Protestant gentry. It was not uncommon for them to attend native amusements or have by their fireside harpists and poets who sang of Ireland's past. Over time they intermarried with the Gaels and had little concern about so doing. Sir William Sarsfield – head of the Lucan branch – wedded his grandson to Eleanor O'Dempsey, the daughter of Lord Clanmailer, and their offspring, also called Patrick, in turn, married Annie O'More, the daughter of Rory O'More, who had been on Crofty Hill.

This connection was significant. O'More was a charismatic figure who owned lands not far from the Sarsfield stronghold at Tully Castle. He sprung from the renowned O'Mores of Laois who traced their ancestry to the fabled Milesians. An ancestor was Rory Óg O'More who had fought incessantly against the Tudor planters in Laois and Offaly. In 1576 he burnt numerous planter townships in Leinster and is described in *The Annals of the Four Masters* as 'the head of the insurgents in Ireland in his time'.[5]

The later O'More was less of an incendiary. His association with the 'Old English' lead to him marrying into one of the leading families of the Pale, that of Sir Patrick Barnewall. Much of his early life was spent in Spain, where he received military training and developed his talents for politics and diplomacy. Whilst away, he kept a keen eye on Irish affairs and returned in 1625, when Charles I came to the throne. He was drawn into the intrigues of the Gaelic aristocracy and with his brother, Lysaght, became convinced that the Catholics should bid for power. They criss-crossed the country in an effort to persuade the Gaelic lords to rise. A sympathetic ally was found in Father Luke Wadding, the head of the Irish Franciscans in Rome. This distinguished cleric, of 'Old English' stock, had the ear of Pope Urban VIII, who was prepared to assist the Irish cause.

O'More was also in touch with leading Irishmen in foreign armies and had tried to induce them to return. One, was Owen Roe O'Neill, the grand-nephew of The Great O'Neill, who had won distinction in

Spain. O'More had successfully interviewed him at Mons in Flanders and at St Anthony's Irish College at Louvain. Wadding provided the funds which brought O'Neill to Ireland in June 1642, and helped him secure men and munitions.[6]

O'More's influence among the insurgents made him a leading light in the Confederation of Kilkenny. During the hostilities he was involved in skirmishes in the midlands and had to go on the run when the Confederate army collapsed. As the enemy closed in he sought refuge on Bofin island, off the coast of Galway, and was last seen escaping from there disguised as a seaman. Earlier, his daughter, Annie – Patrick Sarsfield's mother – was given refuge in the home of an elderly relative in the Fews hills in Co. Armagh.[7]

THE CONFISCATION OF LUCAN MANOR

The struggle did not end until 1649, when Cromwell crushed the rebels. Its outcome was disastrous for the 'Old English' and brought about a new 'settlement' which became the most extensive of the plantations. It embraced the entire island with the exception of four counties west of the Shannon – Clare, Galway, Mayo and Roscommon. Those who benefited were the 'Adventurers' who had financed Cromwell, and his soldiers, whose pay was hopelessly in arrears. The technicalities were laid out in an Act of Settlement passed at Westminster on 12 August 1652. This declared that all Irishmen, irrespective of their ancestry, who could not prove their innocence were to be punished by either loss of life and property, or property alone, according to their guilt.

These developments presented the Sarsfields with problems: they were royalists, but had given aid to the Confederate rebels. Several companies of Confederates had billeted at Tully Castle and, on occasion, Lucan Manor had been used for rebel conferences. All this was well known, as was the fact that Sarsfield Snr had fallen foul of the Dublin parliament in 1642. He had been one of the members for Kildare, but on 22 June was indicted for disloyalty and expelled from the House of Commons. Now when retribution was being demanded from those responsible for spilling Protestant blood, his family was seen to be embroiled with the rebels and connected with O'More.

There was an irony in Sarsfield Snr's predicament, for during the war his fortunes had greatly improved. A cousin had died leaving him the Lucan estate and he had taken up residence there. But the fist of Cromwell would not permit him to enjoy it. On 20 June 1657 he was ordered to quit the property and given a modest holding in Connaught. Protest was useless; he had to bow to the *dictat* of the regime. Lucan was granted to a leading Cromwellian, Sir Theophilis Jones, and Tully Castle allotted to a 'well affected' Dublin Alderman, David Hutchinson. With these transactions the name of Sarsfield Snr disappears from view.

His reduced status helps to explain why there is no record of the birth and early life of his son, Patrick.

The Cromwellians ruled for eleven years. The regime crumbled when the lord protector died and was succeeded by his incompetent son. By this time everyone had wearied of Puritan rule and it was clear that Charles II would be restored. In 1660, General Monk, marching from Scotland, called for a new parliament in London and had Charles proclaimed.

In Ireland, the Cromwellian generals, Coote and Broghill, who had been secretly negotiating with the Duke of Ormonde, the leading Irish royalist – and even with Charles himself – flung off the mask and seized Dublin Castle. In February 1660 a new Irish parliament was called, which acknowledged the king and voted him large revenues.

The fact that Charles' restoration was due, not to royalists, but to former Cromwellians may have influenced his views regarding the redress of Irish grievances. He would have liked, perhaps, to do something for the 'Old English' who had always been loyal. He was not prepared, however, to jeopardise his throne or, as he put it, 'to go on his travels again'.

A Court of Claims was set up which ordered the Cromwellians to surrender one-third of their lands, so that these could be redistributed. But the machinery of the court was slow and only a limited number of claims were examined. Not more than a few thousand of the dispossessed were restored even to a portion of their estates.[8]

One of the first to enter a claim was Sarsfield Snr. As early as November 1660 he petitioned the lord lieutenant and backed it with testimonies from the Lords Donegal, Dillon and Loftus, who vouched for his loyalty. All he received was a curt note saying that his claim would be considered. But he was not to be brushed off; he made further appeals, but still nothing happened. Finally, he petitioned the king and was unexpectedly successful. In 1661, a royal order was issued which returned most of his lands. This went some way towards satisfying him: it dislodged Alderman Hutchinson, but Theophilis Jones remained *in situ*. The old Cromwellian refused to budge as he prized Lucan as a jewel. He was also well connected and tried to frustrate Sarsfield's efforts.

But Sarsfield was not deterred. He solicited the king anew. A further royal order was sent reopening the matter. Wheels were put in motion, and plans made to have Sir Theophilis moved to a new estate. But he remained recalcitrant.[9]

The matter came formally before the Court of Claims on 17 June 1663, and Sarsfield Snr was adjudged to be innocent of rebellion 'because of the king's letter'. This did not settle the matter. Fresh evidence was taken and a complicated legal wrangle ensued. In the end, the court struck a compromise: Sarsfield Snr was refused possession and Jones was allowed to retain his tenure in his lifetime, but an absolute claim was vested in William, Sarsfield's eldest son. This was not, however, to be exercised until the occupant's death. It was a halfway measure, but not wholly unsatisfactory. It meant that in the next generation all the Sarsfield property would again be in family hands. In immediate terms it meant that the future Jacobite leader, now perhaps no more than seven or eight years old, would be brought up at Tully Castle.

2

THE YOUNG CAVALIER

HIS MOTHER'S SON

Life at Tully Castle was regulated and simple. It was a backwater remote from controversy and ideal for the rearing of children. There were four children in the Sarsfield family: William, the eldest, may have been as much as ten years older than Patrick; his two sisters, Frances and Anne, were probably ahead of him too.

Little is known of those early years, but it is not difficult to imagine the children running along the flagged corridors and rush-strewn rooms of the old fortress. Ponies, dogs and other animals would have thronged the courtyard, and music, perhaps, tinkled from inner rooms where solemn little girls played their virginals or learned from their brothers the steps of the necessary dances. Annie O'More Sarsfield presided over all; upright and handsome, innocent alike of pretentiousness or swagger as she busied herself with the chores of a housewife.

Tradition has it that Annie taught her children the native language and that, from her knee, they learned of ancient Ireland. Her son, Patrick is not on record as having spoken Irish, but the proposition that he had at least a smattering of it, is not fantastic. Many 'Old English' families had been imbibing Gaelic culture for generations. To some it was part of the air they breathed, and their children necessarily acquired it. Although the old culture was staggering from the blows of Cromwell it was still vibrant. There were 'courts of poetry' where the time-honoured conventions of rhyme, metre and assonance were practised. Harpers and pipers still played and sang in the halls of the gentry and the Sarsfields doubtless extended hospitality to these minstrels and partook of the idiom of the people.[1]

Outwardly a more settled time had begun. Landowners, old and new, were recovering from the devastating years of war, and were replenishing their crops and herds. Commercial life was rallying, aided by the sprouting of new towns like Charleville, Portarlington and Lanesborough. It is from this time (circa 1665) that the first real expansion of Dublin may be dated. The medieval walls had vanished and quays were built along the river. The decayed timber houses of Tudor times had come down, to be replaced by more elaborate ones. Families like the Sarsfields, although no longer part of the ruling elite, were still sufficiently affluent to acquire such properties. Indeed it is easy to visualise the young Sarsfield strolling through the streets with his father and marvelling at the new, busy, metropolis which was springing up.

Along the quays there was a stir of life almost as great as in Liverpool or Bristol: foreign sailors in outlandish garments, using strange, harsh sounding speech; stalwart fishwives with baskets of herrings on their heads, calling their wares almost inarticulately; stevedores in woollen caps and loose trousers rolled at the knee; peasants in goatskin coats, their wooden shoes clattering on the kidney stones. And sprinkled among this mass, the young Sarsfield may have beheld in sober garments, opulent shipping brokers in long, fur-lined coats and velvet hats and, once in a while, a distinguished nobleman rolling along in his coach and four to the whip-crackings of his coachman.

In spite of the recent building boom some of the old landmarks remained: the castle, built in the days of King John; the two cathedrals of Christchurch and St Patrick's, and the university founded in the reign of Elizabeth. It was a bustling time in which to grow up, and the young Sarsfield, surely, made the most of it.

A CAPRICIOUS LEGACY

The first to leave the family home was the eldest son, William. He was scarcely twenty-one when he attended a ball at Dublin Castle and met a tall, brown-haired girl, not many years his junior. Her name was Mary Walter and she was the ward to Lord Carlington, a friend of William's father. Their attraction was instantaneous and in a short time they were in love and inseparable. Their romance is of interest because of Mary's background. Her mother was the notorious Lucy Walter, an early mistress of the king.

The Walters were a Welsh family who had served the crown for generations. They paid the price when their castle near Haverfordwest in Pembrokeshire, was destroyed by Cromwellians in 1644. Lucy found shelter first in London and then in The Hague; it was there in 1648, that she met the king, possibly renewing an earlier acquaintance. There is no reason to believe that she was Charles' first mistress, nor is it certain that he was not her first lover. Their intimacy lasted with intervals until the autumn of 1651, when Charles acknowledged the paternity of a child born in 1649, whom he later created the Duke of Monmouth.[2]

The king did not acknowledge Mary, who was born in 1651. Her reputed father was Henry Bennet, the Earl of Arlington.[3] The sad thing was that Lucy, after her affair with Charles, abandoned herself to promiscuity, which probably resulted in her early death. Mary was brought up by what might be termed 'friends of the family'. She developed an affectionate relationship with her half-brother, Monmouth, who was given a position at court and treated as royalty.

In 1671 William Sarsfield and Mary were married, and the recovery of the Lucan estate became urgent. They were in strained circumstances and could not await the demise of Theophilis Jones, so William felt that his best bet was to enlist the aid of Monmouth. The young duke had no hesitation in pressing the king to renew his interest in the case. Charles, although weary of the matter, arranged for fresh pressure to be put on Sir Theophilis. This time, the Cromwellian was candidly told to dispose of his life interest, and be gone. But just as Jones was about to yield, tragedy struck. William was laid low with smallpox and died in April 1675. Mary was devastated. She had a three-year-old daughter, Charlotte; a six-month-old son, Charles; and was pregnant again. Her misfortune was compounded when she learned that her husband had made an unfavourable will prior to his death. He had bequeathed almost everything to the Sarsfields, left her only £200 a year, and virtually ignored provision for his children.[4]

The widow's predicament was alarming. She could not believe that William would leave her impoverished and her suspicions were aroused. She had been kept from his bedside because of his disease, but felt that she had been squeezed out of the will by chicanery. She read with astonishment that the prospective rents of the estate were settled on William's mother; that both his sisters were given £350 each, and that young Patrick was granted £150. Further, portions of the lands were divided so that Patrick would later receive £750, and his sisters £3,000 each. More alarming was the disclosure that William's heir – Charles, the six-month-old baby – was to be placed under the guardianship of his grandfather, Sarsfield Snr.

Mary felt hoodwinked, and took the view that the will was a forgery. Anyway, she believed it to be invalid, as the disposition of the estate had not been arranged to benefit the Sarsfield family. She decided to sue, but the whole affair played into the hands of Jones, who refused to budge until the wrangle was sorted out. And there was a further complication, William had died laden with debt: his creditors had begun making claims on the estate; numbered among them were his sisters who asserted that they had lent him sums which had not been repaid.

The whole affair was a shambles and became bogged down in the courts. Mary could not await the outcome. She remarried in 1676 and lived in poor circumstances with her husband, William Fanshaw. They survived on modest, irregular, remittances from the king. Mary had, however, one signal victory: she succeeded in having Sarsfield Snr disqualified as guardian to her son on grounds of religious incompatibility. The child, unfortunately, did not survive infancy. With his loss, his uncle, Patrick Sarsfield – the next in the male line – came to inherit the estate. It was an ill-starred patrimony. Sarsfield never took possession of the property and the legal dispute continued for years.

A BAPTISM OF FIRE

During these contretemps Patrick reached his majority. His aptitude, as far as we know, was always for soldiering, but the career options for young men of his class were restricted. Catholics were excluded from the professions, and even a meaningful career in the army seemed remote, as 'papists' were debarred from commissions. But the keenly motivated hopeful found a way round the stumbling block. Monmouth was colonel-proprietor of a regiment serving with the French army – the 'Royal Anglais' – and through his good offices a blind eye was turned on the prohibition.[5]

Sarsfield was not the first Irish Catholic so favoured; a few years earlier Justin MacCarthy (the son of Earl Clancarthy) enlisted through the influence of his uncle, the Duke of Ormonde. Sarsfield, in fact, was to see his first service under MacCarthy and the two would later become firm Jacobites.

Fortune smiled on the young recruit in another way: his passion was for the cavalry and he received his training at an elite French academy and, for a time, is believed to have been under the tutelage of the renowned Duc de Luxembourg.[6] It is probable that he first tasted combat under this hunchbacked genius, for in 1672 France went to war with the Netherlands, and Luxembourg was assigned to hold the captured city of Utrecht.[7] The French position deteriorated rapidly and the duc was forced to execute a retreat in the face of a stronger enemy. The courage and stubbornness of his troops were praised, and he was given command of the army of the Rhine.

Sarsfield remained, however, in the southern Netherlands and received a commission under MacCarthy whose regiment was engaged in the reduction of towns and fortresses. These campaigns gave the young Sarsfield a baptism of fire and he learned to have no illusions about the hardships and terrors of war.[8]

SARSFIELD IN LONDON

When the conflict entered a new phase in 1673 nothing much was effected by the French, save the capture of Maastricht. Monmouth himself took part in the siege and his courage in storming the walls was remarked on. We may be sure that the intrepid Sarsfield was in the thick of it. By this time, the Dutch had become alarmed at the French advance and opened the dykes around Amsterdam, flooding large areas of the country. Their army rallied behind this 'water line' and French progress was arrested. Thereafter the war languished. Monmouth's regiment could no longer play a useful part, and in England the mood changed. Parliament showed support for an alliance with the Dutch, and thus, a decision was taken to recall the Royal Anglais.

Sarsfield now found himself living in London. His connection with Monmouth was still useful and he landed a commission in the king's life guards, an elite body paid directly from the privy purse. Even a private in this prestigious force was styled a 'gentleman of the guard'.

Life became humdrum and boring. Sarsfield's name began to appear in the army lists, but these reveal little save that he was ranked as a lieutenant.[9] He lodged in the house of a saddler at Charing Cross and spent much of his time jumping horses and engaging in imaginary cavalry charges in the royal parks. It was all very sedentary and, maybe, he felt that he was wasting his time. He was fortunate, however, that plans were afoot for the men who had served with Monmouth. It was proposed that a new regiment be established under Sir Thomas Dongan and sent to France in exchange for a bounty which the king was pocketing from Louis XIV.

Sarsfield was more than willing to serve, particularly when he learned that he was to be promoted to captain. In October 1678 he was interviewed by Colonel Lawrence Dempsey and Captain Dominick Trant at The Sceptre tavern in Piccadilly, and presented with his papers. He was not to know that his new-found status would be short-lived.

THE POPISH PLOT
Shortly before, one of the most bizarre events in English history had set the country agog. Titus Oates, a habitual liar, had 'informed' the privy council of an alleged Popish Plot to kill the king and replace him with his Catholic brother, James, Duke of York. In September, Oates made dispositions to this effect before a well-known London magistrate, Sir Edmundbury Godfrey, who in turn revealed them to Edward Coleman, the secretary to the Duchess of York. The arrest of Coleman for conducting a treasonable correspondence with the Jesuit confessor to Louis XIV, gave some credence to the story. But the whole affair was raised to panic proportions with the discovery of Godfrey's body – transfixed with a sword – on Primrose Hill in Hampstead. To this day his killing remains a mystery.[10]

These sensational events, widely publicised in pamphlets and broadsheets, seemed to confirm Protestant fears of Catholic cabals in high places aimed at subverting the English Reformation. Even the normally judicious diarist John Evelyn, generally sceptical of Oates, assumed that Catholics were responsible for the assassination and wrote: 'The murder of Sir Edmundbury Godfrey … as was manifest by papists.'

Mass hysteria broke out – a wave of irrational credulity swept the country – and any crank or criminal with an anti-Catholic horror story found an appreciative audience. A number of zealous politicians fanned the flames. The king – who maintained a healthy scepticism – found that his ministry had to investigate every petty charge, and a senior figure, Halifax, let the cat out of the bag when he said, 'the Plot must be handled as if it were true, whether it is so or not'.

Eminent Catholics were hounded from office and home, some to the Tower of London. James prudently retired abroad, and Oates added to his allegations by accusing the queen, the 'pious and virtuous' Portuguese Catherine of Braganda, of trying to poison the king. Charles saved her only by dissolving parliament before it could commence proceedings. Even Pepys, the diarist, was accused of being an accomplice in this plot, and was sent to the tower. In the frenzied atmosphere every Catholic were fair game, and a proclamation was issued ordering 'all Papist recusants to leave London and the surrounding districts'.

Irish Catholics in London were immediately put on the suspect list, and even well placed figures like Sarsfield and MacCarthy became vulnerable. Both applied for exemption from the proclamation but were turned down. MacCarthy left hurriedly but was arrested by an over-zealous officer at High Barnet.[11] He was not released until a directive was received from Whitehall stipulating that High Barnet was outside the exclusion area. There was uproar in the House of Commons when it was learned that an Irish officer had been caught fleeing. This clamour was, however, senseless, as MacCarthy was simply adhering to the terms of the proclamation. Sarsfield and others managed to get as far as Chester before being similarly detained. Again, news of their flight led to commotion, and they were held until the local mayor received a letter from the secretary of state, Sir Joseph Williamson, saying:

> His majesty greatly approves of his (the mayor's) care in stopping certain persons passing towards Ireland ... but the writer is commanded to let the mayor know that these particular persons ... have his majesty's leave to return to their own country, being Irishmen and dismissed from his majesty's service.[12]

Astonishingly, it was from this letter that Sarsfield learned of his dismissal from the army. No explanation was given, and he sailed to Ireland gloomily to join the ranks of the unemployed.

TERROR IN IRELAND

In Ireland, Sarsfield became embroiled in the dispute over Lucan Manor, but of more immediate urgency was his empty pocket. He had not been paid for months and embarked on a correspondence with Sir Stephen Fox, the paymaster general for his back money. The Treasury was slow to react and, as often during the early reign of Charles II, was practically depleted. Sarsfield received some interim sums, but a few years later was still pressing for £108, which he claimed to be outstanding.

He found it prudent to keep a low profile. The terror inspired by Oates had crossed the Irish Sea and on 16 October 1677 an order was issued for the expulsion of all popish ecclesiastics from Ireland; and a further proclamation was made, forbidding papists to enter the vicinity of Dublin Castle, or any fort or citadel anywhere. Orders were sent to every market town, commanding that markets or fairs be held outside the walls and that papists be refused entry to the interior. Next, measures were taken to enforce the oath of supremacy in the army and all personnel were placed under surveillance: rewards were offered for details of any officer espied attending mass; there were similar bounties for information on troopers and ordinary soldiers.

On 2 December a search was begun for Catholic clergy who had failed to quit the country. Since the storm erupted most had gone into hiding, including the primate Rev. Dr Oliver Plunkett, of Armagh. But there were informers among the archbishop's flock who gave information to the authorities implicating him in a fabricated invasion plot. On 6 December he was arrested in Co. Louth and arraigned before the Dundalk Assizes. He pleaded not guilty and the case collapsed when the chief witness failed to appear. In London, however, the Popish Plot required fresh momentum, so the archbishop was recharged and transferred there.

He was tried again on 8 June 1681, found guilty, and hanged at Tyburn (near the present Marble Arch). In a long series of judicial murders this was the most scandalous, but providentially also the last. Shortly afterwards the tide of fanaticism ebbed. A reaction set in and wiser counsels were heard.[13]

A CHALLENGE TO LORD GREY
Sometime later, Sarsfield returned to London. The next we hear of him comes from the diarist Narcissus Luttrell who in an entry dated 9 September 1681, says:

> … there has been a tall Irishman to be seen at Bartholomew Fair, and the Lord Grey having seen him was pleased to say he would make a swinging evidence; on which one Captain Sarsfield, an Irishman sent his lordship a challenge, taking it as and affront on his countrymen.[14]

St Bartholomew's Fair was an annual event held in Westsmithfield, near St Bartholomew's Hospital. The fair ground was littered with sideshows and in one of these a giant Irishman was exhibiting feats of strength. A young peer, Lord Grey of Wark, walking among the stalls with his companions was heard to refer to the showman as 'swinging evidence'. This quaint term was meant to convey that the fellow was of a type likely to perjure himself in a witness box. The insinuation was that all brawny Irishmen were liars and had given false evidence during the Popish Plot trials.[15]

Sarsfield – himself a sturdy Irishman – was not present, but on learning of Grey's remarks, was stung. He impetuously challenged the peer to a duel. Grey was amazed, as he did not know Sarsfield and had no intention of engaging with him. He was an influential figure and would not be seen brawling with a lowly Irish captain. He sent a note refusing the challenge, but did not apologise. This was not the end of the matter, for he was sufficiently annoyed to report the incident to Sir Llewllyn Jenkins, the secretary of the privy council, who took a poor view of Sarsfield's behaviour. Duelling had been banned a few years before; besides, Jenkins felt that he could not allow a peer of the realm to be insulted by a junior officer. Instructions were given to the sergeant-at-arms, to take Sarsfield into custody. A few days later, on 14 September Luttrell noted:

> Captain Sarsfield, who challenged the Lord Grey, was arrested, but hath since made his escape out of the messengers hands.

With this entry the information trail unfortunately, dries up. It is not known how Sarsfield escaped, or even if he was ever charged or whether the matter was dropped. It is difficult to understand his incautious behaviour. Why did he offer a challenge for so trivial a slight on an unknown fellow countryman? Was there something else between Sarsfield and Grey which we do not know about? Maybe Grey was one of those cocksure Englishmen whom the Irish detest. Or, perhaps, Sarsfield was just a hot-head who enjoyed spoiling for a fight. The truth will never be known, although the latter seems the likely explanation, given that a few months later we find Sarsfield implicated in an actual dustup. Luttrell's entry for 9 December reads:

> There was a duel fought on the 6th between the Lord Newbury and the Lord Kinsale, as principals (two striplings under twenty), and Mr Kirk and Captain Sarsfield, seconds: the principals had no hurt; but Captain Sarsfield was run through the body near the shoulder, very dangerously.

The main combatants were schoolboys of fifteen and sixteen years of age, but an absurd convention existed which made it obligatory for seconds to engage as well. Sarsfield, it seems, met more than his match and was lucky to come through. Again, it is mystifying why he got caught up in such a silly encounter. Maybe, he was a peppery type who enjoyed a scrap. He recovered with remarkable rapidity, but went to ground for some time. He soon was involved, however, in another ill-advised escapade.

THE MRS SIDERFIN AFFAIR
There is abundant evidence that the period was much given to crime and lawlessness. The diary of Luttrell provides numerous matter-of-fact accounts of criminality and reads like a police gazette of a later age. The speed and number of some of the felonies committed is astonishing. Luttrell records how, in 1693, a man was convicted of rape, sacrilege, highway robbery, burglary and murder, all carried out within twelve hours. In such an age everyone was obliged to carry weapons. The gibbet

and pillory were familiar sights and were employed in punishing even minor wrongdoings.

Some levels of crime were, naturally, less venal than others: duelling was fashionable among the gentry and performed as part of a code of honour; the abduction of young ladies was a malefaction that often evaded the law. It was prevalent in England and Ireland and perpetrated with different degrees of outrage. Sometimes it occurred with the consent of the ladies themselves, seeking, perhaps, to overcome parental strictures. More often the lady was forcibly carried away by a man whom she refused, and compelled to marry him. An unmarried woman with a dowry could be vulnerable in her own home, and dragged away to a hideout in the mountains. Lecky records a typical incident, at Cappawhite, Co. Tipperary, a number of years later, when a wealthy spinster, Rebecca White, was abducted by unknown villains;[16] after great commotion she was found, unharmed, in an adjoining county.

Sarsfield's involvement in two abductions adds to his image as an irrepressible tearaway. In the first incident, his friend Captain Robert Clifford was the chief culprit. In May 1682, Clifford developed an infatuation with a young widow, Ann Siderfin, whose husband, a barrister, had recently died. She was rich, attractive and had a large circle of fashionable friends. In vain did he seek her attentions. His airs and graces made little impression and he imagined that her courtesy towards him betrayed feelings of affection. He was mistaken, but being a dullard sought stratagems to advance his suit. He settled on abduction and invoked the aid of Sarsfield.

He knew his man, for Sarsfield, as we now realise, was not one to turn down a bold enterprise; with another officer, James Purcell, he enthusiastically agreed to help. With a few accomplices, the three began to track Mrs Siderfin's movements and hatched a plot to stop her coach as she journeyed from London to Windsor on 27 May. Everything went as planned, except the unexpected resistance of the coachmen, who were lightly beaten and left gagged as the abductors rode away with their victim.[17]

There was uproar in London and the usual suspects were questioned. The privy council ordered that the lodgings of all Irish cavalrymen be searched. But the birds had flown. The king instructed the secretary of state to use all his resources to locate the whereabouts of Mrs Siderfin and have her returned. Certain sightings had been made. A group of horsemen were seen riding furtively towards the coast, and had crossed to Calais.

The secretary of state was expeditious. He contacted the governor of Calais and requested that a search be carried out. By this time, Clifford, Sarsfield and Purcell – with their distressed captive – had booked into an inn. They had not counted on being espied and were more than surprised when the Calais town guard came banging on their door. They drew their swords and refused to come out, but soon realised that the game was up and escaped through a courtyard under darkness. Mrs Siderfin was liberated, but was in a distressed state when placed in the care of Lord Preston, the ambassador at Versailles. In monarchies, then as now, ambassadors are accredited to courts.

The hue and cry went out for the kidnappers, who split up and went different ways. After some time Clifford's money ran out and, tiring of the life of a fugitive, he gave himself up. On the 21 November he was arraigned, with some of the others, before the king's bench in London. Lord Chief Justice Pemberton directed that he be found guilty. He was sentenced to a year's imprisonment, bound to good behaviour for six years, and fined £1,000. Four others, were given lesser sentences and fines, but Sarsfield was not even charged. This may have been because the evidence against him could not be proven – although this is doubtful when the testimony of Mrs Siderfin's would have convicted him – but, for whatever reason, he got off scot-free. In fact, a few weeks later we hear of him again sending petitions to the Treasury for his back-pay.

THE ABDUCTION OF LADY HERBERT[18]

The dust had scarcely settled when Sarsfield was in more trouble. This time it was an affair of the heart. He had sought for some time to woo Elizabeth Herbert, the daughter of Lord Chandos, and she, it seems, did not find his attentions disagreeable. Her late husband, Lord Herbert, who was a great deal older, had died in 1678, and Sarsfield made her acquaintance through her step-son, whom he knew in France.

Although not in the flush of youth, Lady Herbert was a most desirable woman, and had two further marriages ahead of her. Her affection for Sarsfield may have been motherly; she is known to have visited him when he 'lay ill of his hurts'. His ardour was heightened when he learned that Lord Cholmondelay was also paying his addresses. Lady Herbert had, in fact, recently grown cold towards Sarsfield.

In his lovelorn state Sarsfield threw caution to the winds and abducted Elizabeth. The deed was done at night and the lady was carried off to an unknown location. But Sarsfield's postulations of love served only to harden her heart. After a few days torment he realised that his suit was hopeless and gave up the ghost. But he was prudent enough to save himself from the fate of Clifford. He wheedled Elizabeth into signing a document which stated that she would not take proceedings against him.

But that was not all. A friend, Sir John Parsons, had lent a hand during the abduction and Sarsfield ensured that his name was included on the document. Then, he gave it to Parsons for save keeping. Sometime later he requested its return but Parsons refused on the grounds that it was better off in his own care. The two men argued, but Parsons held his ground. The matter could only be resolved, Sarsfield felt, by a duel and a challenge was given.

The two met on Sunday morning 29 April 1683 behind Montague House, near the Strand. The event attracted a number of onlookers, but the outcome was unfavourable to both. Frank Gwyn, the gossip, recorded what happened:

> … they fought behind Montague House. Sarsfield is run through the body a little above the belly into the lungs, and Sir John into the lungs. They were both thought desperate but today their surgeon … tells me that he has much hope for them both.

Sarsfield had, again, played close to the edge, but both men recovered, the only fatality being their friendship. With this, Sarsfield once more disappears from view, but on 7 April 1684 an incident took place which may or may not have his fingerprints. Narcissus Luttrell mentions it in his diary:

> Captain Clifford sometime since convicted of a great misdemeanour in stealing and carrying away Mrs Siderfin into France had laid for some time in Fleet Street prison. Some gentlemen came under pretence to see him, but rescued him, and carried him away, notwithstanding the endeavours of the officers.

It is, perhaps, idle to speculate, but the question is irresistible: was Sarsfield the 'gentleman' who sprung his friend Clifford from jail?

3

THE MERRY MONARCH AND THE POPISH KING

THE EXCLUSION CRISIS

While Sarsfield was sowing his wild oats in London during the late 1680s, momentous events were unfolding which, in a few years, would rock the monarchy and precipitate profound constitutional change.

Some historians trace the origin of these events to previous reigns, but there is little doubt that their immediate cause sprung from the so-called 'Exclusion Crisis' of 1678–81, which arose from attempts to debar James, Duke of York, from the succession because of his conversion to Catholicism. There was widespread apprehension amongst the duke's enemies that were he to become king, he would inaugurate an 'abso-lutist' Catholic monarchy on continental lines and that the pope would again rule in England. In three parliaments between 1678 and 1681 the discontented Whigs exploited their majority in the House of Commons to promote 'exclusion' measures.

One of the prime movers in this drama was Anthony Ashley Cooper, first Earl of Shaftesbury – half-demagogue, half-philosopher, and the creator of the Whigs. Early in the civil war he had sided with Charels I, but quickly saw that the royalist cause was doomed and switched allegi-ance. Cromwell made him a member of his Council of State but, in time, he became alienated and intrigued to bring the lord protector down. After the Restoration he received his reward, was raised to the peerage, and found himself playing a leading role in Charles II's counsels. 'You are the wickedest dog in England', laughed the king, on learning of one of Shaftesbury's unscrupulous proposals. 'By your word, Sire, I believe I am!' was his unabashed reply.[1]

Wit, debauchery, venomous anti-Catholicism, and a facility for wily designs were the hallmarks of Shaftesbury. It was he who originated the ploy of legitimising Monmouth and spun the tale of a secret mar-riage between the king and Lucy Walter, so that the 'Protestant duke' (as Monmouth was called) could succeed instead of James. During the Popish Plot he fanned the flames, and was the most conspicuous mem-ber of 'The Green Ribbon Club' which met in the King's Head tavern in Chancery Lane, to organise pope-burning processions.

The first Exclusion Bill was brought before the House of Commons in July 1679, but the king – who would not countenance an alteration to the succession – arrested its progress through the prorogation of par-liament. When the new house met in October 1680, it was as determined as its predecessors to oust James. A second Exclusion Bill was introduced, and successfully went through the House of Commons, but was rejected by the House of Lords.

The House of Commons was not, however, to be deterred, and called upon the king to assent to the measure in spite of the lord's rejection. The king refused and for a second time prorogued parliament.[2] For a third time the electors voted in a pro-Exclusion majority. Piqued, particularly by those London members who routinely incited the mob, the king transferred parliament to Oxford.

THE OXFORD PARLIAMENT
On 21 March 1681, parliament met in the Great Hall of Christ Church College, Oxford, and the London MPs arrived, brazenly, with ribands in their hats bearing the slogan 'No Popery, No Slavery!' The sittings continued for a week and the question of the succession was debated in both houses. From the House of Lords came the proposal that Monmouth should be recognised as Charles' successor, whilst the House of Commons considered a compromise involving the separation of the crown from the executive. A third Exclusion Bill was tabled, but before it could be considered a quarrel erupted between the two chambers. Charles, now thoroughly disenchanted, took the opportunity to prorogue parliament again.

This peremptory move incurred great anger among the Whigs. Yet, they took it lying down. Some time later Shaftesbury was arrested and lodged in the Tower of London. As he lay there, one of his Oxford supporters was tried and executed on evidence similar to that which could be brought against him. London was, however, a Whig stronghold and the jury – selected by Whig sheriffs – refused to convict: the ex-lord president fled to Holland to pine and die of heartbreak and dropsy. The king had won. He had faced down his enemies and they had scattered before him.

After this, Charles did not bother with parliaments. His policies assumed a Byzantine complexity. An atmosphere of credulous uncertainty prevailed in which rumour and truth merged with suspicion and doubt. He relied on 'subsides' negotiated with King Louis. These were in fact bribes, but the king accepted them without compunction. He undertook to fight the Dutch – which was Louis' main reason for proffering the bribes – ostensibly to redress a commercial grievances, but really to keep the money flowing.

The king was prepared to live on a knife-edge to overcome his enemies. The Whigs must, he felt, be kept down at all costs. Yet, one man near to him, Monmouth, saw them in a favourable light. He had become puffed up with the prospect of one day wearing the crown, and had begun scheming with the lesser Whigs. To heighten his profile he went on a tour of the midlands and the north-west, but was received indifferently: in Lichfield he was snubbed, in Chester mobbed, and in Stafford, arrested for disturbing the peace. For his father, this was the last straw: the 'Protestant duke' was deprived of his offices and left to cool his heels away from court.

THE RYE HOUSE PLOT

Matters now took a serious turn: a plot to assassinate the king and the Duke of York was uncovered. The royal brothers were to be waylaid as they returned from Newmarket races at Rye House, in Hertfordshire. Fortuitous events stymied the plotter's design. A fire broke out at Newmarket and the king and duke rearranged their schedule. Nothing happened on the homeward trek, but several weeks later one of the would-be assassins spilled the beans. Several small fry Whigs were arrested, tried and executed. But some senior men were also implicated. The treason laws were used to convict and execute Lord William Russell and Algernon Sidney, a well-known Republican.

Panic arose and many, including Monmouth, ran for cover. Lord Grey of Wark – Sarsfield's erstwhile adversary – took off for Holland. Monmouth, being his father's whiteheaded boy was pardoned, but also bolted and became the focus of intriguers who began spawning plots to put him on the throne.[3]

THE KING BOWS OUT

In England the storm blew itself out. With the Whigs routed and scattered, life returned to normal. The king resumed his leisurely ways. He was seen each morning exercising his spaniels in St James' Park and throwing crumbs to the birds. He seemed happy and content, and not unreasonably so. His kingdom was quiet and he had no pressing need for money.

Life at court was again bawdy and decadent. On Sunday 1 February 1685 the Great Gallery at Whitehall was crowded with revellers and gamblers. The king lay on a couch flirting with his ladies and a minstrel warbled a love-song on a lute. Nearby, a party of couriers played baccarat at a small table. In spite of appearances, the king was feeling poorly. That morning he had felt a burning pain whilst shaving, and as the day wore on received no relief. Presently, he could endure it no longer. He rose and asked to be taken to his chamber. It was soon evident that his life was in danger.

On Tuesday, he was bled, cupped and bled again. The brains of an executed felon, fresh from the scaffold, were hurriedly distilled into a potion for his consumption. He drank it obediently. When he grew too weak to hear the bickerings which disturbed his chamber he still submitted to the incredible measures devised to save him. But this prodigious medical ado was futile from the start. At fifty-four he was played out; he had burned the candle at both ends, and could cope no more.

As death drew near, his several mistresses' were ushered away and he was left alone with James. They were joined by Protestant clergymen who read prayers for the dying and beseeched the king to take the sacrament. The duke instructed that they leave. As they withdrew, the Duchess of Portsmouth – one of the king's long-term mistresses' – slipped back in and said: 'I have a thing of great moment to tell you. The king is truly a Catholic, and should wish to die in that creed'.

Shortly, a small table with a solitary candle was placed by the bedside. A side door was opened and old Fr Huddleston, a Benedictine priest came through. For several minutes he knelt as the king confessed his sins. Then he pronounced the Absolution and administered the extreme unction. When he left the candle and table were hurried away.

Minutes later the door was flung open, and in streamed grim-faced courtiers, ambassadors, and members of the household. The death of a king was a public act which had its own protocol. They all stood around in an attitude of noble mourning. When the morning light crept under the curtains, the king murmured that it was time to wind up the great clock which stood nearby. An hour later, he whispered his last pleasantry: 'gentlemen, I am afraid that I am an unconscionable time in dying'.

He lingered a while, and drew his brother to him saying: 'let not poor Nelly starve'. It was a reference to the high-spirited and illiterate fruit-seller who, years before, had won his heart. It was not till noon that he passed away.[4]

The Popish King

James succeeded so quietly it was difficult to imagine that there had ever been Exclusion Bills. Despite the predicted calamities that would befall the country if a Catholic came to the throne, there was a sense of anti-climax. No fires were kindled at Smithfield and no Protestant babies were impaled on spits. Even the pope responded with indifference.

But the new king had none of his predecessor's charm. He lacked a sense of humour, and was stubborn and tactless to a fault. In person, he was tall, elegant, fair haired and bore his fifty-two years lightly. He had shared a number of his father's escapades during the civil war, and following the defeat at Worchester (1657) was lucky to escape abroad.

In the following years he volunteered for the French army and served, with honour, under Turenne. Later, he joined the Spanish army and gave a good account of himself. Later still, he became lord high admiral of England, and was a most competent naval commander.

In private life, James was a notorious womaniser.[5] His appetites were as lusty as those of his brother, but his penchant was for ugly women, whereas his brother always had an eye for glamour. Charles once said of James' mistresses that they must have been given to him as a penance. One of the best known, Arabella Churchill, was the sister of the great Duke of Marlborough, and mother of his son, the renowned Duke of Berwick. During his exile he fell in love with 'ugly Anne Hyde' daughter of his brother's chancellor, Clarendon; their marriage was directly occasioned by her pregnancy.

This lascivious picture makes James' conversion to Rome all the more remarkable. Indeed, the circumstances of his change-over are something of a mystery. What is certain is that it was a gradual process, and that once the decision was made there was no turning back. He was intellectually and morally convinced that the Catholic Church was the one, true Church and became resolute in his beliefs. Ten years later he wrote to his friend, George Legge, who had attempted to undo his turn-about:

> Pray, never say anything to me again of turning Protestant; do not expect it or flatter yourself that I shall do it; I never shall. What I have done was not done hastily, but upon mature consideration, and foreseeing all, and more than has yet happened to me.[6]

Following the death of the Duchess of York in 1671, James found a second wife in the Italian Catholic princess Mary Beatrice d'Este of Modena. In years to come Whig propagandists would mendaciously suggest that this lady was the bastard daughter of Fabio Chigi, the late Pope Alexander VII.[7]

The King's Designs
Although openly acknowledging his Catholicism, James began his reign prudently. At his first Council of State he said:

> I shall make it my endeavour to preserve this government in both church and state as it is by law established. I know that the principals of the Church of England are for monarchy and members have shown themselves good and loyal subjects; therefore I will always take good care to defend and support it.[8]

Reassured, his ministers swore allegiance and were permitted to stay in office for the time being. Few, however, were blind to James' personal faults, but it was felt that a Catholic king would keep his word and maintain the existing constitution.

But James had secretly made another pledge – to advance the rights of his co-religionists. His intent, contrary to what Whig historians have claimed, was not to establish Catholicism as the sole religion of the realm but to put it on a similar footing to Anglicanism. This could only be achieved by repealing the Test Acts of 1673 and 1678, under which, all office holders, including members of parliament, were required to receive the sacrament under the rites of the Church of England and to declare their disbelief in transubstantiation. Once this legislation was undone, James believed that Catholicism would rejuvenate in England on its own merits.[9]

It was not long before the open exhibition of the king's religion began to cause annoyance. On the second Sunday of his reign James publicly attended mass at the royal chapel in St James'. The Duke of Norfolk, who carried the sword of state, stopped at the door. 'My lord,' said the king, 'your father would have gone further'. The duke's rejoinder was: 'Your majesty's father would not have gone so far'.

On 9 November 1685, a parliament was called to renew the revenues which had expired on Charles' death. It was mainly a body of James' Tory supporters and had little hesitation in doing his bidding. A large revenue was voted for life which, with the growth in trade, amounted to the then gigantic sum of £2,000,000 a year. Thus facilitated, he had no reason to doubt his security and preceded with his coronation.

The ceremony was a carefully choreographed spectacle, discharged with traditional pomp. The king refused to take the sacrament and the Protestant features were played down. On arrival at Westminster Abbey he processed to the high altar and was questioned by the archbishop as to his willingness to observe the laws and customs of the realm and asked to promise peace to the Church and justice to the people. He confirmed these promises by oath upon the altar and bowed low as the litanies were sung. Then, following the unction, as anthems and long prayers were recited, his hands, breast and shoulders were anointed with oil of the catechumens, and with chrism. Next, came the vesting and crowning, followed by the conferment of the ring (which he managed to keep through all the vicissitudes to come) and then the sceptre and orb were given to him. After a general homage and the crowning of the queen consort, the archbishop and peers swore fealty to his person and to his heirs.

Thereafter, everyone retired to a great banquet in Westminster Hall. That evening there were firework displays and bonfires. To a Tory royalist it was all very satisfying.

4

THE MONMOUTH REBELLION

THE GENIAL HOSTS

The new king had the briefest of honeymoons. The first to conspire against him were those English and Scottish Whigs who had fled to Holland after the failure of their conspiracies against Charles II. The Duke of Monmouth, initially, stayed aloof from them. Instead, he sought to make the most of his exile and accepted the hospitality of his cousins the Prince and Princess of Orange.[1]

It must not be thought that his hosts were unthinking in the bestowal of their favours. They had their own interests in English affairs, not least that Mary, the Princess of Orange, was James' eldest daughter and first in line to the throne. Her husband, William, was himself third in succession through his mother, who was James' sister.

At one time both the Prince and Princess of Orange had seen Monmouth as an obstacle to their claims, but with the death of Shaftesbury the schemes to legitimise him had collapsed and now, with James on the throne, his opportunity seemed to have passed. Yet, the lesser Whigs still saw him as their best hope.

While Charles lived Monmouth's Dutch cousins had every reason to be hospitable. They knew that the king's affection for him had not died, and that they could expect royal gratitude for their munificence. To their knowledge numerous envelopes in the king's handwriting, addressed to the duke, arrived and Monmouth's spendthrift habits made it easy to surmise that these contained large sums of money. Like everyone else they believed that it was only a matter of time before the duke would be recalled.

These expectations were, naturally, dashed when news of Charles' death reached The Hague. The tidings shook no one more than Monmouth himself. He was inconsolable for weeks. Those who slept next to his chamber told of the wails which came through the partitions at night. New and dismal prospects opened before him, and the Prince of Orange saw the advantages of entertaining him reversed. To continue to accommodate the rash duke would, doubtless, anger King James.

William was disposed to be circumspect, and made a discreet suggestion. In Hungary the war was raging against the Turk, and the emperor – Leopold I – would welcome the sword of a distinguished nobleman. If Monmouth were to repair to Vienna he would be received with open arms, and given an opportunity of fighting for the noblest cause in Christendom.

The duke was tempted, but could not make up his mind. He left for Brussels with his mistress, Baroness Wentworth of Nettlestede – a lady of fortune who was infatuated with him.[2] Under her soothing influence he dismissed all thought of Hungary and Christendom, and began to lend an ear to the small-fry Whig exiles, who saw him as their leader.[3]

MONMOUTH'S RETURN

These Whigs, it must be said, were impractical dreamers and hotheads. Distance lent enchantment to their views and they harboured false impressions of political realities in England. They were a curiously mixed bunch: Nathaniel Wade was a lawyer whose sentiments were more republican than monarchist; Richard Rumbold had long opposed the Stuarts – he had stood on the scaffold when Charles I was executed; Lord Grey of Wark had been a zealous exclusionist and caused a sensation when he eloped with his sister-in-law. One of the most guileful was Rev. Robert Ferguson, a Scot who had lived in England for many years and was the author of violent anti-popish pamphlets which disgusted even his friends. The most important was the Earl of Argyll, the head of the clan Campbell, known in Scotland as MacCallum More. His father had been the chief Scottish opponent of Charles I. The young Argyll was never in good odour with the Stuarts and had been condemned to death on a trumped-up charge by James in 1681, but had escaped to Holland.[4]

These men had, daily, become more desperate and constantly nagged Monmouth to assert himself and make a bid for the crown; they held that a strike should be effected while the embers of anti-popery were warm. After some hesitation Monmouth was won over, and a scheme was worked out. Initially, Scotland was to be raised by Argyll, and then Monmouth was to land in the south of England, where it was expected that all would flock to him. Both plans were bold, but soon James' government learned that something was afoot and went on the alert.

In May 1685, Argyll slipped across to Scotland and tried to arouse the western highlands. It was a doomed enterprise and within days he was captured, tried and executed. Monmouth sailed three weeks later, with no knowledge of Argyll's fate and the most inflated of expectations.

He dropped anchor at Lyme Regis in Dorset, on 11 June. When the perplexed locals saw his ship they ran to the pier with great excitement, and watched as about eighty men come ashore. They gaped as the duke unfurled a large standard emblazoned with the words 'Fear Nothing But God'. In a loud voice he announced that he had come to relieve their tyranny. Then Rev. Ferguson, stepped on a sea-trunk, unrolled a proclamation, and read aloud:

... that upon the decease of our Sovereign Lord Charles the Second, the right of succession to the crowns of England, Scotland, France, and Ireland with the dominions and territories thereunto belonging, did legally descend and devolve upon the most illustrious and high-born Prince James, Duke of Monmouth, son and heir apparent of the said King Charles the Second ...

The townsfolk loved it all and cheered Monmouth to an echo. Soon he was surrounded by a multitude of eager recruits. But there were loyalists present, and news of the landing was quickly taken to London. Parliament was sitting and listened mutely as Lord Sunderland outlined the details of the revolt. It voted the king £400,000 to stamp out the rebellion, and provided £5,000 for the capture of Monmouth dead or alive.

ALL THE KING'S MEN
The life guards and the militia were immediately summoned to the defence of the realm. A Frenchman, Louis Duras, recently created Earl of Faversham, was put in charge, and Lord John Churchill appointed second-in-command. Six troops of horse and five infantry companies were dispatched, under Churchill, to the West Country.

Sarsfield could not contain his excitement. He felt fortunate to be in London and although he owed much to Monmouth, he would not countenance treason and unhesitantly unsheathed his sword. He briskly offered his services as a 'gentleman volunteer' and was assigned to a troop of horse under Colonel Theophilis Oglethorpe which was given patrol duties. They left London, ahead of Faversham, to reconnoitre the enemy.

Meanwhile, a section of the Dorset militia deserted and joined Monmouth. As he marched from Lyme a number of others caught the rebellion bug and tagged along. Some had fowling pieces, others swords, but most were armed with clubs or pikes fashioned from scythes. Each wore a green bough in his hat to denote that he was marching for Liberty and Protestantism.[5]

Everything depended on Monmouth's ability as a commander. One of his options was to quickly engage Churchill and destroy him before Faversham's army arrived. But knowing his opponents, and being unsure of his own greenhorns, he held back and marched into the town of Taunton.

The civic authorities came out to greet him, and young girls spread flowers in his path. He seemed to be a new Messiah, and paraded at the head of his cohorts. Under the shadow of the old stone cross in the market square, the cavalcade came to a halt. Here, to a hushed silence, followed by a rolling of drums, he proclaimed himself James II, by the grace of God, king, et cetera – and every knee was bent before him.

He had not, himself, been in a hurry to adopt the regnal title, but

Ferguson and Grey had insisted. They feared that the gentry, who so far had held aloof, were concerned that a Cromwellian-type republic was about to be foisted on them. It was thought that in the event of failure, their followers would be treated less harshly if serving a king – even if not a *dejure* one – than a mere rebel leader. But treason could not be so easily veiled, and Monmouth knew it.

With his invisible crown on his head he marched from Taunton to Bridgewater, a known centre of Protestant support. From there he planned to carry on to Bristol, the second richest city in the country. If he could gain this prize it might be a prelude to greater things.

OGLETHORPE'S ATTACK

At this point a whiff of reality began to encroach on the duke's dreams. Colonel Oglethorpe and Sarsfield had been hanging close to him for days. On the evening of 25 June they watched his rag-bag army march into Keynsham, a village about five miles from Bristol. They seemed a dishevelled lot, more like a multitude of yokels out on a revel than an army.

Despite his slim numbers Oglethorpe decided to charge through the village and catch them by surprise. He dashed from his cover with lightening speed, his men slashing with their sabres. The surprise was total and the rebels did not know what hit them. Before the withdrawal signal was given about a dozen were cut down.

Sarsfield, however, ran into trouble and was nearly overpowered, but with his excellent horsemanship, managed to pull out. His only injury was a slashed hand.

THE DUKE WEAKENS

In the succeeding days Oglethorpe, and Sarsfield – who was the colonel's right hand man – continued to dog the rebels and became not only aware of their movements, but of their problems.

The duke's objective was still Bristol, but when he reached the outskirts he became faint-hearted and hung back. During his hesitancy a detachment of royal troops entered the city, making his prospects of taking it problematic. His supporters urged him to press ahead but he lost his nerve. He must have realised that his position was hopeless.

Although he had the support of five thousand peasants, none of the gentry came forward. There had been a shift in mood during his exile. Without the support of the Whig gentry he could not succeed. And the news of Argyll's failure in Scotland did not cheer him. His indecision had cost him Bristol and if he did not do something quickly he would be caught in a pincher movement by Churchill and Faversham.

He decided to retreat to Bridgewater and escape encirclement by heading for Cheshire. But deep down he wanted to make a run for it. Grey and Ferguson were appalled by such treacherous notions. Grey urged him to stand and fight like a man. After a dressing down he resolved to stay. A fellow named Godfrey ran up and said that the royal army had moved into Westonzoyland, a village a few miles from Sedgemoor, a low-lying moor a few miles away. He also disclosed, that the royal army was getting roaring drunk on local cider and was in no condition to fight; further, they were careless and had not posted sentries.

To confirm the story, the duke was taken to the tower of Bridgewater church – said to be the loftiest in Somerset – where he could see the disposition of the enemy. All around was marshland, criss-crossed by wide ditches dug in ancient times as drainage systems to prevent the local hamlets from flooding.

Monmouth made an audacious decision. He decided on a night-time ambush on Faversham. He did not know that not far away, on Knowle Hill, Oglethorpe and Sarsfield had their field-glasses trained upon him.

The Battle of Sedgemoor

That evening the rebel army lined up in Castle Field in Bridgewater, sustained by the delusion that they could destroy the royal forces. They were to march to the enemy lines with the utmost silence; anyone making a sound was to be immediately stabbed by his neighbour. They knew that the ditches, known locally as rhines, constituted the greatest hindrance to their plans. If they could cross these without alerting the enemy, they would have a chance of victory. They felt fortunate in having Godfrey as their pilot as he appeared to know the lie of the land.

At 11 p.m. they moved, like mice, and took a circuitous route which went within half-a-mile of Oglethorpe's sleeping patrol which was not awakened. Within the hour they were on the open moor; between them and the enemy lay four broad rhines filled with water and mud. Three of these, the Black Ditch, the Langmoor Rhine and the Moor Drove, were successfully crossed at fords known to Godfrey. But the fourth one, the Bussex Rhine, lying immediately in front of Faversham's camp, puzzled him. He was unsure of how to steer across it. As they stealthily approached, their luck ran out: a pistol abruptly discharged. It may have been fired by Oglethorpe's patrol, alerted to their movements, or an act of treachery from within their own ranks. Whichever, it caused an alarm: the royal army was instantly aroused.

Half-awakened sentries leapt to their feet and bugles pierced the air. The men of five battalions drew up directly facing the rebels. But it was the rebels who initiated the action. Grey's horse came dashing from the perimeter of the moor, but made the mistake of presenting its flank as a target for the royal infantry. Under fire the horses bolted and went stampeding back through the lines of their advancing foot. Next, the infantry was caught under a hail of grapeshot. With the advantage of surprise lost, they were doomed by the superior fire power against them.[6] Individually the rebels showed magnificent courage and returned a good quantity of shot. Grey even tried to rally his horse, but again it was scattered. For a while Monmouth himself fought pluckily, side-by-side with the foot, but on seeing an opportunity, fled.

The gallant rustics fought on, but their destruction was inevitable. Oglethorpe made a vigorous attempt to break them by charging obliquely but was beaten back. Sarsfield repeated the exercise but was also repulsed. As he wheeled his horse in a scuffle he was struck by a musket butt on the skull and thrown to the ground. In the heat of battle he was left for dead.

The rebels could withstand little further pressure and broke. The royal infantry poured over the ditch and a great butchery ensued. Within half an hour more than a thousand rebels were killed, and double that number wounded. The Battle of Sedgemoor was over, and an eerie silence hung on the moor.

Monmouth's Fate

A few days later, Lord Faversham wrote to Sunderland, the secretary of state, saying:

> I do not believe that we have lost fifty men … nearly two hundred were wounded. There was only one ensign killed; two captains, six lieutenants and six ensigns were wounded …

Sarsfield's standing was indicated by a special mention. Faversham said:

> Sarsfield was wounded but not mortally.

Monmouth escaped a murderous round-up by Colonel Kirke's dragoons. But his hope of absconding came to nothing. Within days he and Grey were arrested by the Sussex militia. They were found hiding in ditches, disguised as shepherds.

On 15 June 1685 Monmouth went to the block. He died terribly after a number of blundering blows failed to decapitate him. For years afterwards wild stories circulated in the West Country: it was said that a man resembling Monmouth had died in his stead, and that the 'Protestant duke' would come again to deliver Zion and make war upon Babylon.

The Bloody Assizes

The sequel added a horrible footnote. The chief justice, Lord George Jeffreys, was dispatched to the West Country to dispense the king's justice. He bore himself so brutally that his name became forever associated with 'The Bloody Assizes'.

Two or three hundred unfortunates were hung or chopped before it was realised that such slaying was a waste of valuable material. Slaves were urgently required in the plantations, and a healthy man could fetch up to fifteen pounds. Eight hundred souls were parcelled out to well-connected traders who grew rich by trafficking in human flesh and blood in the colonies.[7]

5

THE TOTTERING CROWN

CLIMBING THE LADDER

That Sarsfield played an energetic role in Monmouth's downfall c̣
be doubted. It may well be that this role was greater than the reco.
suggest, for not long afterwards his career was boosted and he obtaineu
at least one tangible reward. A document on file in the old public records
office in Dublin dated 8 June 1686 *Anno Secondo Regis Jacobi* showed
that he was granted lands by the crown in the barony of Offaly, Co. Kildare.[1]

The king also took a personal interest in him: an entry in the royal
diary following Sedgemoor described how he was clubbed and knocked
from his horse. In the same year his name appeared twice in the army
listings, each mention showing a different status. Initially, he was described as a major, and then as a captain. In earlier mentions he was
shown as a Catholic who had not conformed to the Test Acts. This now
seemed a technicality as it was the king's ambition to abolish these acts.

James had not been impressed by the militia during the rebellion,
and held that the security of the realm required a strong permanent army.
When parliament reassembled in November he announced his intention of augmenting the existing forces and of retaining the Catholic officers who had enrolled during the emergency. Both proposals caused panic. The question of military authority had long been a contentious issue
between the crown and parliament. There were those who felt that if the
king was given control of a regular army, he would use it to render parliament ineffectual.

Underlying this fear was the prospect of a royal praetorian guard
made up of Catholics divorced from popular English sentiment. Even
a number of James' Tory friends backed away and the House of Commons
demurred. It refused to grant supplies while illegal commissions were
in place. The House of Lords took a similar line: its protest backed by
the strong opposition of the Anglican episcopate, particularly by Henry
Compton, bishop of London. James lost his patience and prorogued
parliament.

The king's new resolve called for fresh tactics. What parliament
refused, he undertook to obtain through the judiciary. First, it was necessary to remodel the bench. He dismissed four judges who disagreed
with him; their successors connived in bringing a test case known as
Godden V. Hales before the king's bench – Godden sued his employer,
Sir Edward Hales, a Catholic, for breaking the Test Acts by failing to
take the sacrament prior to accepting a royal appointment.

;ht to grant Hales a dispensation under
.t right which allowed the monarch to
.de parliament. In his summation the lord

The cour'
the royal Rwhatsoever but may be dispensed by the supreme law-
stultify s'
chief j .ig) ... the laws of England are the king's laws.

.on opened the way for Catholics to join the armed forces and
.an civil posts, and James set about appointing them to remuner-
.ve positions without delay.[2]

SARSFIELD AT LIME STREET

Sarsfield was an early beneficiary of these developments and was given
a commission in a newly raised regiment of horse under the Catholic,
Lord Dover. As his lordship was not a professional soldier the day-to-day
running of the regiment devolved on Sarsfield. His men began to participate in the great parades which were held regularly on Houndslow Heath,
involving large numbers from all ranks.[3]

Fashionable London turned out to see these spectacles, although
some were dismayed to find on the parade ground – 'between the horse
and the foot' – a great wooden chapel on wheels where popish priests
offered mass each morning, whilst their co-adjutors moved among the
troops on proselytising missions.

Sarsfield's regiment saw little real action, save when called out in
April 1687 to protect a Catholic chapel in Lime Street, which was being
consecrated. From early morning a Protestant mob had gathered and
shouted abuse at the congregation. A small party of militia were posted
at the gate, but as the morning wore on was overpowered, and the mob
streamed into the building, smashing statues and crucifixes.[4]

When Sarsfield's men arrived the militia was standing by helplessly. They had to force their way in with drawn swords, but within
minutes managed to corral the mob and frogmarched the ring-leaders
out. They then compelled the rest to withdraw and disperse. The incident is significant in that it illustrates the prevailing depth of anti-Catholic feeling, and because it convinced James of the necessity of having
Catholic troops at the ready.

Months later, during a rationalisation, Sarsfield's regiment was disbanded and the men transferred to a new, mixed force known as The
Fourth Troop, with Sarsfield again in a senior position.

THE TIGHTENING SCREW

The international situation at this time was tense. Across the channel,
Louis XIV had sent shockwaves through Europe by his treatment of the
Huguenots. Since 1598 they had enjoyed freedom of worship under the

Edict of Nantes. But the French Catholic Church had resented this accommodation and wanted it ended.

Louis was not inattentive to the Church, and felt that the existence in his realm of a large nonconforming body was an irritation. Besides, he badly needed the *ex-gratia* funds which the Church paid into his coffers and was prepared to be obliging. Further, he wished to redeem his reputation in the eyes of Catholic Europe for refusing to take up arms against the Turk.[5]

A reign of terror was opened against the Huguenots. Their churches were burnt, their schools closed and their charitable institutions transferred to the Catholic Church. They were barred from different employments and spies infiltrated their congregations: if they uttered any criticism of Catholicism, they were indicted of blasphemy. Their persecution reached its height with the notorious dragonnades – the forced billeting of troops in Huguenot households.[6]

This persecution rebounded in England. Fleeing Huguenots arrived with tales of terror, murder and torture. The old cry of 'no popery!' rang out, and James' Tory friends grew alarmed as their popularity wilted. There was a warning in this for the king, but he failed to heed it. Having used his prerogative to secure Catholic appointments, he pressed ahead by granting a declaration of indulgence, allowing his co-religionists and dissenters religious tolerance. This further use of the prerogative was seen as autocratic and reinforced fears that he intended to negate parliament and undermine the rule of law.

Anxieties were increased when borough charters were remodelled and Catholics appointed as local magistrates. An ecclesiastical commission was established to act as a court for Church affairs with powers to make and unmake appointments. This commission was soon used to expel Fellows from Magdalen College, Oxford, and replace them with Catholics. For James this was, perhaps, a means of creating equality and redistributing privilege. To the increasingly alienated Protestant establishment it was an attack on their tenure and entitlements.

The anger created was predictable, even if its precise outcome was not. In 1688, James imprudently renewed the declaration of indulgence and ordered it to be read in every church on two consecutive Sundays. Of all the events leading to his undoing this one was pre-eminent, for on 17 May 1688, William Sandcroft, the archbishop of Canterbury, and six of his fellow bishops protested against reading the declaration. James saw their protest as tantamount to rebellion. At once, and without legal advice, he prosecuted the bishops for seditious libel, and made every effort to secure a conviction. But they were acquitted, and the people of London danced on the streets with delight.[7]

On the same evening, 30 June, a messenger left London for the Dutch Republic. Admiral Arthur Herbert disguised as an ordinary seaman carried a letter signed by seven great leaders of public opinion, both Whig and Tory. It was addressed to the Prince of Orange and invited him in the most unequivocal terms to bring an army to England and overthrow the popish king.

The letter was treasonable and those who signed it concealed their identity with code. The signatories, known to history as 'The Immortal Seven' included: the Lords Danby, Sidney and Lumley, Bishop Henry Compton and Edward Russell (a cousin of the Russell executed for his part in the Rye House Plot) and the earls of Shrewsbury and Devonshire. They boldly claimed to speak for the people of England and wrote:

> 'Your highness may be assured, there are nineteen parts out of twenty, throughout the kingdom, who are desirous of change', and added, 'we who subscribe to this document will not fail to attend to your highness on landing'.[8]

The Warming Pan Baby

That the invitation was dispatched on the day of the bishop's acquittal was a mere coincidence. The immediate reason was because, twenty days earlier, one of James' greatest dreams was realised. His queen, Mary Beatrice, had given birth to a son. This event killed all hopes that James' reign was no more than a temporary affliction which would die with him.

News of the queen's pregnancy had been a surprise. She had never borne a healthy child and now the arrival of a popish heir was too much for people to accept. Some refused to credit what they did not wish to believe. A tale was spun that the baby was the son of a washerwoman named Mary Gray and had been slipped into the queen's bed in a warming pan. The fabrication gave the lampoonists a field day: in the hands of James' enemies, it became a powerful weapon against him. The only plot, in fact, was to disrupt the lawful succession.[9]

The invitation to William was no surprise. It was a carefully devised piece of sophistry to lend respectability to an act already decided onpon. For months, even years, he had been conniving with James' enemies and had already begun his preparations for an invasion of England. He had opened a propaganda campaign in Europe to justify his intent and informed the pope and the emperor that he had no wish to bring harm to James' Catholic subjects.

The Whig version stresses that the invitation was from 'the people of England'. It was not. William, in fact, invited himself. No parliament summoned him and those who did, however eminent, had no authority to do so. He could have had no illusion but that he was engaging in a blatant usurpation, and no pious platitudes about the 'freedoms of England' could conceal that his real intent: to secure the resources of the Three Kingdoms for his struggle against Louis XIV.[10]

It was not until 19 October that William put to sea. Immediately he ran
into trouble; his fleet was driven back by heavy gales and there were
fears that the enterprise might have to be abandoned. He ventured again
on 1 November and aided by the famous 'Protestant Wind' smoothly
entered the channel. His armada consisted of fifty war-ships, twenty
frigates, four hundred transports; it carried 14,000 men, with arms and
equipment for hundreds more. The van was commanded by Admiral
Herbert and the rear by Vice Admiral Evertzen, with William and his
high command in the centre. Each vessel flew the flag of England, and
the prince's own frigate could be identified by a huge banner emblazoned, on top, with the words:

Pro Religione et Libertate
For Religion and Liberty

and on the bottom, with the device of the House of Nassau:

Je Maintiendrai
I Will Maintain

By noon the fleet had entered the Straits of Dover with its canvas spread
to a favourable wind; it sprawled to within a league of Dover to the
north and Calais to the south, and saluted the fortresses on both sides
with staccato blasts from its cannons.

On board were English, Irish and Scottish Whig refugees, and a
dozen or so Huguenot officers, the principal of whom was Marshal Freidrich von Schomberg, one of the great soldiers of the age. This old veteran was the son of a German father and an English mother and had served the House of Orange during the Thirty Years War and later gave distinguished service to the kings of Portugal and France. In 1685 he was
one of eight marshals of France appointed on the death of Turenne, but
in protest against the Edict of Nantes, he returned his baton to Louis and
went to serve The Great Elector, Friderich William of Brandenburg. He
had recently been seconded, with a Prussian force, to William. Accompanying him was his son, Count Meinhard Schomberg and notables such as
Callemote and his brother Ruvigny; Mellioneire, Cambon and Tetteu,
all men of proven military capacity.[11]

On Sunday 4 November the cliffs of the Isle of Wight came into
view, and the sail was slackened so that divine service could be held on
each ship. In the afternoon and during the night the fleet held its course;
next morning, at sunrise, it put safely into the harbour at Torbay in Devonshire.

As William watched his troops disembark, he turned to his chaplain, Bishop Gilbert Burnet, and said, with a knowing wink: 'Well, Doctor,
what do you think of predestination now?'[12]

Those who first encountered William (shortly to become known in Whig lore as 'The Great Deliverer') in Torbay saw a spare man of middle size, whose long upper lip and acidulated gaze gave an impression of egotism. But he was not conceited. He was brusque in manner, careless in dress and revealed none of the condescension of seventeenth-century monarchs. 'In youth,' Macauley says, 'his face had been fixed into a mask of immobile, almost repulsive coldness'. In manhood, these lineaments remained unchanged. Yet in that baleful gaze, that thin straight

William

mouth and pinched face, lay something compelling even to the most indifferent beholder. The man fascinated as well as repelled.

He was born at The Hague a few days after his father's death – his mother was Mary, daughter of Charles I of England. His father attempted a failed coup which had promised him supreme power. Before he could renew his effort, he contracted smallpox and died. With no one to reconstruct his audacious policy, it melted, and William from early childhood lived among men who hated his father's memory. The control of the Dutch Republic passed into the hands of John de Witte, leader of the trading and moneyed interests, who were traditionally hostile to the House of Orange. William was made a 'Child of State' and grew up suspicious, cautious and tight-lipped. Circumstances forced an early maturity on him and much of his youth was spent pondering ways of restoring the power and titles of which he had been deprived.[13]

Louis XIV, as we have seen, flung an army into Dutch territory in 1672. The preparations which de Witte had made for his country's defence were inadequate. As the French achieved success after success the Dutch people grew angry with the reverses, and threw over de Witte. The states general called up the Prince of Orange and proclaimed him, *stadholder*, captain general and admiral for life.[14]

Equipped with this new authority, and cheered by the news that The Hague mob had dispatched de Witte, the young *stadholder* addressed himself to ridding his country of the invader. Immediately his courage and ability became apparent. Determined to 'die in the last ditch' – he coined the phrase – he opened the sluices and flooded huge tracts of the countryside to check the French advance. He campaigned so hard that by the spring of 1674 the last French soldier had retreated over the border.

Three years later he married Mary, eldest daughter of James and Anne Hyde. Thus he acquired a claim, besides his maternal one, which put him in line to the English throne.

From his wedding day onwards William kept a keen eye on English affairs. For years he had hoped that his father-in-law would join the League of Augsburg – a confederacy which he had formed against the rapacity of Louis. But he had come to see that this was a pipe-dream. Practical in all things, he therefore began to ingratiate himself with those in England who wanted to be shut of James.[15]

At Torbay, William was not received with enthusiasm. The people of the west, remembering Jeffreys, were apathetic or afraid; they watched curiously as the army of Dutch and foreign mercenaries floundered over the rough country roads, but made no effort to join them.

It was the anniversary of the Gunpowder Plot,[16] and William availed of the anti-Catholic mood which this event aroused to proclaim his mission of protecting the Reformed Faith. This did not have the effect which he expected, and feeling somewhat disconcerted, he marched his army to Exeter. Here, finding that the Anglican clergy had fled at his approach, and that none of his conspiratorial friends had come to meet him, he began to think that he had been deceived by false promises. But that evening the Lords Colchester and Godfrey fled London and joined him; others followed, and with an army which daily began to receive more support he marched towards London and the throne.[17]

SARSFIELD REMAINS LOYAL

When James learned of the invasion he mustered 30,000 men and marched to Salisbury to meet the invader. On the way Lord Cornbury, under the pretence of attacking an Orange outpost, took his regiment and three others over to the enemy. Soon afterwards, the Duke of Grafton, Colonel Barclay and Lord John Churchill openly defected. A few hours later, the royal army began to crumble, and Sarsfield and other officers tried to stem the tide, but Whig propaganda had already undermined the loyalty and confidence of the men. Soon it was apparent that the royal cause was in jeopardy. The king retired to Andover, where his son-in-law, Prince George of Denmark, also defected.

Sarsfield remained firm, and was maddened by the treachery which he saw around him. Earlier, he had been instructed to scour the countryside for information on enemy movements. All sorts of rumours were flying. One was that a troop of Orange foot had entered the village of Burton, near Wincanton, seeking horses. He went to investigate and found the story to be true. About thirty Scots from General Hugh Mackay's regiment (which had been serving in the Netherlands), were scavenging.

Their leader, Lieut Campbell had spent the night in the village, and was still there when he received a tip-off that Sarsfield's patrol was on his heels. He had to make a quick decision. He did not know the size of Sarsfield's patrol: if it were small, he would stay and fight. If it were large he would leave. He decided to stay and deploying his men in the ditches near the village, he awaited Sarsfield. To get to the village, and on to Wincanton, the patrol would have to pass this cunningly-laid trap.

As Sarsfield and his men approached, Campbell jumped out and shouted, 'Stand! For who are ye?'

'For his majesty the king,' replied Sarsfield, adding, 'and for who are you?'

'I am for the Prince of Orange'.

'God damn you!' said the hot-headed Sarsfield, 'I'll prince you!' At this, the Scots opened fire and one of Sarsfield's troopers fell. There was panic. The patrollers tried to wheel their horses; but Sarsfield bellowed at them to stay. They did, but as they surged forward, a huge tree was felled in the their path, and their horses reared.

In seconds they steadied themselves and surged forward, skirting the obstacle. Campbell was unfortunate to find himself in Sarsfield's pathway, and following a sabre trust, fell and was trampled. When another Scot went under the hooves, those remaining scurried to the hedge-rows.

Sarsfield knew that he had to run a gauntlet to reach the village and was about to do so when someone rushed up to him shouting. His informant said that a huge contingent of Orange horse was approaching and that he should withdraw. Whether or not this was true, we do not know, but Sarsfield took it seriously and decided to pull out. As he took off, the bushwackers broke their cover and fled.[18]

It was a minor skirmish and is only worth recording because it was one of the few encounters between the rival forces.

THE KING'S FLIGHT

Overwhelmed by desertions and suffering from stress-induced nose bleeds, James was on the verge of a nervous break-down. He decided to return to London. In Whitehall a further blow awaited him. His younger daughter, the Princess Anne, pretending to fear his wrath because of her husband's defection, had left the palace and taken refuge with his enemies. He had always been affectionate towards her; that she should also spurn his cause hurt him. Like King Lear, he cried out: 'God help me, my own children have forsaken me'.

The queen and her infant now took his attention. He placed them in the care of a French courtier, the Count de Lauzun, who rushed them to France. Not knowing where to turn he dispatched Lord Faversham to negotiate with William, and remained in London to await the outcome.

William received the envoy politely and listened to his arguments, but showed no interest. In the meantime the palace at Whitehall was surrounded by an advance party of Dutch blue guards, and James was notified that he must quit London by noon, next day. He did, but his attempted flight to France was arrested when fishermen at Faversham, near Rochester, detected his identity and blocked his passage. In utter misery he was returned to London to be greeted, to his amazement, by

cheering crowds. When William learned of th⌐
culated the news that the king had been ca⌐
from his realm.

This was the final blow to the king's re⌐
for the London mob to engage in an orgy ⌐
'Irish Night' erupted, when, fed on bog⌐
that Irish soldiers were being let loose ⌐
everyone.

But it was only Catholics who suffered. ⌐
destroyed and a score of their chapels set ablaze. The nou⌐
ish and Florentine envoys were gutted; the French embassy was ⌐
only because the ambassador had doubled the guard. Yet, in spite of the
havoc and burnings, it must be said, there was remarkably little blood-
shed. The only man who came near to being lynched was Jeffreys, who
had been loathed since the 'Blood Assizes'. He had attempted to disguise himself by cutting off his prominent eyebrows and donning the
garb of a sailor. He was spotted as he waited for a boat to Wapping, and
thrown into the Tower of London. By nightfall bonfires appeared all over
the city and mobs marched up and down Piccadilly yelling to their hearts
content and carrying Orange flags.

Yet James had not quit his realm. His presence in London was an embarrassment to William who was still some distance away. From Winsor,
where he had pitched his camp, he issued instructions that the luckless
king should be allowed to 'escape' once more.

The following day, shortly before noon, in drenching rain, James
descended the steps at Whitehall for the last time. He entered the royal
barge, and sailed down the Thames as hundreds of Londoners watched
in silence. Their mood was strange, given the jubilation of the previous
days. Lord Clarendon summed it up, remarking:

> The treatment which the king had received from the Prince of Orange, and
> the manner in which he was driven from Whitehall, moved to compassion
> even those who were not very fond of him.[19]

Bishop Gilbert Burnet had the same impression:

> Compassion had begun to work, especially since the prince sent him word
> to leave Whitehall.

On learning that James had definitely gone, William set out to complete
his journey. By late afternoon he entered London and found it in a fes-
tive mood. James' departure was forgotten and the crowds were again
jubilant.

At Hyde Park Corner, the prince was officially greeted by the Sheriffs
of London and Middlesex. The bells of the city rang out as he reached
St James' Palace. But despite the hurrahs, bonfires and jubilation, the

y – an astute commentator – noted that some were dis-
even angry. The size of this group is queried, but the cause
temper is known: they felt that an anointed king had been
lly brushed aside. Among them was Sarsfield.

DUTCHMAN TAKES THE CROWN

n Wednesday 13 February 1689, the precincts of the palace at Whitehall were filled with onlookers. The magnificent Banqueting House, the
masterpiece of Inigo Jones, so beautifully embellished by Rubens, was
prepared for a great ceremony.

The walls and corridors were lined with yeomen of the guard and
near the northern door the lords spiritual and temporal had assembled.
On the left were members of the House of Commons and the speaker;
before them stood Black Rod, with the mace on his shoulder. The southern door opened: and the Prince and Princess of Orange entered, side
by side, under the gold-brocaded canopy of state. As they approached
both houses bowed low, and received in return the merest of courteous
nods.

When they reached the dais, Lord Halifax came forward and spoke.
He asked in the name of all the estates of the realm, that the prince and
princess accept the crown of the kingdom. William, in his own name,
and in that of his wife, replied: 'we thankfully accept what you have
offered'. With these words shouts of joy went up, and were echoed by
yells of acclaim from the streets below.

As the House of Lords and House of Commons retired, the kettle
drums rolled and the trumpets blasted. The great herald came on the
balcony and to a hush, proclaimed to all who could hear him, that the
Prince and Princess of Orange were King and Queen of England. From
that moment, he said, all subjects were charged to bear true and rightful allegiance to their new joint sovereigns.

It is doubtful whether Sarsfield actually heard this proclamation
although he was still in London. Two months earlier his troop of horse
had been disbanded. He was, again, unemployed and, under the new dispensation, probably unemployable. His mood was sullen and it is known
that he expressed violent views against the new king: word of his incautious remarks reached William, with advice that he should be arrested, lest he try an assassination attempt.

William could not arrest all who opposed either his person or his
government. He replied: 'let him do it, if he dares'.[20]

6

'BONNIE' DUNDEE – THE SCOTTISH SARSFIELD

I fought at land, I fought at sea
At home I fought my Auntie, O
But I met the devil and Dundee
On the braes o' Killiecrankie, O.

BURNS

SARSFIELD'S VIEWS

Whether Sarsfield planned to assassinate William we shall never know. The reports are insubstantial and there is insufficient knowledge of his mental state to say whether he was disposed towards such a deed. He may well have been. He was quick-tempered with a reckless streak and much of his world had collapsed. To him the Dutchman was a usurper and he must have been appalled at the ease with which the crown was transferred.

Moreover, more than most, Sarsfield would have seen that the 'revolution' was a stage managed affair instigated by a small group of Whigs who felt threatened by a reforming, if blundering, monarch. They had cunningly organised disaffection in the army and whipped up the London mob with crude anti-Catholic slogans. There was no nationwide uprising and the great majority of citizens had remained indifferent. No shift had occurred in the social or economic structures nor was one intended. The 'revolution', in fact, was a good old-fashioned palace coup.

It is not preposterous to suggest that had the hapless James shown greater resolution or ignited the instinctive English dislike for foreigners, there would have been fewer army desertions and, hence, he might have overcome his adversary. Instead his vacillation ruined everything. The man who had earned the praise of Turenne for his valour, who had charged the famous *tercios* of Spain and the redoubtable Ironsides of Cromwell had abandoned the campaign because of nervous tension and a nose bleed!

If Sarsfield found the collapse at Salisbury inexplicable he, doubtless, found the policies of the king of France less so. It had been in Louis' power to prevent the invasion. A French army was ready for war and could have thwarted William by marching to the Dutch border. Instead it was directed to attack the empire on the Upper Rhine. The reason is not hard to find: for years Louis had sought to neutralise England by encouraging its domestic disputes. Now he could claim to have embroiled it with the Dutch – for his diplomats had never ceased to encourage James in his lunacies – thus affording himself a free hand else-where. A military man, like Sarsfield, would hardly have been unap-preciative of the Machiavellian calculations of Louis.

In all this, Sarsfield's personal position was straightforward. He was a Stuart loyalist and could scarcely be otherwise. Under James his career had snowballed. In Ireland the prospects for Catholics were better than at any time since the Reformation and the detested act of settlement, which had almost ruined his family, was likely to be repealed. Was all this to be lost, because of the usurper? Sarsfield did not think so. A fea-ture of his day, as of our own, was that political upheavals were gener-ally followed by reactions. Already there were those who planned to send the Dutchman packing and restore James. Shortly such people would be given the generic name of 'Jacobites'. One of the earliest of them was a young man whose temperament and loyalties were similar to Sars-field's. His name was John Graham of Claverhouse, known to history as 'Bonnie' Dundee.

THE REVOLUTION IN SCOTLAND

Dundee was a resourceful cavalry officer, who had come to promi-nence years before during the campaigns against the Covenanting radi-cals. With the Earl of Balcarras, James had given him great power in Scotland and made him a viscount immediately prior to the *debacle* at Salisbury.[1]

When news of the projected invasion had reached Edinburgh, Dun-dee cold-shouldered the Scottish Whigs, mustered an army, and marched south in defence of the crown. After a few days in London he trans-ferred to Salisbury to link up with the royal army. He quickly became troubled with the king's lack of enterprise and urged him to take the of-fensive, as William had only by this time advanced to Axminister and appeared vulnerable. When it became clear that James lacked stomach, Dundee implored him to withdraw to Scotland and fight a rearguard action. But James refused to listen. When the royal army disintegrated, Dundee drew off his men.

Following James' aborted flight, Dundee and Balcarras were given an audience in Whitehall. Again, they counselled that a stand be made, but James was not hopeful of success. He took them for a walk in the Mall and said:

> I see you are the men I always took you to be; you shall know all my inten-tions. I can no longer remain here but as a cyper, or to be a prisoner of the Prince of Orange, and you know that there is but a small distance between the prisons and the graves of kings. Therefore, I go to France immediately: when there, you will have my instructions. You, my Lord Balcarras, shall have a commission to manage my civil affairs, and you, my Lord Dundee, to command my troops in Scotland.[2]

A few hours later James had left Whitehall forever, and Dundee returned to Scotland with those of his men who had not drifted away.

He found the situation in Edinburgh changed. During his absence, the Scottish Whigs had virtually taken over the country. The Scottish council had not, however, made any formal move to transfer the crown. It had, as yet, only requested William to administer the country until it could decide for itself.

In May, William summoned a convention of estates in Edinburgh. Both he and James sent letters setting out their respective positions. William was tactful and conciliatory, James considerably less so. It appeared as if the crown of Scotland was up for auction, and the Dutchman raised the stakes by dispatching General Mackay's veterans to ensure that it was knocked down to himself.

For a time Dundee took part in the convention, but when it became obvious that there was a majority for William he stormed out. With seventy followers he rode to Sterling intent on establishing a rival convention. His plans were frustrated when Williamite soldiers took over the town, and posted notices declaring him a fugitive and a rebel.

By now the convention had ruled that James had vacated the Scottish throne and therefore forfeited his right to it. It was formally offered to William and Mary, but with strings attached. As if preparing a new lease for an incoming tenant, a 'Claim of Rights' and 'Articles of Grievances' were drawn up, listing the offences of the retiring tenant and imposing fresh conditions on the newcomers. The new sovereigns were asked to protect the law, religion and liberties of Scotland, and to root out the enemies of the Kirk. Their agreement was automatic and within days the regalia of Scotland was shipped to London. In a quaint ceremony in Whitehall the joint monarchs modestly took their Scottish coronation oaths.

The northern kingdom, so casually assigned, was now ready for war. Dundee raised the Jacobite standard in the city of his title, but it caused little stir. Undaunted, he rode to the highlands and rallied the clans. The MacDonalds of Keppoch were indifferent to the claims of either dynasty and agreed to fight for James on the promise of reward. The Camerons of Lochiel declared similarly, as did the Stewarts and the Macleans. Dundee's great charm persuaded them all to set aside their feuds and strike in the new cause.

But fate had dealt Dundee a poor hand. The clans were completely undisciplined and although they contained some of the best fighters in Europe it was difficult to keep them in order. His hand was also held by James, who instructed that no decisive action be taken until the arrival of forces from Ireland. Accordingly, while the highland host was assembling Dundee could mount only minor raids on the enemy. Yet, Perth, Aberdeen and Inverness all felt the weight of his arm.

Archibald Campbell, the new Earl of Argyll had become one of the most powerful men in Scotland. When he returned from the coronation in London he was in a fighting mood. In his pocket he held a commission from William to put down the rebels, and he instructed General Mackay to march against them.

The two armies met at the Pass of Killiecrankie near Pitlochry on 27 July 1689. The day began with Dundee deceiving his opponent as to where the battle would be fought. He sent a small party of highlanders along the road from Blair to Killiecrankie and fooled Mackay's scouts who assumed that the battle would take place on low ground near the river Garry.

Dundee's intention was otherwise. He gained the heights overlooking the pass on the northern side and took Mackay by surprise. When the Williamite general raised his eyes he found the crest above him alive with the enemy. Dundee gave the enemy plenty of time to realise the seriousness of their situation and then, as the sun dipped, he waved his bonnet and the men dropped their plaids. At a further signal they came rushing at the enemy with a frightful yell. Their heavy claymores felled their opponents before they could fix their newfangled plug-bayonets and it was all over within minutes.

"Twas a fine tussle,' said old Ian Luim, the bard of Keppoch, 'many a cocked hat and dainty perwig were thrown to the ground, blood flowed like waves over the grass and more than a thousand spades were used to level the graves of the enemy.'[3]

The victory was a pyrrhic one. In the mighty, triumphant, downhill charge Dundee was fatally struck. He had taken his place in front of the cavalry and rushed forward with them. Standing on his stirrups and waving his sword, his armour rose and a freak shot hit him in the loin. His horse plunged into a cloud of smoke and nobody saw him fall. Minutes later, a clansman named Johnson spotted him. His end had all the ingredients of a melodrama. The dying man asked, 'How goes the day?'

Johnson replied 'Well for King James,' and added, 'but I am sorry for your lordship'.

With a last gasp Dundee's final words were: 'If it is well for him, it matters the less for me'.[4]

His body was wrapped in plaids and carried to the castle of Blair. Next day, he was laid to rest amid the tears of the clansmen. For years afterwards highland hearts would swell with pride at the mention of his name. Today, a rude stone on the field of honour marks where he fell.

Dundee has sometimes been seen as the Scottish counterpart of Sarsfield. Petrie says:

Dundee was the typical 'Beau Sabreur' in which he resembled his contemporary Sarsfield, and the skill which he displayed in his last campaign affords ground for the supposition that, had his talents ever enjoyed wider scope he might have attained an international military reputation, and that, too, in an age of such soldiers as Marlborough, Eugene and Berwick'.[5]

DUNKELD

Their leader's death spelt catastrophe for the highlanders. Colonel Cannon, an Irishman, was appointed in his place, but was not in the same class. He led the grieving clansmen southwards to the cathedral town of Dunkeld in an effort to consolidate Dundee's victory.

A surge of support increased the host's numbers and Cannon had almost 5,000 men when he met 1,200 well dug-in Williamites, mostly Cameronians, under the youthful Colonel William Cleland on 21 August 1689. The Battle of Dunkeld took the form of a brief siege and afforded the highlanders no opportunity for the type of headlong charge which had unnerved the Williamites at Killiecrankie.

After four hours of sniping and sorties, the clansmen withdrew. Both sides claimed a victory which neither achieved, but it was a turning point. The Jacobite rising lost its impetus and morale slumped. The spirit of faction among the highlanders which Dundee had dampened surfaced again and within a month all resistance had melted away.

GLENCOE

Although resistance ceased many of the clans remained sympathetic to James, and the highlanders, who were mostly Catholic, demurred at taking an oath of allegiance to an anti-Stuart, anti-Catholic and anti-French king. But William sought to pacify them and promised payments to the clan chiefs if they swore loyalty by 31 December 1691 – a date which was fixed as the deadline for submission.

Alexander MacDonald of Glencoe made it a point of honour to delay his oath until the last moment, but then made the error of presenting himself to an official at Fort William who was not authorised to take the submission. He then set out for Inverary to swear in the presence of the sheriff – although it seems likely that he may have been deliberately misinformed as to where to go – but bad weather delayed him and it was not until 6 January that he was able to go through the formality.

This technical infringement was seized on by the under-secretary of state for Scotland, Sir John Dalrymple, master of Stair, as a pretext to make an example of MacDonald. In the old manner, letters of fire and sword were issued against the chieftain's clan with a view to dispersing them. The task was entrusted to troops under the Campbells of Glenlyon. For two weeks the Campbells enjoyed the rude hospitality of the MacDonalds, and then, during the night of 12–13 February killed about forty of their hosts in their beds. The homes of the rest were torched and their animals driven to the hills. A Lieut Lindsay was responsible for dispatching old MacDonald himself. The ailing chief was shot in the back as he rose from his bed.[6]

Few in Scotland doubted that William was behind the outrage, although he may not have specifically prescribed the methods employed. Yet an inquiry exonerated him for it was said that he frequently signed documents without reading them. The blame was put on Dalrymple who was forced to resign his office. But this was a mere technical rebuke. In 1703 he was rehabilitated and William gave him an earldom.

Throughout the highlands the Dutchman's name was spat upon. Besides, Scotland did not thrive during his reign. His campaigns against France ruined the country's commerce with its best trading partner. The period became known as the 'Seven ill years of King William's reign'.[7] And, then, a succession of bad harvests sent grain prices above the reaches of the poor. Scots in their thousands died of hunger and disease. By 1699 it was estimated that one in six was reduced to begging. It was little wonder that James Hogg, the shepherd-poet, wrote:

> And curs'd be they who helped on
> That wicked revolution
> Curs'd be the parliament, that day
> Who gave their confirmation
> And curs'd be every whining Whig
> And damn'd be the whole nation.[8]

7

THE NEW LORD DEPUTY

THE RISE OF TYRCONNELL

Circumstances in Ireland during the early months of 1689 were more favourable to James than in either of the kingdoms he had lost. The country was predominantly Catholic, and the great majority liked him for being of their own faith.[1]

Life had been relatively quiet in Ireland during the first few years of James' reign. The harshness which had characterised Cromwellian times had given way to a more tolerant period under Charles II, save during the Popish Plot, when fanaticism was rife. The land question had dominated public debate for years and its resolution had satisfied few. The Cromwellians felt disgruntled in being deprived of one-third of their holdings, whereas the Catholics were aggrieved to end up with 30% less than they held in 1641. The Protestant landed class monopolised office at all levels and were, until the accession of James, secure. To Catholics the advent of a monarch of their own religion seemed an opportunity to turn the tables on their oppressors.[2]

James had little regard, however, for the Irish people but thought it improper that Catholics should be excluded from office on religious grounds and was prepared to alleviate their grievances provided it did not greatly alienate Protestant opinion. His Irish revenue was derived mainly from Protestants and he was aware that if Catholics became too powerful, commercial confidence would slip and his yield diminish. Also, he knew that any signs of a Catholic advance in Ireland would alarm his English subjects and make them reluctant to acquiesce in changes at home.

There were cogent reasons, therefore, why Irish affairs had to be handled with caution and these were continually stressed by James' English advisors. These counsellors had not, however, reckoned on the skills of a man who had given almost thirty years service to the Stuarts and won the trust and respect of James. This was Richard Talbot, a self-confident and forceful politician who could advance his arguments with conviction.

There has been much dispute about Talbot's character and some about his abilities. Whig historians have abhorred him. 'He was,' says Macauley, 'one of the most mercenary of mankind', adding: ' … a cold blooded, far-seeing sycophant'. Bagwell found him: 'a canny, dissembling courtier'.[3] If all we read about him is true, he stooped particularly low in 1660 to curry favour. This was when he asserted that it was possible that he was the father of Anne Hyde's first (unborn) child. The allegation was made so that the Duke of York – had he wanted it – could escape the consequences of his own imprudence. This willingness to take the rap for James was, doubtless, the basis of the two mens' life-long friendship, and the key to Talbot's influence.

On the score of family background there is little to be said against Talbot. He was born in 1630 to an 'Old English' family of similar status to that of the Sarsfields. His father was a landowner and lawyer who gained sufficient favour with the ruling elite to be granted a baronetcy and lived comfortably at Carton, Co. Kildare, where Richard was brought up. Imbued with the values of the 'Old English' gentry, Richard was twelve when the strategic defence of these values necessitated the alliance negotiated on Crofty Hill.

As a young man Talbot served in the Irish army of Charles I and was unfortunate to be in Drogheda on the 10 September 1649 when the town was sacked by Cromwell. During the butchery he was injured and left for dead. The experience left him with a deep hatred for the 'New English'. Later, he turned up in Spain, and for years earned his living as a mercenary.

In 1653 he made the acquaintance of James in Flanders and both hit it off. Talbot's breezy, personable manner – and his propensity for boozing, whoring and duelling – impressed James, and he cut a dash around the Stuart court-in-exile. That he was a reckless type there can be no doubt. On one occasion he hatched a plot to assassinate Cromwell and travelled to London to execute it. He was betrayed by a double-agent, arrested and brought before the lord protector himself. Cromwell sought to impel him to reveal the names of his co-plotters, but Talbot remained silent. He then threatened the rack and said that he would spin the truth out of his bones. 'Spin me to a thread, if you like,' was Talbot's reply, 'I have nothing to confess, and can only invent lies'.[4] At that, the baffled dictator ordered that he be taken away. Later, on being transferred to the tower, he managed to bribe his guards and 'escaped' on a Thames boat. Thereafter, he went from strength to strength. Following the Restoration, he emerged as spokesman for the Irish Catholics, and became their champion.

'LILLYBURLERO'
One of James' initial acts on becoming king was to recall the Duke of Ormonde, the long serving Irish lord lieutenant. This move alarmed Protestants who felt change in the air. Their fears were heightened when Talbot was appointed commander-in-chief of the army and given a free hand in the administration. Earlier, James' brother-in-law, Lord Clarendon, a staunch Protestant, was made lord lieutenant. This was a disappointment to Catholics who had hoped for Talbot, but, in fact, Talbot behaved as if he were top dog and walked roughshod over Clarendon.

His first move was to remodel the army. He replaced Protestant officers with Catholics, who in many cases, were unqualified. Next, he appointed Catholics to positions on borough councils and other areas of authority. Clarendon offered little resistance and believed that Protestants had little to fear as long as the land settlement remained intact. He put his trust in James' assurances on this point. On arrival in Dublin in January 1686, Talbot had announced:

> I have the king's command to declare upon all occasions that, whatever imaginary apprehensions men may have, his majesty, hath no intention whatsoever of altering the land settlement.

But whatever James' intentions were, Talbot made no secret of his own. 'By God, my lord,' he exclaimed to Clarendon, 'these Acts of Settlement are damned things', and began a campaign to influence the king. The matter became live and a clamour was raised for repeal. Judge Rice said that he could drive a coach and six through the respective Acts and Sir William Petty compared them to St Sebastian, punctured with holes.

In January 1687, James reshuffled his privy council and among those to go was Clarendon's brother, the Earl of Rochester, the lord treasurer. In Ireland, Clarendon was removed, and to the consternation of Protestants was replaced by Talbot who was ennobled as Earl of Tyrconnell. The new appointment was not everywhere popular. The diarist, John Evelyn wrote:

> The Lord Tyrconnell has gone to succeed the lord lieutenant in Ireland to the astonishment of all sober men and to the evident destruction of the Protestants of that kingdom.[5]

Tyrconnell, as we now must call him, was sworn-in on 12 February 1687, and was immediately dubbed by Protestants 'Lying' Dick Talbot. He was also lampooned in a ditty called 'Lillyburlero' written (or at least published) by the Whig politician Lord Thomas Warton, which became popular:

> Ho brother Teig, dost hear de decree
> Dat we shall have a new deputy;
> Ho by my soul, it is Talbot
> And he will cut de English throat.

The words were a take-off of Irish brogue and enraged Catholics. The last verse was particularly insulting:

> Dare was an auld prophesy found in a bog
> That Ireland would be ruled by an ass and a dog
> And now the auld prophesy has come to pass
> For Talbot's a dog and James is an ass.

Tyrconnell was indifferent to the maledictions of his enemies and set about speeding up his pro-Catholic policies. He discerned that James' tenure was likely be short and realised that he must move quickly. His main bugbear was the Acts of Settlement. In a effort to abolish them he sent two Catholic judges – Rice and Nugent – to London to put the case for repeal. The London mob chased them through the streets with long sticks, on top of which potatoes were stuck; they mockingly cried out: 'make way for the Irish ambassadors'.

Tyrconnell was not put off. The judges reported that the king had heard them sympathetically and appeared convinced, but was dissuaded from acting by the privy council. Tyrconnell set about devising fresh tactics.

THE PROTESTANT REACTION

In all this, what were Irish Protestants to do? The tables had turned against them. The Catholics for so long shut off from power were at last making headway. In comparison the Protestants were small in number and could not hope to hold out against Tyrconnell.

The situation became volatile. Commercial life began to falter and in some areas industry ground to a halt. Rumours began to fly, and day after day wild and contradictory stories were heard. One day, it said that the Catholics were intent on avenging past wrongs and planning to destroy Protestants. The next, it was broadcast that the Catholics were to be the victims. Many began to fear for their lives. Protestants began to band together for their protection.

This was in the summer of 1688, around the time that Tyrconnell first received information of the conspiracy against James. He communicated his intelligence to the king, who received it incredulously. The Earl of Sunderland described it as nonsense and advised James to take it with a pinch of salt. 'How could your majesty believe that your affectionate son-in-law, who cast out Monmouth, could be of such evil intent?' was Sunderland's comment. But James was no fool, and was moved to take precautions. Tyrconnell was instructed to dispatch 3,000 troops – virtually half the Irish army – to England to strengthen the royal defences. This only exasperated English opinion, for a rumour circulated that the Irish had been sent across to massacre Protestants. The point seemed confirmed when a number of Irish soldiers became involved in riots and, mindlessly, attacked a Protestant church in Portsmouth. Their deployment also alienated the royal army, who saw them as barbarians and refused their company.

In Ulster the Protestants were privy to the moves taking place in The Hague. Their leaders – Blaney, Rawdon, Skeffington, Keames and Walker – felt that the time had come for action. They promoted the canard that the Catholics were about to repeat the attacks of 1641. The ruse they employed took the form of an anonymous letter planted in the street of Comber in Co. Down. It was addressed to a local nobleman and written in a semi-literate hand. It said:

> To my lord, this deliver with haste and care. Good my lord. I have written to let you know that all Irishmen Through Ireland is sworn that on the ninth of this month are all to fall on, to kill and murder, man, wife and child, and I desire your lordship to take care of yourself and of all others that are judged by our men to be heads, for whosoever of them can kill any of you, are to be given a captain's place.
>
> So my desire to your honour is to look to yourself and give other noblemen warning and go not out either night or day without a good guard with you, and let no Irishman near you.
>
> So that is all from one who was your father's friend, and is your friend and will be, though I dare not be known as yet for fear of my life.[6]

Similar letters were 'found' elsewhere, but were unquestionably hoaxes. No evidence has ever come to light of a planned attack on Protestants, but the anxieties aroused had the intended effect.

The Protestant leaders broke cover and called their able bodied to arms. A meeting was held at Hillsborough, Co. Down, and an 'Antrim Association' formed to 'protect the lives, property and religion of Protestants from the imminent danger indicated by the increase in popish levies'. This last point was a reference to Tyrconnell's efforts to strengthen his ranks following the dispatch of men to England.

Other counties followed: Protestants in Armagh and Monaghan organised under Lord Blaney of Castleblaney; those in Derry, Donegal and Tyrone came together under Major Gustave Hamilton, a recently dismissed officer. In Cavan, they organised under local leaders and in Sligo and Leitrim chose the Honourable Childley Coote and Lord Kingston as their commanders.

Each county had its own control structure, but all came under a general council at Hillsborough, chaired by Lord Mount-Alexander. The mobilisation was not confined to Ulster, although elsewhere Protestants were too few to combine effectively. In Bandon and Kenmare they were strong enough to take control of the towns, and sizeable groups in Mallow and Charleville were active.

These moves were not unforeseen by Tyrconnell. In January 1689 he issued warrants for 40,000 new levies and Catholics enthusiastically responded. Their numbers presented him with a problem: he had insufficient uniforms and weapons to go around. Many were given antique pikes and wooden staves. His officers came almost exclusively from the 'Old English' class and were often decidedly amateurish. Sarsfield was brought from London, and with Lieutenant-General Justin Mac-Carthy and a few others, tried to separated the wheat from the chaff. By year-end, the listings showed forty-five infantry regiments, eight of dragoons, seven of cavalry and a life guard. The quality of all, with the exception of the horse, was poor.

Tyrconnell now had a great need for money. There were insufficient funds to maintain a large army and the men were often unpaid. In order to keep body and soul together they were allowed to fend for themselves and frequent complaints of plundering and cattle-driving were heard. When an envoy from Enniskillen complained about the indiscipline of the levies in Fermanagh he was told that the lord deputy could not prevent unruly types from looting and that people should look to their own defences.

Towards the end of February there were rumours of a planned Protestant 'coup' and Tyrconnell set about disarming the 'disloyal' of Dublin. Protestants were ordered to hand-in their weapons or 'run the risk of the ill consequences which may fall from disorderly soldiery'. A search of Trinity College and other 'suspect' centres yielded a number of weapons and these were distributed among the levies. With these supplies Tyrconnell was anxious to continue recruiting and sought financial assistance from Whitehall. When Sarsfield returned to London on 2 October he carried a letter from Tyrconnell to James. This has not survived, but is referred to in a bulletin dispatched a day later, which said:

> I have writ at large by Sarsfield to Yr Ma'ty yesterday and will not give your Ma'ty any other trouble in this but to beg you to read my letter of this day's date to my lord president, and to consider well the necessetye thear is for yr. Service, of dispatching with all good speed what I desired in it: as well as what I writ Yr Ma'ty yesterday, being much the same thing.
>
> I beg Sir, I may have a quick dispatch to my letters, for noe time is to be lost in raising new forces: I shall make them subsist as well as I can, tho the revenue do fail, w'ch it will clearly doe out of hand, for all trade is now given over here … but we have plenty of meat and drink here …
>
> The Lord Jesus bless you and preserve you from the power of yr enemies.[7]

But time was running out for Tyrconnell. A few weeks later, William disembarked at Torbay and the 'Glorious Revolution' became underway.

Ireland's fate was now balanced on a knife-edge. It was said that strange omens were seen in the sky. No less a figure than Lieutenant-General Justin MacCarthy was reported to have seen two armies fighting in the clouds over Dublin. Few doubted that this was a portend of things to come.[8]

8

A WINTER OF DISCONTENT

When James II sailed down the Thames for the last time on 18 December 1688 he was to all intents and purposes a prisoner. The royal barge which took him to Gravesend was accompanied by vessels containing Dutch soldiers. He was taken to Rochester and placed under house arrest. The queen and her infant had already escaped to France and it was known that James wished to join them. This suited William admirably, for as long as the king remained in England he could claim to be the *de facto* monarch and demand the right to be heard in any political settlement. If he left, it could be argued that he had abdicated.

At Rochester James was given every chance to slip away. On the evening of 22 December he was joined by his eighteen-year-old illegitimate son, James FitzJames, Duke of Berwick, and after bedtime the guards looked the other way as they slipped down to the waterway where a sloop was waiting. Soon they were on the ship, *Henrietta*, and making their way from English waters. The vessel was so modest that they were lodged in a cabin with scarcely room to sit. Berwick later wrote:

> … yet there was cause for mirth when Captain Trevanion went to fry the king some bacon, for by misfortune the frying pan having a hole in it, he was forced to seal it with a pitched rag, and to tie an old can with cord to make it hold the drink put in it; however the king never ate or drank more heartily in his life.[1]

After a wretched crossing the *Henrietta* arrived at Ambleteuse on Christmas Day, and Berwick was dispatched to Versailles to announce to the king of France that his Britannic majesty had arrived. Louis extended a warm welcome and made much of the exiled monarch. Weeks earlier when the queen and her infant arrived he had placed the palace of St Germains, outside Paris, at their disposal. On the dressing table Mary Beatrice had found a casket containing 6,000 pistoles (£20,000 at 1688 values) – a present from Louis, who even laid on toys for the infant.

Ever gentlemanly, Louis went to St Germains to greet James on arrival, and after the two monarchs had embraced, he took his guest to the room where Mary Beatrice was, announcing: 'I bring you someone who you will be pleased to see'. When the time came for Louis to withdraw, he refused to allow James to see him to the door. 'This is your house,' he said, 'and when I come here you will do the honours to me, just as I will to you, when you come to Versailles'.[2]

James did indeed go to Versailles on numerous occasions both to dine with Louis and to attend the entertainments which were regularly held there. He appeared, however, to take greater pleasure from the stag and wolf hunts arranged for him in the forest at Marly, and he was always in front with the dogs.

But James was never the same after he left England. He underwent a physical and mental deterioration and seemed permanently perplexed by his plight. He developed a marked stammer and lost his facility to speak French fluently. Also, he became convinced that his downfall was due to God's displeasure and began to spend hours in religious meditation, beating his breast and praying for consolation. The traits which drew most comment were his indifference to all that had happened, and seeming lack of determination to recover his crown.

But if James was morose and lethargic there were some around him who were the opposite. William's coming had induced a number of the king's lieges to flee to France and from the beginning they were persistent in seeking French help to put him back on the throne. It was noted that the queen was more active in this regard than her husband, and that she firmly intimated a resolve to return to England.

A court-in-exile was established but it was beset by financial problems, for James and Mary Beatrice were virtually penniless. The queen had brought away some of her jewels, but James had come with practically nothing save his coronation ring. The *pistoles* had to be used to replenish their wardrobes and to provide the basics for their courtiers. In the circumstances, Louis granted James a pension of fifty thousand francs a month, but it was scarcely enough. The court had to be run on the most economical lines, and those who dined at the king's table remarked how frugal it was. Still in the opening months of 1689 the situation was far from discouraging. In Scotland the highlands were in arms under Dundee, and Tyrconnell controlled the greater part of Ireland. Everything depended on the attitude of the French. James could not be restored without their assistance, but the problem was that although Louis was willing to be a genial host he was not prepared to compromise the French interest for cousinly sentiment.

The man with the greatest influence in France, at this time, was François-Michel le Tellier, the Marquis de Louvois. He was, after Louis, the most powerful figure at court. As minister for war he had perfected the military machine which held half of Europe in dread. Unfortunately, he had a low opinion of James and was not impressed by his retinue. The exiled monarch, in his view, was a busted flush. It would, he figured, be foolish to risk too much for him.[3]

Yet, de Louvois saw advantages for France in James' predicament and was willing to suggest limited assistance. The exiled king could usefully keep Ireland and Britain in turmoil without the French having to make a commitment to a Stuart restoration. Moreover, France could negotiate a *quid pro quo* for any outlay which she may incur. On de Louvois' advice, therefore, a bargain was struck. Louis agreed to lend his cousin a contingent of troops to assist him in Ireland, but only on condition that an equal number of Irishmen were enlisted in the service of France. To this, the Jacobites agreed.

SHUTTING OF THE GATES

In Ireland the 'Comber Letter' and its replicas had achieved their purpose. News of their content spread through a gullible Protestant population. The 'Letter' itself transferred to Belfast and from there to George Canning in Garvagh, Co. Londonderry, who passed it to Colonel George Phillips, an ex-Mayor of Derry, who lived at Limavady. Phillips read it with alarm, as on that very day – 6 December 1688 – there was more than a little local commotion. An unruly regiment of Catholic troops (known as 'redshanks' from the colour of their stockings) had entered the town accompanied by a camp-following of ill-disciplined youths and unsavoury women, and created an uproar. They were under the command of the Earl of Antrim and en route to Derry. Phillips grew suspicious.

In Derry – a Protestant city which had been at loggerheads with James – matters were unsettled. Twelve months earlier, its charter had been revised and a predominantly Catholic corporation appointed. It is not definite whether its new mayor, Cormac O'Neill was a Catholic, but his wife certainly was. Until late autumn, it had been garrisoned by Protestant troops, under the command of Lord Mountjoy. The Protestant citizens had seen these men as their protection from Catholic marauders who roamed the countryside. To their dismay Tyrconnell suddenly recalled the men to Dublin. The city was to be re-garrisoned with a force under the Earl of Antrim which was scheduled to arrive on 20 November. But the earl would only recruit six-footers and had difficulty in finding his requirements. The delay meant that the new garrison was unavailable when Mountjoy's men left. The citizens were thus unprotected at a time of mounting tension. Several public meetings were held in the city and a lawyer, David Cairns, argued that the citizens should provide for their own security.

In Limivady, Phillips watched the antics of the redshanks with increasing alarm and wrote to a friend in Derry, Alderman Samuel Norman, advising him of what to expect. He recommended that the alderman 'should consult with the sober people of the town and set out the danger' before admitting the rabble. A courier was dispatched, riding at night, to deliver the message.

On reaching Derry, the horseman found one of the leading citizens, Alderman Tompkins, reading a document from the steps of the market house to an exited crowd. It was the 'Comber Letter' which had been received earlier. When the letter was read, the crown froze. The news that a horde of virtual desporados were about to descend upon them seemed to confirm their fears. Were they to be massacred? Did not the 'Comber Letter' predict their fate? Soon the streets were filled with exited, panic-stricken people anxiously discussing their fate. The leading citizens went into consultation, while some of the younger bloods argued that the gates should be immediately closed. Others counselled caution.

What was to be done? Was the threat real? What would be the consequences of refusing to admit the king's troops? Around midday, a sentry shouted that the redshanks were approaching. It was only an advance party who had arrived on the east bank of the Foyle. The citizens watched as two men, a lieutenant and an ensign, rowed across the water. They had come, the lieutenant announced, to make arrangements for the reception of King James' new garrison.

A technical hitch in their warrants – they were unsigned – allowed the citizens to play for time. The leaders continued to confer, some arguing for the exclusion of the redshanks, some not. Dr Ezekial Hopkins, the Protestant bishop of Derry, was asked for his advice. The old prelate, temperamentally cautious, and by vocation against resistance, preached peace and submission, and advised that the troops be admitted.

By now more redshanks had crossed the river and were within a few hundred yards of the Ferryquay gate. At this critical moment, nine apprentice boys, tired of the argument and indecision going on around them, sprang to action. Lead by young Henry Campsie they drew their swords and rushed to the main guard house, forced the guardsman to hand over the keys and then closed the Ferryquay gate in the face of the oncoming soldiers. Then, joined by four others, they sped to secure all the gates. The people's relief was palpable and a huge cheer went up. A soldier, James Morrison, jumped on the walls, and shouted to the redshanks to be off. They began to hector and hurl abuse, but when he trained a gun on them, they fled.

The Citizens' Defence

Not everyone was happy with the action taken. The deputy mayor and two sheriffs urged that the gates be reopened, and upbraided one of their colleagues, Alderman Horace Kennedy, for inciting the impetuous youths. They ordered that the ammunition magazine, located at the old medieval towerhouse, be secured. They were outmanoeuvred by the Apprentice Boys who reached it first. It was guarded by a Catholic called Linegar, who fired at them, hitting young Campsie in the arm. This inflamed the situation and the guardsman was seized and beaten.

The fact that Linegar was a Catholic drew the mob's attention to his co-religionists. A few days before it had been rumoured that the

Catholic clergy had urged their congregations to pray for 'a secret intention'. It was remembered also that a friar had preached from the steps of the Market House on the theme of Saul's Destruction of the Amalekites and on the iniquity of saving those whom the lord had doomed. A wave of anti-popish hysteria swept through the mob and all Catholic residents were expelled from the city. They hurried through the gates with abuse ringing in their ears.

Others also left. One was Bishop Hopkins who warned that James' wrath would befall those who rebelled. Next, a citizens coup established an all-Protestant Corporation and John Campsie – the father of the Apprentice leader – was appointed mayor and issued a proclamation:

> We have resolved to stand upon our guard and to defend our walls and not to admit any papist whatsoever to quarter among us.

The new leaders lost no time in warning Lord Antrim against a further approach and David Cairns organised the menfolk into military units. The following week he set out for London to solicit help from William.

When news of these events reached Tyrconnell, he immediately instructed Lord Mountjoy to return to Derry and restore royal authority. Soon he received a curious letter from the new corporation which ascribed everything to providence. They said that God had intervened and stirred up the people for their own safety. The letter pleaded that the closing of the gates did not impinge on their allegiance, and ran:

> It pleased God, who watches over us, so to order things that when (the 'Redshanks') were ready to enter the city, a great number of the younger and some of the meaner sort of inhabitants ran happily to the gates and shut them, loudly denying entry to such guests, and obstinately refusing obedience to us. At first we were amazed at the enterprise and apprehensive of the many ill circumstances and consequences that might result from so rash an undertaking; but since that … we began to consider it as a special instance of God's mercy towards us, that we were not delivered over as a prey onto them and that it pleased Him to stir up the spirits of the people so unexpectedly to provide for their and our common safety, and preservation: Wherefore we do declare and remonstrate to the world, that we have resolved to stand upon our guard, and to defend our walls, and not to admit any Papist whatsoever to quarter among us, so we are determined to preserve in our duty and loyalty to our sovereign lord the king.[4]

Tyrconnell was not deceived by this sophist document and was confident that Mountjoy would bring the rebels to heel. But Mountjoy got a mixed reception. As a Protestant, he was admitted to the city with two Protestant companies under the command of Colonel Lundy; his Catholic companies were refused entry and had to go into quarters at Strabane. Negotiations began, and after much wrangling an agreement was reached. It provided for the permanent exclusion of Lord Antrim's troops, the installation of a Protestant garrison, and the appointment of Lundy as governor. When Mountjoy returned to Dublin, he incurred the lord deputy's displeasure. Tyrconnell suspected that he had conspired with the enemy.

The citizen's defiance continued. A committee was formed to raise money for arms and an agent dispatched to Scotland to purchase some. In February 1689 when William and Mary were proclaimed in London, the news reached Derry within hours. There were whoops of joy and people danced in the streets. The corporation formally announced that it had changed its allegiance.

ENNISKILLEN RESISTS

On the day that Derry closed its gates – 7 September 1688 – a copy of the 'Comber Letter' reached Enniskillen. Built on an island between Upper and Lower Lough Erne it consisted of about eighty houses clustered around an old castle. Since the days of the plantations it was predominantly Protestant and had successfully resisted attack during the rebellion of 1641.

As in Derry, the 'Comber Letter' provoked alarm. This was intensified when a communique was received from Dublin saying that two companies of infantry were to be quartered in the town. Immediately everyone became keyed-up. Three men, William Browning, Robert Clarke and William MacCormick – shortly to be joined by James Ewart and Allan Carthcart – came together to oppose the proposal. They knew that William was about to land in England and surmised that this would spark a civil war in Ireland. Enniskillen, they felt, would then be of vital strategic importance. If its militia could hold the line with Ballyshannon to the west, it could effectively block incursions to Ulster from the southwest.

To deny admission to Tyrconnell's infantry was the immediate task, but the town was poorly equipped. Its arsenal held only ten barrels of powder and twenty firelocks, moreover fewer than eighty able-bodied men could be mustered. Besides, not everyone was in agreement. Captain Corry, a retired army officer, was vehemently opposed to any move to exclude the infantry.

On Wednesday 12 December, a tip-off was received from Clones, Co. Monaghan, that a Captain Nugent and a number of officers had arrived en-route for Enniskillen. This brought matters to a head, but there was an argument before it was decided to seek the views of Gustave Hamilton, the most influential man in the area, who lived outside Enniskillen. MacCormick was detailed to ride out and put the views of the opposing parties to him. Hamilton unhesitatingly came down on the side of resistance and undertook to lead the citizens.

On Sunday 16 December, information was received that the infantry had reached Lismella, a few miles from Enniskillen, and were advancing apace. Most of the townsfolk were attending divine service, but broke from their worship and ran to arms. Hamilton counselled that the best form of defence was attack, and mustered a force to march out to meet the infantry head-on. They must have looked formidable because on seeing them, the infantry turned and fled in the direction of Maguiresbridge.

During the remaining weeks of 1688, the Enniskilleners organised themselves. In the New Year, Hamilton was appointed governor and announced that he 'would admit no popish army'.

The men took an oath:

> I … do hereby testify, and upon the Holy Evangelists swear, that I will own and acknowledge Gustave Hamilton Esq., chief governor of this town and shall give due obedience to him and my superior officers in all his and their commands, and shall to the utmost of my power and ability, defend him, them, and this place, with the country adjacent, together with the Protestant religion and interest, with my life and fortune, against all that shall endeavour to subvert the same. So help me God and the holy contents of this book.[5]

Tyrconnell Plays his Cards

Tyrconnell resumed recruiting. He appealed to the heads of the old Catholic families and their response was instinctive. They rushed to his colours and in a short time regiments of O'Reilly, MacMahon, MacGuinness, Maguire, O'Donnell, Nugent, O'Neill, O'More and O'Dempsey and others were in the field – totalling nearly 20,000 and all recruited from their respective hinterlands. Having been deprived of bearing arms for so long, and thus unprovided with them, the new recruits had few weapons. Some were equipped at the expense of their commanders, but it was impossible to supply everyone. It was rumoured (and believed), however, that an immense armament was being prepared in France and that its arrival would rectify everything. All that came, however, was a communique from James, addressed to Tyrconnell, delivered by an emissary called Rooth. It said:

> I send this bearer, Captain Rooth to you to give you notice of my being here, and to be informed of how things are with you, so that accordingly I may take measures; hoping that you will be able to defend yourself and support my interest till Summer at least. I am sure that you will do it to the upmost of your power, and I hope that this king here (a reference to Louis) will so press the Hollanders that the Prince of Orange will not have men to spare to attack you. In the meantime, all I can get this king to do is to send 7 or 8,000 muskets; he not being willingly to venture more arms or men till he knows the condition you are in, so that it will be absolutely necessary that you send back this bearer as so as may be … For more I refer

you to this bearer, who will give you an account of how we all got away and how kindly I have been received here.

Jacobus Rex[6]

There was little in this of practical benefit to Tyrconnell. If he were to hold out he needed munitions and money. In his reply he showed his political skills by stressing the urgency of his needs, and adding:

if your majesty will in person come hither ... I will be responsible to you, that you shall be entirely master of this kingdom and of everything in it, and, Sir, I beg you to consider whether you can with honour continue where you are when you may possess a kingdom of your own.

This was an adroit call to James to accept his responsibilities. And it was timely, as James was being pushed similarly by his hosts. A French emissary, called de Pontis, filed a report which stated that the Irish Jacobites could not hold out without aid and added: 'should sufficient men, money and arms be provided they, so strengthened, could even carry the fight into England'. In the French naval archives there is a memorandum, evidently based on this report, entitled: 'Reasons why the king of England should go to Ireland'. It describes the favourable psychological effect which James' presence would have on the Irish and says that it may even divide his opponents, some of whom 'still render nominal allegiance to him'.

When writing to James, Tyrconnell hit upon a ploy to get rid of Mountjoy, whom he did not trust. He proposed that Mountjoy should bring his letter to St Germains and explain to James that conditions were such in Ireland that the administration had no alternative but to come to terms with the Prince of Orange. This view accorded with Mountjoy's sentiments and he was pleased to do Tyrconnell's bidding.

But Mountjoy fell into a trap. Tyrconnell sent a second envoy, Sir Stephen Rice, in whom he had full confidence. Both left Dublin on 20 January. When they reached St Germains, Sir Stephen handed James a secret note from Tyrconnell, which stated that Ireland was overwhelmingly loyal but that Mountjoy was covertly supporting the enemy and should be detained. James, knowing Tyrconnell well, had no reason to doubt him, and Mountjoy was thrown into the Bastille.

The recommendation that he should travel to Ireland himself was less well received by James. He felt that he was being invited to an unattractive land that he did not know. Madame de Sevigne wrote:

He seems to prefer to remain where he is, and dislikes any idea of going among the Hibernians.[7]

Louvois and his friends also put heavy pressure on James. Vauban, for instance, took the view that going to Ireland was a responsibility which

James could not avoid.[8] Yet James dithered and there was much speculation about his intentions. As the days passed it was said that he was abusing French hospitality and being timorous in pressing his own affairs.

One evening Louis was holding a court in the great Apollo drawing-room at Versailles when a messenger arrived with a letter from James. Louis glanced at it, and, wishing to give those present the latest news, passed it to the archbishop of Rheims to read aloud. The prelate began spiritedly but suddenly stopped short. He had come to a private passage, and being a man of tact tried to skip it. Louis, realising his problem, snatched the paper, and those present were more curious than ever to learn its contents. They were not informed at the time, but James had finally made up his mind to go to Ireland.

JAMES LEAVES FRANCE

Sarsfield, who had been at St Germains since Christmas, was busy preparing for James' departure. In February he was involved in moving troops belonging to James to the coast and in picking men for various posts. Meanwhile, Louis himself was selecting the officers who would have over-all command. The first chosen was Marechal de Camp Maumont de Fontage (known simply as 'Maumont') a major general of considerable merit, who was promoted to lieutenant-general. Next, came Pusignan and Lery, brigadiers, raised to major generals, and Boisseleau, a captain in the guards, to act as adjutant general; also chosen was L'Estrade of the life guards, who was to be quartermaster-general of the cavalry. Among the Jacobites, were the Duke of Berwick, who since leaving England had acquired considerable influence over his father; and his brother, Henry FitzJames, the grand prior. Prominent among the Irish contingent were two Hamilton brothers and Sarsfield.

An interesting appointment was that of General Conrad von Rosen, a Livonian, with twenty years service in the French army. He was known to be a good cavalry officer, but had not impressed as a general. His appointment as commander-in-chief was a surprise. The command had been intended for Lauzun, but he had fallen foul of the court. It has been said that Louis could not have made a worse choice. Von Rosen was lacking in capacity and, as Berwick later wrote: 'was subject to passion … even to a degree of madness'.

While this was in progress, a fleet under Admiral Gabaret was assembled at Brest. On 25 February, James went to Paris to offer prayers at the cathedral of Nôtre Dame. Then, he drove to Versailles where Louis received him for the last time. The court had assembled and both kings wore violet in mourning for the queen of Spain who had just died. When the time came for James' departure, Louis rose and said:

I hope, Sir, never to see you again. Never-the-less, if fortune decrees that we are to meet, you will find me always the same as you have found me.[9]

A few days later James left for Brest. As soon as it was known that he had quit St Germains, the frigate *Soleil d'Afrique*, with Lord Dungan on board, was sent to Ireland to announce his prospective arrival. It was assumed that his fleet would follow closely, but contrary winds entailed a delay. On 15 March all seemed well and the anchors were raised. But the departure was again delayed. In a sharp gale James' ship collided with another and her bowsprit was carried away. This necessitated a repair and the fleet did not finally put to sea until 17 March 1689.[10]

HAMILTON TURNS HIS COAT

Not long after Tyrconnell had written to James, a not dissimilar letter was dispatched by the Hillsborough council to William. Captain Baldwin Leighton took it to London and urged the Irish Society[11] (whose members were Williamites to a man) to use its good offices with the new king. A few weeks later William replied, but his response, while encouraging, only amounted to a promise. He wrote:

> We are resolved to imply the most speedy means in our power to rescue you from the oppressions and terrors which you live under … in the meantime … We understand you are putting yourself in a position of defence … We are persuaded that there are even of the Roman Communion many who are desirous to live peacefully and to not approve of the violent and arbitrary proceedings of some who pretend to be in authority.[12]

Leighton, however, brought back other news. He had been told that 15,000 men were being held in Liverpool in readiness for Ireland. But William, as yet, appeared reluctant to commit troops as communications were being opened with Tyrconnell. There was speculation that Tyrconnell might betray James and come to terms with William. It was known that people close to the lord deputy advocated this course and that Tyrconnell himself had, obliquely, given the impression that he was prepared to do a deal. John Keating, one of the few Protestant judges on the Irish bench, was given the task of putting out 'feelers' to London. He wrote to Sir John Temple, the Irish solicitor-general (who was in London), and who had contacts with William through his brother, Sir William Temple, a former ambassador to The Hague.

Keating intimated that in certain circumstances Tyrconnell could be persuaded to yield his authority and disband the Irish army. The letter was taken seriously, and an emissary was picked to go to Dublin on William's behalf. The man chosen was Richard Hamilton who had commanded one of the Irish units sent to England. Since the coming of William, Hamilton had been a prisoner but, because of family connec-

tions – and friendship with Tyrconnell – was deemed suitable to negotiate, besides, he had indicated a will to win Tyrconnell over.

On reaching Dublin, Hamilton turned his coat. He urged Tyrconnell to reject William's pledge that under the new dispensation Catholics
in Ireland would be allowed the freedoms which they had in the reign
of Charles II. Tyrconnell, by this time, had come off the fence, and was
not interested in a deal. He welcomed Hamilton and applauded him.
The Earl of Danby had earlier advised William to have no truck with
Hamilton and suggested that a squadron of ships dispatched to Dublin
would be a more effective way of winning Tyrconnell's co-operation.

THE PACIFICATION OF MUNSTER

Outside of Ulster, Ireland was virtually under Tyrconnell's control. In a
few areas, like Cork and Kerry, small numbers of Protestants offered
resistance. The strongest resistance was in Bandon – then known as
Bandonbridge – about twenty miles from Cork city. The town dated
from the Desmond Rebellion of 1583 when the land in the region was
sequestered and given to settlers. Its walls enclosed about thirty acres
on both sides of the Bandon river, and its most imposing building was
the Anglican church which had the distinction of being the oldest post
Reformation church in Ireland. The town had always been violently
anti-Catholic. A sign on one of its gates bore the legend: 'Turk, Jew or
atheist may enter here – but never a Papist'. A Catholic wit, not to be out-
done, was said to have scrawled underneath: 'whoever wrote this wrote
it well – for the same is written on the gates of hell'.[13]

In 1687 a new charter was imposed on Bandon and a fresh garrison stationed there. This had an uneasy relationship with the townspeople and when William became king, the Bandonians were among
the first to declare for him. They disarmed the garrison, killed a soldier,
and ran up a flag with the words: 'No Surrender' (they were the first to
use the phrase). Tyrconnell confronted them by dispatching Lieutenant-
General Justin MacCarthy to clean out 'that nest of rebels'. The Bandonians were defiant but MacCarthy's men marched in on a Sunday
morning whilst they were at divine service and affected a take-over.
Two Jacobite pipers strode up the aisle and struck up 'The Humours of
Bandon' and 'The King Shall Enjoy His Own Again'. MacCarthy demanded that the rebel leaders be identified and handed over. The townsfolk refused – an incident still commemorated by the inscription *Ne Cede*
on the towns coat of arms – and MacCarthy decided to chastise them.
He burnt much of the town, installed a new garrison and withdrew.

The next day – known as 'Black Monday' – the Protestants rose again,
killed eight of the new garrison, and put the rest to flight. MacCarthy
was halfway to Cork when he heard the news. He returned immediately and crushed the revolt. This time a number of leading townsfolk

were rounded up and were about to be hung when a young clergyman named Nicholas Brady came forward and pleaded for their lives. He must have been persuasive for MacCarthy held his hand. Some of the citizens – though not the ring-leaders – were pardoned on paying an indemnity and promising restitution to the bereaved. MacCarthy wanted more, and ordered that a further section of the town be put to the torch. But Brady intervened again, and mollified him. MacCarthy settled for a promise that a section of the walls be demolished, and hit on the bright idea of allowing the main rebels to plead for their lives before the king.

If MacCarthy was lenient in Bandon, he was less so elsewhere. In the following days he suppressed a revolt at Castlemartyr, led by Captain Henry Boyle, the father of the Earl of Shannon (and a relative of the Earl of Cork). Next, he put down an uprising by William O'Brien, the second Earl of Inchiquin, son of the infamous Murrough O'Brien, known as 'Murrough of the Burnings'. These operations added to MacCarthy's reputation and he became known as the 'Pacificator of Munster'.

THE BRAKE OF DROMORE

Following these incidents, the struggle took off in earnest. The logistics seemed to favour the Jacobites. In the north they held Carrickfergus and Charlemont and in the south, all the forts on the Shannon from Lough Allen to Limerick. Each was reinforced and put on a defensive footing. Kilkenny, Waterford and Cork were given stronger garrisons and towns like Dundalk were secured from incursions by insurgents from Armagh and Monaghan. Having distributed men to these posts and elsewhere, Tyrconnell found that he had only 6,000 or so left. These he split into three corps: one, to remain in Munster under MacCarthy, the others to be deployed in the northern zone. Of the latter, one was placed under Lord Galmoy and charged with reducing Williamite strongholds in the north-west, principally in Sligo, Fermanagh and Cavan; the other, under Lieutenant-General Richard Hamilton, was to penetrate Ulster from the north-east.[14]

The Williamites had already made an assault on Carrickfergus. A friar named O'Heggerty had witnessed this action and reported that the Protestants were, for the most part, short of arms and that many were 'unfit for service'. Tyrconnell instructed Hamilton to move against them. He sent a Presbyterian clergyman, Alexander Osbourne, to Hillsborough to offer the council terms. In return for their surrender and the handing over of weapons and horses, he said he was prepared to grant a pardon. He made sure to stipulate the alternative: should they resist, they would be crushed.

Osbourne arrived to find the council in session. In an act of double-dealing he urged its members not to accept the offer. They had little difficulty in agreeing with him and sent Tyrconnell a defiant reply. Their purpose, they said, was to defend their religious and civil liberties and they would not lay down their arms until these were secure.

But events overtook the council. Hamilton's army was virtually upon them. He left Drogheda on 8 March with 2,000 men and a few days later swept through Dundalk and Newry. Soon he was between Loughbrickland and the river Bann, and sent his second-in-command, Colonel Butler, to make a reconnaissance of enemy positions. Butler reported that the Williamites were entrenched near the village of Dromore (then known as Dromore-Iveagh), on the northern side of the Lagan; their numbers were greater than those of the Jacobites and they were under the command of Lord Mount-Alexander.

Hamilton was unperturbed by their strength and decided to attack. He broke camp on 14 March, crossed the Bann, and moved towards them. Mount-Alexander drew up his cavalry in readiness, but following a lightening charge by Hamilton's dragoons, the Williamites fell back in confusion. By this time, Hamilton's infantry, which had hung behind, crossed the Bann and a further charge was ordered. The Williamites did not fight but fled towards Dromore. Half-way through the village they were overtaken by Hamilton's cavalry and cut to pieces. Four hundred lost their lives, and the rest fled in all directions. The rout became known as 'The Brake of Dromore'.

The Protestant Flight

Lord Mount-Alexander did not break breath until he reached Hillsborough. He threw his badly bruised survivors into the defence of the town and instructed that, if overpowered, they should fall back on Coleraine. Believing his cause to be in ruin he left for Donaghadee and took a ship to England.

Meanwhile, Hamilton allowed his men 'to secure the prizes of victory', and they ran amuck in Dromore. Then, they rested for twenty-four hours before pushing on to Hillsborough. The town collapsed quickly and, predictably, 'the council' vanished. Soon news was received that Sir Arthur Rawdon (known as 'The Cock of the North') and 4,000 Williamites were approaching from the direction of Lisburn. Hamilton was again unperturbed by enemy numbers (although, this time, they were exaggerated) and drew up his men. But Rawdon failed to arrive. He had a change of heart on meeting some of the Hillsborough garrison escaping the town. They told him that Hamilton's army was too strong and too well entrenched to be dislodged. Judging prudence as the best policy, Rawdon drew off and headed for Coleraine.

The taking of Hillsborough was a boost to the Jacobites. It was not only the headquarters of 'the council', but an entrepot for stores and munitions which Hamilton wanted to get his hands on. By the end of the month all of Down and Antrim were under heel and droves of refugees were rushing to the seaports. More than sixty years later, John Black, a Belfast merchant, recalled the Protestants' exodus:

> My father's family by a night-time alarm at Belfast, left their furnished house, when a horseman came with the news that the Irish were upon us, sparing neither age nor sex, and intent on putting all to the sword. I was put aboard my father's ship, the *John* which immediately set sail.[15]

Further accounts refer to the ports of Larne and Portstewart being 'black' with people as men, women and children sat huddled on the beaches waiting for any form of sea transport.

THE STRUGGLE FOR CROM CASTLE

In the north-west Lord Galmoy's force was less successful. His area of operations was uninviting. The terrain held numerous lakes and tributaries and was so studded with islands and marshland that it was virtually impassable in bad weather by any but locals.

Galmoy wanted to seize Enniskillen, but in recent months it had been strengthened by Protestants from Sligo, Leitrim and Cavan. Besides, it had found an able commander in a young man named Thomas Lloyd, from Croghan, near Boyle, Co. Roscommon, who was dubbed 'Little Cromwell'.

Knowledge of Galmoy's approach preceded him, and advance parties on both sides began to haggle when he issued a threat to hang Enniskillen's clergymen 'higher than Harmen' – an altitude (according to the *Book of Ester*) of some fifty cubits. During the parlay an exchange of prisoners was agreed. Captain Brian Maguire, whom the Enniskilleners had captured some time before, was to be swapped for Captain Woolston Dixie, the son of the dean of Kilmore. Maguire was handed over, but Galmoy broke his word. He had Dixie and another Protestant officer court-martialled for possession of Williamite documents. Both were hung from signposts in Belturbet. Nothing could be more calculated to infuriate the Williamites, who now resolved to oppose Galmoy tooth and nail.

To take Enniskillen, Galmoy had first to seize Crom Castle, an outpost about 20 miles south. This fortress was impregnable to light infantry; so he opted for a rather quaint ploy. He constructed fake cannon – improvised from tin and bound with buckram – and placed the apparatus within range of the walls. The ruse fooled nobody. The defenders trained their long guns – normally used for duck shooting on Lough Erne – on the Jacobites and picked off several of them. Galmoy was also taken by surprise when the Williamites sallied out and drove his men from their trenches, killing about forty. His position became untenable when he learned that 'Little Cromwell' and about 200 horse were on their way to relieve the castle. He raised the siege and withdrew into Co. Cavan. This round, decidedly, went to the Enniskilleners and left them free to develop into 'rough riders' – mounted guerrillas, whose *modus operandi* entailed going on lightening raids into enemy territory to disrupt lines of communication. In the months ahead they would be a major thorn in the side of the Jacobites.

9

THE KING'S OTHER ISLAND

A KING'S WELCOME

James arrived in his Irish kingdom on 22 March 1689. He landed at Kinsale accompanied by about 400 French officers, a few hundred Scotch and English Jacobites and numerous Irish exiles. He also brought modest amounts of arms, ammunition and money.

He did not disembark at once as local accommodation had not been arranged, besides, there were no horses to draw his carriage. When the French tried to requisition their requirements the peasantry angrily drove their animals into the hills. Two days passed before he could leave for Cork, where his reception was more cordial. Everyone, one account says, 'poured forth' to greet him. MacCarthy, who held the Munster command, laid on a military extravaganza and Tyrconnell was present to kiss the royal hand. After the formalities, the lord deputy gave an account of his stewardship. James was pleased and, there and then, raised Tyrconnell to the rank of duke. MacCarthy's services were also recognised: he was created Lord Mountcashel and promised a place on the privy council.

Before the courtesies ended the Bandonians were brought forward to plead for their lives. James jumped at the opportunity to show his goodwill towards his Protestant subjects and ostentatiously granted them pardons. In the hearing of all he announced that he had been lenient to show that they 'may know that they had a generous king'. He used the occasion to present himself in a favourable light at home. In a decla-

James landing in Kinsale

ration to his English subjects he said: 'The calumnies of our enemies are now shown to be false, for since our arrival in Ireland we have made it our chief concern to satisfy our Protestant subjects'. It is doubtful whether those sentiments cheered the Bandonians. Shortly afterwards about thirty of them crossed to Bristol never to return.[1]

But James did excite the enthusiasm of others. After a brief stay in Cork, he set out for Dublin. As he processed through the country he was met with a continuous ovation. His journey is described by the author of *A Light for the Blind*:

> All along the road the country came to meet his majesty with staunch loyalty, profound respect, and tender love as if he had been an angel from heaven. All degrees of people and of both sexes were of the number, young and old; orations of welcome were made to him at the entrance to each town, and rural maids danced before him as he travelled.[2]

Everywhere men took off their coats and laid them in the mud before his horses' hooves. In Carlow he 'was slobbered with the kisses of the rude countrywomen, so that he was forced to have them kept away from him'.

Dublin showed similar delight. It was Palm Sunday and at the gates two venerable harpers played heartily as young girls danced an ancient *rince*. Embroidered cloths, silks and tapestries hung from balconies; the streets were freshly gravelled; bells were rung and royal salutes pierced the air. The mayor and corporation presented the city keys and the Catholic primate, crowned with his mitre, waited to give his benediction. As James approached everything came to a halt. To a hush, he knelt, bareheaded, and kissed the cross. Then, rising from a long genuflection, he acknowledged the salutations of the crowd and walked into the royal chapel at the castle. Overhead, the white standard of the Stuarts broke to the breeze. It bore the motto: 'Nor or Never; Now and Forever'.

A wild cheer – deep and fervid – burst from the multitude. The disinherited king symbolised the hopes of a downtrodden people.

SARSFIELD AT BIRR

The next day James installed a new administration and issued proclamations. The first, commanded Protestants who had recently quit the kingdom to return under penalties for refusal; the second, was against marauding and ordered all subjects not in uniform to give up their arms; a third, called upon the peasantry to provision the army; a fourth, promiscuously raised the value of money; a fifth, summoned a parliament to meet in Dublin on 7 May.

Sarsfield, although in Dublin, had little concern with these measures. His interest lay with the composition of the army command. Unsurprisingly, the French held most of the senior positions, but Tyrconnell and his commandants were represented, as were some of James' English adherents. Prominent among those in the king's favour were John Drummond, first Earl of Melfont and the Comte d'Avaux, an experienced envoy whom Louis had appointed to keep an eye on James. This diplomat's dispatches provide shrewd insights into the problems facing the Jacobites and show that he had no illusions about the predicament they faced.

In his first dispatch dated April 1689, d'Avaux was upbeat about the Jacobite army; he said: 'I believe that there are nearly 40,000 of the finest possible troops, but the greater part of them need to armed and properly drilled'.[3] But, apart from the men's quality there were far too many of them. Tyrconnell's recruiting had gone too far. The government's resources were simply insufficient to maintain such large numbers, besides some did not even have a musket and others were without uniforms nor boots. It was agreed that the numbers should be reduced. Sarsfield was the obvious man to undertake this task.

He began in the midlands. In April he arrived in Birr and found the place in turmoil. The townsfolk had risen against the local Protestants and placed the town's Cromwellian proprietor, Sir Lawrence Parsons, under lock and key. This was a surprising turn of events for a man of such barometric instincts. A few years before Parsons had seen the way the wind was blowing and departed with his family for England. He left his affairs to his estate manager, Heward Oxburgh. This trusted retainer was authorised to collect his rents, discharge his debts and transfer the surplus to Parson's address in Cheshire. Everything went smoothly for a time, but then the sums transferred became modest and dried up. Parsons grew anxious and returned to Birr to see what was going on. What he found alarmed him. His retainer had gone over to Tyrconnell and was using the rents to underwrite a troop of horse and a regiment of foot which he had raised. Parsons protested. But Oxburgh was unmoved; he replied that the security of the country had necessitated his actions. When he announced his intention of billeting the men in Birr Castle (which was owned by his employer) Parsons fumed and made an indiscreet remark about Tyrconnell and King James. This was the opportunity Oxburgh wanted. He had the incautious old Cromwellian arrested and charged with treason. The bigoted Catholic judge, Sir Henry Lynch, had little sympathy with Parsons and ordered him to be slung into the dungeon of his own castle.[4]

When Sarsfield arrived he had little interest in the case. He felt obliged to intervene, however, when Parsons smuggled a note to him, begging an interview. Sarsfield consented, and was concerned that Parsons had been put on starvation rations. He took the matter up with Oxburgh who advised that there was scarcely enough food for the king's friends, not to mind his enemies. This was unacceptable to Sarsfield. He ordered that monies be allocated towards the prisoner's rations and that application be made to Dublin Castle for reimbursement. There the matter ended. The story is worth mentioning only because it illustrates the chaotic manner in which the law was administered.

Sarsfield reviewed twenty-two companies of recruits in a meadow outside Birr, and found them a dismal sight. Most were without weapons, uniforms or boots. He picked out the fittest and dismissed the rest. Then some of the men began to panic when rumour was spread that they were to be sent to beseige Derry. Two threw down their muskets and bolted down the meadow. Sarsfield was not amused. He cast off his jackboots and sped after them, dragging them back by the scruff of their necks. The spectacle was watched by Mrs Oxburgh and her two daughters, who rushed from their carriage and begged Sarsfield not to punish the fellows. After good-hearted banter he bowed to their wishes. It was said that 'the two beauties so melted his heart that he overlooked the knaves' transgressions'.

LADY HONORA BURKE

That Sarsfield had a keen eye for the ladies cannot be doubted. It was at his next port of call that he met the love of his life. And this time he married her: a gentle and beautiful girl called Lady Honora Burke, the teenage sister of the seventh Earl of Clanricard.

The Clanricards lived in Portumna Castle on the Connaught side of the Shannon, and Lady Honora's younger brother, Lord Galway, had raised one of the largest regiments in the country. Sarsfield had come to cut it down. Lady Honora had helped her brother in recruiting and spent long hours with him trying to knock the men into shape. She had a keen eye for a dashing cavalry officer, and despite the disparity in their ages, was attracted to Sarsfield. He returned her interest and romance blossomed. We have no details of their courtship, save that it was a whirlwind affair. They were married shortly after meeting, probably at Portumna.

Two portraits of Lady Honora survive and show her as striking. As a matrimonial proposition she was 'a catch'. Her pedigree was distinguished; her family – whose name is spelled, variously, Burke, Bourke, De Burgos, De Burgh and Burk – professed descent from Pepin I, Carolinian king of Acquitaine (died 838 AD); her forebearers fought with The Conqueror at Hastings, and reaped a handsome reward. The family first appeared in Ireland – contemporaneously with the Sarsfields – in 1172, but (unlike the Sarsfields) were part of the Norman nobility. It was a de Burgh who formally received the submission of Roderick O'Connor, last high king of Ireland. Little is known about Lady Honora's interests or personality.[5]

It was at Portumna that Sarsfield learned of his election to parliament as a member for Dublin county. Given that Tyrconnell had manipulated the borough charters, the news was hardly a surprise. Despite this, the new parliament was more representative of public opinion than any previous one. It was overwhelmingly Catholic, and its election was not less democratic than others of the period. For the time being, however, few eyes were on parliamentary matters. The immediate task was to crush the Ulster rebels.

THE BATTLE OF THE FORDS

Since the 'Brake of Dromore' Protestant resistance had floundered. Coleraine held out briefly only to collapse demurely. Having sat before the town for a week, Hamilton began to flush the rebels out. He started to plug the crossings on the river Bann to cut off escape routes to Derry. The garrison spotted his move and made a dash for it. Hamilton entered the town without opposition and installed a small force to prevent it being retaken.

A day or so later, he was joined by Major General de Pusignan, who had taken Moneymore, Magherafelt, Dawsons' Bridge and other towns east of the Bann; together they marched to Strabane. On 11 April they learned that between 7,000 and 10,000 Williamites under Colonel Lundy had taken up positions along the rivers Foyle and Finn, their aim being to prevent Jacobite forces from moving towards Derry. Despite their numbers, Hamilton, with only 600 horse and 350 infantry was undaunted. With the Duke of Berwick (who had just been given the rank of major-general) he decided to move against the enemy.

On 14 April the sides faced each other across the Finn at Claudy and there were sharp exchanges. The river was of considerable volume and fords difficult to find, besides, the Williamites had destroyed the only bridge and thrown up breastworks on the far side. Hamilton decided to force a crossing and ordered that planks be laid over a broken archway. Two dozen infantry set about laying timbers, as their colleagues provided cover. Hamilton took part of his cavalry along the riverbank in search of a crossing. On finding one, his men made their way over the water despite heavy fire. The infantry accomplished their object too: they settled the planks, dashed pluckily across and dislodged the enemy. The combined feat unnerved Lundy who fled towards Raphoe six miles in the rear. The Jacobites went in hot pursuit, and Berwick later wrote:

> we killed about 500 of them, but the rest being favoured by local morasses, escaped.

When Lundy returned to Derry he doubted whether the city could be defended. Some agreed with him, including two colonels – Cunningham and Richards – who had arrived from England with a small relief force, and who now undertook to withdraw. It was decided to parlay with Hamilton and a delegation was sent to St Johnstone, where he had set up camp.[6]

Hamilton had scarcely unrolled his maps when he saw the Derry-men approaching with a white flag. They were courteously received, but Hamilton laid down strict terms. He informed them that the citizens of Derry would be allowed to live in peace, provided they handed over their arms and any horses suitable for military purposes. They were given until next day to make up their minds. In the meantime Hamilton agreed not to come closer to the city.

CABALS AT THE CASTLE

While these events were taking place the Jacobite leadership at Dublin Castle was losing its cohesion. Two cabals emerged: there were those who wanted to use Ireland for the sake of James and those who wanted to use James for the sake of Ireland. One was identified with Lord Melfont, a Scot, who hoped that James' restoration would come about by the efforts of his countrymen, and urged that the king transfer to Scotland. He pleaded that James should move to Ulster to be favourably positioned and when Derry fell to skip across the channel. James was inclined towards this view and saw eye-to-eye with Melfont on most things.

Tyrconnell disliked Melfont and was chaffed by his closeness to James, besides, he held opposing views: it would, he felt, be madness for James to leave Ireland before all the Ulster rebels were crushed – a prospect he felt to be unlikely. Furthermore, he thought it incumbent on James to remain in Dublin to open the new parliament on 7 May. Melfont would hear none of this. He was suspicious of Tyrconnell and suspected that he wanted James to remain to consent to pro-Catholic measures that would be ill-received in England.

In these squabbles Melfont was supported by his own countrymen and the English; Tyrconnell by the Irish and French. D'Avaux saw little prospect of James being restored from Scotland and had no illusions about his attitude towards the Irish. In fact, d'Avaux favoured an Ireland freed from English control and put under French protection. Louvois agreed with him, and wrote:

> We must forget that he (James) was once king of England and Scotland, and think only of what may benefit Ireland and improve subsistence there.[7]

D'Avaux accurately depicted James' attitude when he wrote:

> His Brittanic majesty's heart is too English for him to agree to anything which might displease his English subjects, as he still counts on being re-established in that kingdom … and will do nothing to remove Ireland's dependency on England.[8]

Melfont's influence, d'Avaux thought, could ruin everything; he wrote to Mary Beatrice suggesting that she dissuade her husband from taking

Melfont's advice. But nothing could rent James from Melfont's spell and few were surprised when he announced his intention of going to Ulster.

He left Dublin on 11 April with Von Rosen and their journey northwards was unrelievedly depressing. The rain fell; the wind blew; and the horses could scarcely make their way through the mire on the dirt roadways. All around lay a wilderness as the crops and cabins of the poor had been devastated by both sides. 'This,' said one of the French officers, 'is like travelling through the deserts of Arabia'. On the 40 miles to Omagh only a handful of sound cabins could be counted; for the rest, the roofs were burned, the windows broken and the doors knocked in.

At Omagh, they learned that 13 war-ships were en-route from England to aid Derry. The news halted James' progress and he needed little persuasion to do an about turn. When he reached Charlemont (in Co. Armagh) he was given a letter from his son, Berwick, which told a different story: it made no mention of a relief fleet and said that rebels had fled before the Jacobite army at Claudy. This put a new complexion on things and moved Von Rosen to urge James to resume his journey to Derry where, he felt, his presence would induce the rebels to surrender. James again ordered his coach northwards, but took a strong escort of dragoons.

He appeared before Derry on 18 April, at precisely the hour when Hamilton was in conference with Lundy's envoys at St Johnstone. Being unaware of the agreement that the army should not move beyond St Johnstone, he summoned the city to surrender. The men on the walls were astonished, and suspected treachery. Their reply was a cannon blast which struck one of the king's aids. The alarmed monarch quickly retreated. The sequel was predictable. The negotiations were broken off and the citizens stiffened their resolve to resist. Further talking was useless. Yet the bewildered king stayed in the saddle all day in pouring rain and without food, hoping that his presence would bring his rebellious subjects to their senses. Next morning, he quit and gave orders for the city to be invested.

THE SIEGE OF DERRY

The campaign in Ulster had made the Jacobites confident that Derry could be taken easily. The city's governor, they knew, regarded the place as untenable. But they did not know that Lundy's views were unrepresentative and that popular feeling was for resistance. Following the defeat at the fords, a suspicion had grown in Derry that Lundy was in cahoots with the enemy, and that he was not the man to conduct the defence of the city. An anti-Lundy faction sprung up, led by Adam Murray, a farmer from the Faughan valley, and it swept the governor from his post. Two determined men took over: Major Henry Baker, a professional soldier from Co. Louth, and Rev. George Walker, a gun-tooting rector from Donoughmore, Co. Tyrone.

Tyrconnell's scepticism about Derry falling was borne out. The Jacobites were ill-equipped to take the city. They had no artillery heavy enough to breach the walls; their troops, poorly trained, were incapable of a serious assault, and suffered heavily from sorties made by the garrison. Yet they rained dozens of shells over the walls and exacted a high toll. Their real hope lay in reducing the city by famine. With 30,000 people crowded within the walls, it could only be a matter of time before supplies ran low. Then hunger would grip the famished citizens and force them to open their gates. In a diary entry for 25 July, Governor Walker set down the high costs of the miserable fare on offer:

Horse flesh	1 shilling 8 pence per pund
Quarter of dog	5 shillings 6 pence
(flattened on the flesh of the slain Irish)	
Dog's head	2 shillings 6 pence
A cat	4 shillings 6 pence
A mouse	6 pence
A rat	1 shilling.[9]

A few weeks before, Walkers colleague, Baker died of pneumonia, caught it was said, from manning the walls in all weathers. Colonel John Mitchelburn, another professional soldier, was appointed in his place.

From outside, Hamilton adopted a conciliatory tone and sent messages to win over the garrison by friendly persuasion: they reminded him of his treachery to the Prince of Orange and refused to listen. Von Rosen grew impatient and thundered terrible menaces, thus steeling their resolve further.

Maddened by their obstinacy the Livonian issued an edict declaring that if surrender did not come by a certain hour, he would drive all the Protestants of the surrounding districts – young and old, women and children – beneath the walls to be left to starve. Next day, he carried out the threat and large numbers were herded to the walls.

The garrison looked on, helplessly. But the new governor, Mitchelburn, resolved to meet terror with terror. He erected a gallows in full view of the Jacobites and sent word that all prisoners would be executed unless the captives were set free. A war of nerves ensued and Catholic priests were given access to the city to administer the last sacraments; but Von Rosen was unmoved. It was fortunate that news of his scheme travelled to Dublin. The Protestant archbishop of Meath, Dr Anthony Dropping, remonstrated with James, and the popish king did not conceal his contempt for Von Rosen's actions. He described the Livonian as a 'wild animal' and immediately issued instructions that his Protestant subjects be freed.

The garrison continued its defence, and hunger continued to take its toll. Then, an empty shell containing a note offering terms was fired over the wall. Walker took it and went to the cathedral to pray. On the altar his eyes fell on a passage in the open Bible. It was Psalm 37:

> Fret not thyself because of evildoers, neither thou be envious against the workers of iniquity. For they shall soon be cut down like the grass and wither as the green herb; trust in the Lord and do good, so thou shall dwell in the land verily, thou shall be fed.

Outside, he gazed at the red flag flying from the roof of the cathedral. It had been placed there by Mitchelburn in defiance of the enemy. Its distinctive colour, symbolic of blood and sacrifice, aptly depicted the spirit of the resistance. Again, the answer was, no surrender.

THE RELIEF OF THE CITY

On the evening of 7 June great excitement arose on the walls: someone had spotted ships on Lough Foyle. Soon, one, the *Greyhound* came up to Culmore fort and engaged in an exchange of gunfire. Jacobite cannon struck it below the water-line; it had to discontinue the engagement and limp away. Hamilton, noting the incident, sent French engineers to erect a boom across the river. Heavy timbers were joined together in iron clamps – similar to rods on a curtain rail – and strung from bank to bank making a formidable obstacle to shipping reaching the city.

Shortly afterwards, other ships were seen on the Foyle – a fleet sent by William, laden with food, men and munitions. Its commander was General Percy Kirk, but he shrank from challenging the boom, and sat before it nonchalantly. The garrison watched in despair. They were now hit by pestilence and ravished with fatigue and hunger. To their amazement they saw Kirk sail away. Yet they were not abandoned: Kirk planned to return. He cut around the coast of Donegal to supply the Enniskilleners through the river Erne and then engaged in a diversionary tactic to draw the Jacobites from Derry. He landed men on Inch Island in Lough Swilly. The manoeuvre failed, as the Jacobites would not be lured from the walls.

Conditions in Derry were now desperate. For a few, resistance became possible only when a baker, James Cunningham, discovered a method of making a pancake by mixing starch and tallow; but these materials ran out. It was then that Kirk reappeared, and Mitchelburn, knowing that the citizens were nearing exhaustion, flashed signals saying that a break-through must be attempted or all was lost. All eyes watched the flag on the cathedral roof being dipped up and down. Then the cannon was discharged eight times. The fleet answered with similar signals which were taken to mean that an attempt would be made at high tide.

It was. The Ulster-owned vessel, the *Mountjoy* rode straight towards the boom. The huge timbers cracked and gave way, but the thud was so great that the vessel rebounded and became stuck in mud. A shout of elation rose from the Jacobites, who rushed to their boats in an attempt to board. But a second vessel, the *Dartmouth* came forward and discharged a broadside which scattered them. The tide was rising fast and enabled the *Mountjoy* to move. It cut through the splintered timbers and advanced towards the city. At this moment tragedy struck. As the captain of the valiant ship directed his crew, a shot rang out and struck him. A Jacobite sniper had hit his target and Captain Michael Browning lay dead. Macauley caught the poignancy of the moment when he wrote:

> ... he died the most enviable of all deaths, in the sight of the city which was his birthplace, his home and which he had saved by his courage and devotion from the most frightful form of destruction.

Other vessels moved past the shattered timbers and made their way towards the city. It was 10 p.m. when all arrived at the quay and the whole population were present to greet them. The author of *A Light for the Blind* wrote bitterly:

> What shouts of joy the town gave ... you may easily imagine, and what pangs of pain it gave the loyal army you can easily conceive.[10]

The siege continued a few days more but on the third night flames were seen rising from the Jacobite camp. On 1 August, the defenders watched their tormentors march off in the direction of Strabane. Derry had endured for 105 days, and Protestant Ulster had its epic, complete with Homeric heroes. The Maiden City, was, in the words of the poet '... a maiden still'.[11]

BANTRY BAY

The failure at Derry was a turning point. It ended the string of successes which had marked the Jacobite campaign and killed all hope of an early transfer to Scotland. It provided the Williamites with a morale booster and gave William a bridgehead which he would exploit with effect.

But, as yet, it was far too early for either side to speak of success or defeat, and the Jacobites were not wholly misfortunate. On 29 April they received reinforcements from France. Admiral Chateaurenault put in to Bantry Bay with 24 ships-of-the-line and two frigates carrying 3,000 men of infantry and cavalry units, together with a quantity of arms and ammunition. He had set his course for Kinsale a week earlier but was forced to play cat and mouse with an English fleet under Admiral Herbert.

The winds had been contrary and took him further west than he had planned.

Herbert had received warning of the French fleet's movements and was determined to stop it, but was wrong-footed by the diversion. By the time his scouts sighted Chateaurenault it was too late to prevent him landing. Herbert was, however, prepared to give battle in Bantry Bay. He arrived on 1 May, saw the French at anchor and noted that their number was less than his own. His presence was spotted and Chateau-renault took up the challenge and hastened to engage him. A mile or so out, both fleets opened up on each other and the confrontation lasted from 11 a.m. to 5 p.m., when, abruptly, the English withdrew and head-ed for the Scillies. The French followed, but, failing to make ground, went back to Bantry Bay.

Both sides claimed victory. But the French, in truth, had the greater success. The estimated casualties were: French: 40 killed, 93 wounded; English: 96 killed, 240 wounded. Neither side lost a vessel, but the damage sustained by the English was extensive.[12] When the news reached Dub-lin, the Jacobites were jubilant and a *Te Deum* was sung in St Patrick's cathedral. Everyone seemed pleased but James. As a former lord admiral of England he found it hard to swallow an English naval defeat, even if it were in his own cause. When d'Avaux described the manner in which the English ships had fled, he retorted: '*C'est bien la premier fois donc*' (It is the first time then). He took the view that the English had pulled their punches in loyalty to him. James' capacity for self-delusion was almost infinite.

THE JACOBITE PARLIAMENT
The scene now shifts to the opening of parliament in Dublin on 7 May. This was an event without precedence for the Lords and Commons who assembled at King's Inns, near the present Four Courts, could claim – more reasonably than earlier parliaments – to represent a majority of Irish people.[13] Most of the surviving information on the parliament comes from Williamite sources and is heavily biased. The fullest account is that of Dr William King, a Protestant archbishop of Dublin, who had been imprisoned by the Jacobites and held a deep animus against them.

In his book, *The State of the Protestants under King James' Government* (Dublin, 1691), King relates the slippery methods employed when the election writs were dispatched to the various sheriff and mayors; they were accompanied by notes from Tyrconnell recommending the return of particular candidates. In the event, the election was uncontested ex-cept, as far as we know, in a single constituency. There was a competi-tion in Dublin city where, King says, Gerald Dillon 'a most furious Papist' failed to be elected because he had purchased an estate under the Act of Settlement and was therefore thought likely to oppose its repeal.[14]

In the lower house, two members sat for every borough and county. In the house of peers there were 11 Protestants, including 6 Church of Ireland bishops; this house had a number of names of distinction, in many cases of men who were destined to be the last of their line. These included, the Earls of Clancarthy (MacCarthy), Clanricard (Burke), Antrim (MacDonnell); the Viscounts Roche of Fermoy, O'Dempsey of Clanmailer, Maginnes of Iveagh, Mountcashel (newly created title of Justin MacCarthy), Clare (O'Brien); the Barons Plunkett, Fitzmaurice, Fleming, Birmingham and an array of Butlers and various Burkes. Sarsfield, however, did not take up his seat. During most of the sitting – from 7 May to 18 July – he was conducting military operations in Connaught.

The members of both houses were devoid of experience in public affairs. Some were the offspring of old proprietors who had lost their lands under the Act of Settlement and whose motives were to reverse this, and other wrongs. The opening session was full of pageantry. The presence of a king was itself unique (and did not recur until 1921 when George V opened the Northern Ireland parliament). He appeared fully robed and wearing a crown made for the occasion. All possible courtesy was given him and he sat on the throne to read the gracious speech. This was bland and predictable:

> The exemplary loyalty which this nation expressed to me at a time when others of my subjects so undutifully misbehaved themselves to me, or so basely betrayed me and your seconding of my deputy in his bold and resolute asserting of my Right, in preserving this kingdom for me and putting it into a posture of defence, made me resolve to come to you in defence of your liberties and to my satisfaction I have found you ready to serve me, and that your courage has equalled your zeal ...
>
> I have no doubt of your assistance in enabling me to overcome the designs of my enemies, and to encourage you the more to it, I would mention the great generosity and kindness of the Most Christian King who gave a sure retreat to the queen, my son the Prince of Wales, and myself when we were forced out of England and sought protection in his kingdom. He embraced by interest and gave me such supplies as have enabled me to come to you ...
>
> I should conclude as I have begun, and assure you that I am as sensible as you desire me to be of your loyalty and shall make it my chief study, as it has always been, to make you and all of my subjects happy.[15]

James stumbled through the reading and every head was bowed as he left the chamber. The members of the House of Commons withdrew to their own house and set about their purpose in earnest.

Their work was neither characterised by tranquillity or moderation. There was much ranting as bills were brought forth for consideration. Macauley, a hostile source, says that it was painful to hear member after member talking nonsense about his losses and clamouring to take possession of some estate. He mentions 'a violent storm which broke forth' when a member named Daly was ordered to the bar of the house to be disciplined for some procedural transgression:

> ... but just when he was at the door, one of the members rushed in shouting, 'Good news: Londonderry is taken'. The whole house rose. All hate was flung in the air. Three loud huzzahs were raised. Every heart was softened by the happy tidings. Nobody could hear of punishment at such a moment. The order for Daly's attendance amidst cries of 'No submission, No submission, We pardon him'. In a few hours it was known that Londonderry had held on as obstinately as ever. This transaction, in itself unimportant, deserves to be recorded, as showing how destitute that House of Commons was of all qualities which ought to be found in the great councils of a kingdom.[16]

The writer of this burlesque does not detail his sources and a survey of the membership of the House of Commons fails to uncover anyone called Daly.

Despite the sneers of its contemporary critics – who were more numerous than in Macauley's day – the parliament achieved its purpose: it repealed the Acts of Settlement outright, and an Act of Attainer was passed against the 2,000 land-owners who had left the country in the recent exodus or were otherwise absent. Their property was vested in the crown and they were ordered to return or prove their loyalty by certain dates. These dates afforded them little time, and the act was seen by many as manifestly unjust. It infuriated Protestants and was later used as a template for reprisals against Catholics. But other views were heard: its apologists said that English and Protestant parliaments could, and often did, pass unfair legislation that Catholics had to swallow. Yet, when a Catholic parliament enacted measures of dubious merit, there was uproar.

Other legislation was less controversial. An act was passed which enabled Catholics and Dissenters to remit tithes to their own clergy rather than to those of the Established Church; another declared that Irish courts of law were independent of courts outside the jurisdiction. But one 'constitutional monstrosity' remained . This, was 'Poynings Law'[17] which every Catholic wanted destroyed; but James dug his heels in, and would not countenance its repeal. In all, the king was little pleased with his parliament. It voted him no worthwhile revenue and as a political exercise it turned out to be more pro-Irish than pro-Stuart.[18]

SARSFIELD MEETS 'LITTLE CROMWELL'

Among the parliament's critics were those who took the view that it was foolhardy for the Jacobites to dissipate their energies in a talking shop when there was a war to be won. During the sittings the rebels at

Derry were defying every effort to dislodge them, and the Enniskilleners were destroying Jacobite lines of communication. The latter had become 'rough riders' and not unlike the modern guerrilla, constantly ambushed, harassed, confused, exhausted and demoralised the enemy. The metaphor of fleas constantly trying to bite a dog to death aptly describes them. On one occasion their raiding parties penetrated as far as Co. Meath and returned with a large herd of cattle and quantities of wheat, oats and barley. Yet, a contemporary source notes how ragged they were:

> They were in a destitute condition. Some had no boots; others boots – but they had no carbines; some had one pistol and a carbine without a sword; others had none of these equipments, only a fowling piece and a firelock. Most of their horses were small and poor. Their uniforms bad; but their fighting was good, although military regularity was absent. They were attended by their favourite preachers who encouraged them to purge the land of idolatry. They attacked with utmost impetuosity, and were rarely deterred by inequality of numbers.[19]

Another account emphasises their role in deflecting the Jacobite forces from Derry:

> During the whole of that long siege the men of Enniskillen kept at least one half of the Irish army from coming to Derry … by so doing they made the siege a great deal easier for the besieged. And, therefore (as those who are best acquainted with the affairs of the place confess), Enniskillen does deserve no small part of the honour of that place's preservation.[20]

Following Galmoy's retreat from Crom Castle the Enniskilleners' numbers were swollen by Protestants from Sligo who had attempted to join Lundy at Claudy but who were cut off, and therefore diverted to Enniskillen. These newcomers enhanced 'Little Cromwell's' forces at a time when his reputation was ascendant. Plainly, something had to be done about this fellow and the obvious person to tackle him was Sarsfield, who had been at Athlone. He was now sent to the north-west with four troops of dragoons and cavalry and five infantry companies; in all, 2,000 men, probably the largest force he had commanded.

He arrived in Sligo on 1 May and found the town in the hands of a colourful character called 'Blind' MacDonough – a one-eyed Catholic lawyer – who, following the Protestant evacuation, had raised a few companies of volunteers. Sarsfield liked the fellow and was content to leave Sligo to him, his own purpose being to get to grips with the Enniskilleners. To achieve this, he knew that he must first reduce Ballyshannon, on the mouth of the Erne, through which provisions were reaching Enniskillen. The problem was that Ballyshannon was well fortified and its garrison aware of his coming. Captain Henry Folliot, the commander, had prepared a hot reception by covering the approach from Sligo and by stationing men in an old fort on Fish Island, an islet in the estuary. He left little to chance: suspecting that Sarsfield had sufficient numbers to overwhelm him, he sent to Enniskillen for help.

When Sarsfield drew near he learned of Folliot's strong disposition with some surprise. 'Blind' MacDonough, who accompanied him, had earlier reported that his scouts had found the town's defences inadequate. This was obviously incorrect, and Sarsfield became aware of the weakness of his own position. He guessed that Folliot had sent for help, and suspected that if he entered Ballyshannon he would be sandwiched between two dangers: Folliot's garrison and the oncoming Enniskilleners. His problems were compounded by a third danger: four miles east (towards Enniskillen) lay the village of Beleek, and ten miles further on was Castle Caldwell, a Williamite stronghold held by Sir James Caldwell with a Protestant force 200 or 300 strong.

Sarsfield pondered on whether to dig in around Ballyshannon and take on the combined forces of the enemy, or to avoid the town and march east and engage the Enniskilleners alone. He chose the latter, and split his men so that the main body advanced towards Beleek, whilst a smaller force kept Folliot pinned down in the rear. 'Blind' MacDonough was given responsibility for the latter operation.

Folliot's appeal for help was responded to in Enniskillen. The governor, Gustave Hamilton, ordered 'Little Cromwell' to relieve Ballyshannon. Twelve companies of foot and a few of horse left Enniskillen and took the road along the southern bank of the Erne. They were unaware that Sarsfield was close by and had positioned himself advantageously behind breastworks near Beleek, away from the Caldwell threat. His position was strong, with his flanks protected by the Erne and a bog which ran for miles. It was 'Little Cromwell' who was now approaching a danger zone – a funnel in which his lines could easily be cut to pieces by enemy fire. But as he approached, he fortuitously spotted Sarsfield's scouts and halted.

'Little Cromwell's' had to do some quick thinking. His immediate problem was estimating Sarsfield's strength; he ordered his men to cut shrub from the ditches for faggots to lay on the bog so that he could approach at an angle and get some idea of enemy numbers. Both forces, at this time, were almost within earshot of each other, and the Jacobites shouted taunts to entice the Enniskilleners to attack. 'Little Cromwell' may have taken this bait, had he not been fortunate. One of his troopers, when scouring the bog, had come upon a peasant who claimed to know of a pathway through and who undertook to help.

The offer was accepted and in minutes the Enniskilleners could be seen diverting leftwards, and moving arc-wise through the bog. Initially, the Jacobites thought their enemies were refusing battle, and shouted abuse accusing them of cowardice. They soon realised that the operation was a diagonal movement designed to outflank them. Sarsfield and the horse were on high ground too far back to see what was afoot. By the time 'Little Cromwell's' manoeuvre was spotted it was too late. In minutes the Enniskilleners had reached firm ground and were charging at the Jacobite infantry. With the horsemen bearing down on them – their sabres pointing at their chests – the unfortunate infantrymen panicked and ran. But a further surprise was in store: Sir James Caldwell and 300 men suddenly appeared from the direction of the Erne and were coming at the Jacobites on the other flank.

By now Sarsfield was awake to what was happening and shouted to his men to run. It is doubtful whether anyone heard him. His entire force – both horse and foot – was in trouble, and every man intent on saving his own skin. Sarsfield wheeled his horse and took off as quickly as its legs would carry him. So too did the other cavalrymen. The Enniskilleners sped in pursuit and several skirmishes broke out on the road to Ballyshannon. Sarsfield and a section of the horse escaped and the episode became known as the 'Break of Beleek'. It did not cover the Jacobite commander with glory.

Within an hour, the 'Siege' of Ballyshannon was raised, and 'Blind' MacDonough taken prisoner. The old veteran was seen by the Williamites as a trophy; he was put in irons, taken to Enniskillen and thrown into a dungeon.[21]

The arithmetic showed that the Jacobites had lost up to 1,000 men, and that 'Little Cromwell's' losses were negligible. It was also reported that the Enniskilleners 'were puffed up because of their success against Sarsfield'.[22]

10

'DEAR NOTORIOUS'

FREEING 'BLIND' MACDONOUGH

Sarsfield soon snapped out of any despondency which he may have felt following the 'Brake of Beleek'. He was not one to fret and, besides, regarded the affair as a setback rather than a defeat. He sought to regain the initiative and within days was drilling new volunteers in the grounds of Sir William Gore's estate at Manor Hamilton. Shortly, he was sending raiding parties against enemy positions along the Erne and even called upon Sir James Caldwell to surrender Caldwell Castle. The old Cromwellian fumed and told Sarsfield that he should accept that his goose was cooked.

The gibe went unheeded, although there was one matter which made Sarsfield angry. This was the capture and detention of 'Blind' Mac-Donough. The old veteran was held in high regard and Sarsfield came under pressure to effect his release. But what could be done? The obvious course was to offer an exchange of prisoners with the Enniskilleners. But would they treat? It was well known that they were infuriated by the treachery of Lord Galmoy and his execution of Captain Woolson Dixie; besides, why should they trust Sarsfield?

The problem was compounded by the small number of prisoners Sarsfield had and there being nobody of distinction among them. The matter may have passed had not news been received that Sir Thomas Southwell, a former sheriff of counties Kerry, Clare and Limerick was being held at the king's pleasure in Galway Jail. This old Cromwellian had been arrested for acting for the Hillsborough council. He was seen as a big fish and the Jacobites were pleased to have bagged him. Sarsfield, seeing his opportunity, instructed that the prisoner be transferred to Sligo, and had his name placed on a list which he dispatched to Gustave Hamilton, the governor of Enniskillen, with an offer to treat.

Hamilton, unhesitatingly, said 'no', and sent Sarsfield's messenger away with a rebuke. Sarsfield was not prepared to take 'no' for an answer. Peeved, he decided to take measures to force Hamilton into an agreement. Acting like Von Rosen at Derry he ordered that Protestant civilians in the outlying areas of Sligo be taken into custody and lodged in the town's jail and a fresh list of prisoners was sent to Hamilton, with an note saying that Sarsfield could not be held responsible for their safety unless an exchange was effected. Hamilton declared that he would not negotiate under pressure and accused Sarsfield of dishonour and perfidy.

Sarsfield turned the screw tighter. The rations of the male captives were reduced and the womenfolk released, but told that their menfolk would be allowed to starve if Hamilton did not yield. The women were persuaded to take a petition to Hamilton, imploring him to save the lives of the men. In their anguish, they set off on foot over the hills to Enniskillen.

When they arrived at the town's gates they were a dreadful sight: cold, hungry and worn out. The Enniskilleners received them compassionately and met their corporeal needs, but Hamilton refused to consider their petition. The sight of the women so moved the townspeople that they begged Hamilton to concede. The matter could not be resolved and a public meeting was called in the market place. For two hours arguments were tossed to and fro. In the end, Hamilton succumbed and an exchange was agreed, which included the 'Blind' MacDonough.

But the Enniskilleners remained wary of Sarsfield. They marched the prisoners from the town under the supervision of Colonel Francis Gore – a relative of the owner of the estate at Manor Hamilton – and arranged for the switch to take place at a spot halfway between Enniskillen and Sligo. In the event, the exchange went without incident, but when Gore was invited by Sarsfield to join him in a glass of brandy, he turned on his heel.[1]

CHALLENGING THE ENNISKILLENERS

Whether Sarsfield intended to carry out his threat against the Sligo captives is a matter for speculation. Arguably, he acted with greater cruelty than Von Rosen at Derry, and with less purpose. The least that can be said of his behaviour is that it showed a cruel streak.

To date, he had achieved little in the north-west. The Enniskilleners still held the line of the Erne and continued to disrupt Jacobite lines of communication, particularly those which ran through Strabane, Omagh and Dungannon. They still required to be dealt with, and the Duke of Berwick was sent from Derry in the later part of June, with a 'flying camp' – a mobile force of 400 cavalry and dragoons. He established headquarters in Stranorlar at a house owned by Lord Mountjoy. His route took him through Barnesmore Gap to Donegal town which was held by 300 Williamites. He arrived in the town at dawn, burnt it, but failed in taking the castle, to which the garrison retreated.

Berwick now planned to move against Enniskillen. In the first week of July he transferred to Trillick, about 12 miles north-east of Enniskillen and was preparing a plan of attack when he was abruptly recalled to deal with a Williamite force which had entered Lough Swilly (part of Kirk's fleet). Enniskillen, thus, escaped his attention.[2]

Soon afterwards a force under Henry Luttrell undertook to probe nearer Enniskillen. It took possession of an old mill a quarter of a mile on the outskirts, but within cannon range. It was spotted, and the Enniskilleners began pounding the mill and planned to sally out. They were too slow; Luttrell had anticipated the cannonade and took his men out of range. He also anticipated the sally, and put his men in an attacking posture. When the sally came, he ordered a charge against it. The clash was head-on, and the Enniskilleners came off badly: they broke during the first sweep, and fled. Luttrell could do no more; his horse dare not challenge the town's cannon. He returned to base, satisfied with having inflicted a defeat on the enemy.

This feat altered nothing. Ballyshannon still provided a lifeline to the Enniskilleners and they continued to create havoc. Von Rosen instructed Berwick to contact Sarsfield and instigate a combined operation to cut off the supply line. Berwick was to return to Stranorlar and Sarsfield to move up from Bundrowes, where he had 4,000 men. Berwick wrote to Sarsfield, addressing him as 'Dear Notorious'. Simms says that this nickname implied an already high reputation in the field; unfortunately, no other example can be found, and Sarsfield's reputation (since returning to Ireland) cannot be said to have been distinguished. In ordinary meaning 'notorious' refers to someone who is publicly known in a bad or disreputable sense. Could it be that Berwick used the tag to describe a raffish notoriety which Sarsfield had acquired following his behaviour at Sligo? The letter ran:

> Dear Notorious,
>
> This is to give you notice that Marshal Rosen and I will march within three or four days from this place to Ballyshannon so that if you look out sharp this way you may see us laying on these rebelly and cowering rogues; which may give you also an opportunity to attack on that side of the water to make a diversion. I am afraid that the siege of Derry will be raised and I thank God that I have not nor ever will give my consent to it. I will say no more of this till I meet you at Ballyshannon. In the meantime, I remain, Dear Notorious.
>
> Your Friend and Servant,
> Berwick.[3]

Sarsfield complied with the request and marched to within a few miles of Ballyshannon, but Berwick failed to turn up. He received fresh instructions to stay in Derry where matters were coming to a climax.

Meanwhile, Lord Mountcashel was advancing towards Enniskillen from the south with 3,600 men. Plans were made for him to be joined by a force of dragoons under Major General Anthony Hamilton – Richard's brother – and by a mixed force of Ulster Catholics under Conconnacht Mór Maguire. With such power, it seemed likely that he could give the Enniskilleners a knock-out blow.

The Battle of Newtownbutler

Mountcashel's instructions (from James) were that, before advancing on Enniskillen, he should reduce Crom Castle, the outpost 20 miles south-east, where Galmoy had earlier suffered humiliation. He arrived on 28 April and invested the castle from the eastern side. Two days later he had driven the pickets from the outworks – though not without loss – and opened a cannonade. During the firing he received news that the garrison was about to receive help. The Williamite, Colonel Berry was advancing from Lisnaskea with 800 regulars, followed by larger numbers under Colonel William Wolseley and Gustave Hamilton. Without raising the siege, Mountcashel withdrew part of his force and took up a fresh position two miles eastward at Newtownbutler. On learning that the enemy had amalgamated, he felt that he would be too weak to meet them in open country, and sent Anthony Hamilton with a regiment of dragoons to hold them back temporarily, while he withdrew towards Belturbet. But Hamilton was drawn into an ambush, by Berry, near Lisnaskea and wounded. A retreat was ordered but not before 230 Jacobite dragoons were slain or wounded.

On learning of this disaster Mountcashel halted his retreat and advanced to meet Berry with his own horse. Berry was repulsed, but Mountcashel then spotted Wolseley, with a force of 8,000 coming up on Berry's rear, and had little alternative but to retreat again. Berry and Wolseley pursued him and he made a fatal decision: he stopped to fight rather than continue his retreat. He drew his men up about a mile south of Newtownbutler and waited for the enemy.

What ensued was catastrophic for the Jacobites. Opposed by more than double their number, and attacked in the front and on the flank, they were caught in a pincher; but they fought bravely. The battle might, in fact, have gone their way but for an unfortunate blunder. The infantry misconstrued Mountcashel's orders; its lines became tangled and panic arose. A rout ensued, and the waters of Upper Lough Erne and its tributaries cut off their escape. They were hemmed in and cut to pieces. The casualties came to over 2,000, of whom 400 were killed and the rest either massacred later or drowned trying to escape.

Mountcashel was wounded and taken prisoner. Tradition has it that he had a hair's-breadth escape, when a Williamite bullet, which would have been fatal, was deflected by his pocket watch, and when an Enniskillener was about to club him, he hurriedly revealed his identity.[4]

Retreat from Sligo

Following this defeat the Jacobites lost their grip on Ulster. They went on the defensive and Sarsfield thought it too hazardous to make an unaided attack on Ballyshannon or, indeed, to continue exposing himself around the Erne basin. He retreated to Sligo.

But the Enniskilleners kept their eye on him. Colonel Francis Gore with three troops of horse was detailed to track him. Early in August they reconnoitred Sligo to see if it could be taken. The story told is that when Gore came within six or seven miles of the town, he took a Jacobite prisoner who, almost implausibly, turned out to be his foster-brother – the son of his wetnurse. The relationship did not endear the fellow to Gore, and he threatened to hang him – but then pretended to be overcome by appeals for mercy. He agreed to spare the fellow if he would carry a message to Sligo and warn half a dozen of Sarsfield's officers – Gore's former friends – that a 20,000 strong Williamite force was due to descend on them the next day. The idea was that Gore was sending a tip-off to his old pals.

The foster-brother agreed, but could not hold his tongue until he reached Sligo: he aired the story on the way and was widely believed. Many became terrified and rushed to leave the area. Sarsfield was alerted and tried to discover the source of the story. The foster-brother was brought before him and questioned. The fellow's gift of narration must have been impressive, for Sarsfield himself became convinced that Sligo was about to be overwhelmed and gave orders for its evacuation.

Soon afterwards Gore and his modest force entered Sligo and had a hearty laugh at the success of their ruse. The Jacobites left in such a hurry that their cannon was intact and a good supply of provisions were found in the storehouses. The episode sounds incredible and cannot be verified. There is no doubt, however, that Sarsfield and his men retired quickly from Sligo.

'THE BREAK OF BOYLE'
A few weeks later 'Little Cromwell' took formal possession of Sligo, but felt insecure there. Reports were received that the Jacobites had gathered in Boyle and were building up under the command of Colonel Charles O'Kelly to retake Sligo.

O'Kelly was of the Catholic gentry and joined the army as a young man and served with distinction in Ireland and the Low Countries. Although now aged 68 he was vigorous and the keenest of Jacobites. In later years he would write the only account of the war by an Irish Catholic participant. This work, *Macaria Excidium or the Destruction of Cyprus*, is a 'secret history' depicting the principal actors with names from classical antiquity and the author himself set down as one Philotus Phiyocypres ('A Lover of Country').[5]

O'Kelly's main problem at Boyle was that his men were poorly armed and trained. Yet, 'Little Cromwell' saw him as a threat and decided on a pre-emptive strike. Under the cover of darkness he got as far a Ballinafad and sent a scouting party ahead who surprised O'Kelly's lookouts on the Curlew Mountains, killing three or four of them.

O'Kelly had been preparing his men in a deer park owned by Lord Kingston. With his lookouts neutralised he received no warning of 'Little Cromwell's' advance. When the attack came, it was devastating. O'Kelly's foot were trapped by the walls of the deer park and utterly destroyed. The old veteran himself was lucky to get away; it is said that he rode, helter-skelter, through Boyle roaring obscenities at his enemies. Within an hour, the 'Brake of Boyle' was over and the town fallen. 'Little Cromwell' took possession of O'Kelly's personal portmanteau which the old man left behind in his haste.

But Boyle was not held for long. As 'Little Cromwell' was enjoying the fruits of victory he learned that Sligo was under renewed threat: Sarsfield had returned. In the days following his evacuation Sarsfield had gone to Dublin for consultations, but was back, refreshed, with 2,000 'choice men'. Included were infantry under Colonel Oliver O'Gara and Colonel Charles O'More (Sarsfield's uncle) and, at Athlone, he was reinforced by dragoons under Sir Neal O'Neill and cavalry under Henry Luttrell. This time, he was determined to clear the Williamites, bag and baggage, from Connaught.

The first point of attack was the Williamite stronghold at Jamestown. Its garrison gave only token resistance before fleeing to Sligo under Colonel Theodore Russell. Sarsfield was in a hurry to advance on Sligo and covered the distance in under five hours, picking up Colonel Charles O'Kelly, Ulick Burke and other commanders with small companies on the way. He now had about 4,000 men and was unimpeded until he came to Ballysodare about five miles from Sligo. A Huguenot commander, St Sauveur, had blocked the roadway with a troop of grenadiers. They had broken a bridge and taken up positions behind a fast-flowing river. It looked as if Sarsfield would have to retrace their steps and make a detour to reach Sligo from the Lough Gill side. Then, a stroke of luck similar to that which favoured the Williamites at Beleek, came his way: a local man told him of a ford a couple of miles upstream. Sarsfield ordered Luttrell to take 300 infantry and 70 horse and cross the river while the main body kept the Williamites occupied with musket fire at the broken bridge. St Sauveur and his men were tough opponents and exchanged fire until their ammunition ran out and then retreated. Upstream, Luttrell made the crossing, but was too late to attack St Sauveur from the rear, which had been Sarsfield's plan. Shortly afterwards the entire Jacobite force made its way to Sligo.

THE RE-TAKING OF SLIGO

The town was badly fortified. It had no walls and its main defences consisted of two forts. One, a stone fort, was of comparatively recent origin, built 25 years before. The other was a derelict structure on high ground, at the far end of the town, known as the green fort; also, near the town centre, was a ruined castle capable of providing cover. Details of the struggle for Sligo are conflicting.[6] One account, from Captain Richard Smith, a Williamite (who brought reinforcements from Ballyshannon) says 'Little Cromwell's' men held the green fort, and describes how they sallied out until driven back by the Jacobites. The account goes on:

> … in the meantime our foot got into the castle and the enemies foot drew up in the market place … the castle being crasie (crazy) and not thought tenable, our men quitted it and got into the fort which they held for five days so long as they had any ammunition left.

Simms says that this reference to the castle indicates that it was occupied first and later abandoned for the stone fort. The account continues:

> One remarkable stratagem made use of by the Irish for storming the fort was, they built a box of timber as high as the wall, with stairs, through which they might ascend to the top of the wall without danger.[7]

Here, Smith is alluding to an item of siege equipment known as a 'sow', used for surmounting walls. It was a hand-made contraption with wheels and a tower which when pushed against a wall enabled the besiegers to reach a parapet without exposure. The 'sow' used at Sligo is described as of 'very strong timbers bound with iron' and 'covered with two rows of hides and as many sheepskins which rendered "her" proof against musket ball or steel arrows'. It was countered by the defenders throwing out bundles of straw and setting these alight at the foot of the contraption: a man was lowered by rope to ignite the bundles but – the story runs – on his way back up, his rope was cut by a bullet and he fell again, only to be pulled to safety on a second attempt.

Rev. George Story says that St Sauveur defended the stone fort with great courage and being fearful that it might be taken after dark 'got a great many fir deals and dipping the ends of them in tar they made such a light when set on fire that … they burned the engine'. Like most accounts, Story fails to give a clear picture of what actually happened. 'Little Cromwell's' genius, it seems, did not lie in holding fortifications: he fought his way out of the green fort and fled, with little loss.[8]

St Sauveur, in the end, surrendered on honourable terms. Sarsfield allowed the enemy to march out with their muskets. Captain Smith was gracious enough to pay a tribute to Sarsfield: he said that he kept faithfully to the terms and entertained enemy officers following the signing of an agreed document. Story says that as the Williamite garrison left, marching over the bridge, Sarsfield stood nearby holding out a purse full of coins; offering 5 guineas, a horse and arms to anyone who would change sides. He says that all but one rejected the offer because they would never consent to fight with papists.[9]

The retaking of Sligo was a feather in Sarsfield's cap, and not long afterwards he swept the few remaining bands of Williamites from Connaught. James, however, was not now favourably disposed towards him. On hearing the news, he is reported to have remarked: 'Sarsfield is a brave fellow, but scantily supplied with brains'. D'Avaux had a different view and admired Sarsfield's ability. He wished to have him appointed commander of the brigade which was ear-marked for France under the agreement of the year before. Having approached James on the matter, he wrote to Louvois on 11 October saying:

> I have asked the king of England's permission to allow a certain Sarsfield to go to France as one of the colonels to command his corps. Sarsfield is not a man of noble birth like my Lord Galway or MacCarthy but he is a gentleman who has distinguished himself by his ability and whose reputation in this kingdom is greater than any man I know. He is brave but above all he has a sense of honour and integrity in all he does. He is a man on whom the king can count and will never leave his service.
>
> I think he will be very useful because he is a man who would always be at the head of his troops and who would take great care of them, and if MacCarthy could not leave prison you would always have a good commander in Sarsfield, who other first-class colonels would keenly obey, something they would not do for anyone else.[10]

Faced with the prospect of losing Sarsfield, James changed his attitude. He walked three times around the room and accused d'Avaux of trying to take his best officers away. 'I bore it all meekly,' said d'Avaux, in a further letter to Louvois, adding:

> The king is now so pleased (with him) that when I asked for Sarsfield, he told me he would not give him to me and that I was unreasonable …[11]

MOUNTCASHEL DEPARTS

On not obtaining Sarsfield, d'Avaux put other names to James, including that of Sarsfield's cousin, Dominick, Lord Kilmallock. Eventually, it was agreed, that the command should go to Lord Mountcashel, who managed to 'escape' from Enniskillen under controversial circumstances. These are worth mentioning. In October a plan to rescue Mountcashel came to nothing. The Jacobites then requested that the prisoner, who had suffered injury, be allowed parole until his health recovered. The Enniskilleners refused. Next, the Jacobites proposed that he be exchanged for Lord Mountjoy who was held in the Bastille, but got no response.

Then, Lord Shrewsbury, the secretary of state, in London – an old friend of Mountcashel's – intervened. He gave his backing to the exchange proposal, but the negotiations dragged on for weeks. Mountcashel grew weary and decided to make an escape. He was allowed the freedom of Enniskillen while on parole, but was placed on his honour not to leave its precincts. This arrangement infuriated him, so he ingeniously concocted a rumour that he intended to compromise his honour and make a run for it. At this, his guard was doubled and he no longer considered himself bound by the parole terms. He bribed his guards and was permitted to 'escape' by boat. The Enniskilleners accused him of dishonour. His actions were later vindicated by a French court, but he could not avoid the taunt that he had contravened his parole, and, vainly used sophistry to vindicate himself.[12]

In Dublin Mountcashel's escape was well received. He spent his remaining days in Ireland at Cork where he took up his new command. When his brigade was ready for transfer to France, a French exchange-force, over 6,000 strong, arrived. On 16 April, Mountcashel's men (5,387 strong) left Ireland on the French vessel's return voyage. His brigade was the first contingent of the famous 'Wild Geese' – that great host of Irishmen who would fight in Europe under different flags.[13]

11

THE DUTCHMAN COMETH

ENTER MARSHAL SCHOMBERG

Jacobite moral plummeted following the recent reverses. On 27 July 'Bonnie' Dundee lost his life at Killiecrankie; three days later the Williamite vessels relieved Derry; on this latter date Mountcashel's army was routed at Newtownbutler. These were devastating blows but did not constitute a knock-out, and there were many – Sarsfield included – who felt that everything was still to play for. The Jacobites still controlled most of Ireland and had the support of its Catholic population. French involvement was set to increase and it was not improbable that the Williamite rebels could yet be brought to heel.

In England the conflict had been watched with increasing anxiety. The presence of James in Ireland, with French support, seemed to underscore the view that the revolution had not yet been accomplished. William, although on the throne, looked vulnerable: sections of the army – the remnants of James' force – had mutinied; the French had declared war; the Scots clans were hostile; parliament was fractious and a number of Anglican bishops had refused to take the oath of allegiance to William and Mary.

Despite these concerns William was able to send aid to Derry and Enniskillen, and in August 1689 he landed an army at Groomsport, Co. Down. This force was commanded by Marshal Schomberg, who on arrival, met little resistance. His patrols found that Belfast was undefended and he was given a great reception when he arrived there. He moved quickly to Carrickfergus and summoned its garrison to surrender. The MacCarthy Mór and Cormac O'Neill held the castle with 800 men. They were poorly armed, badly provisioned and burdened by the local Catholic population who had sought refuge within the walls.

Schomberg showed that he meant business. He opened a heavy cannonade which continued around the clock. A stubborn defence was made, but on the second day the walls were breached. The defenders had recourse to a curious stratagem: the cattle inside the walls were slaughtered and their carcasses thrown on the breach, with earth and stones placed around them. How this aided the garrison is not clear but it scarcely mattered; their ammunition ran low and a frantic attempt was made to tear lead from the castle roof for conversion to ball. But soon the powder ran out.

MacCarthy Mór surrendered on honourable terms, which were violated. The unarmed garrison was assaulted as it evacuated. Rev. George Story tells how women were separated from men and dishonoured by the 'Scots Irish' (500 horse from Derry and Enniskillen had joined Schomberg). The old vetern had to intervene to prevent a massacre and rode up and down, pistol in hand, threatening to shoot the revengeful Protestants.[1]

In a day or so, Schomberg marched to Loughbrickland where he was joined by further 'Scots Irish', increasing his numbers to 20,000. He then advanced on Carlingford to find the town burnt. The Jacobites were operating a 'scorched earth' policy before quitting Ulster. Schomberg remained on their tail and advanced towards Newry in the belief that he had secured his northern base.

The Dundalk Stand-Off

Schomberg's arrival in Ireland was received by the Jacobites with consternation. There appeared little prospect of resisting a commander of such fame. He seemed intent on taking Dublin and if it fell, James felt, all of Ireland would follow. The French said that James was too weak to hold Dublin and recommended that his army retire to Athlone and try to hold the line of the Shannon until reinforcements arrived. James rejected this and resolved, as he put it, 'not to be walked out of Ireland without a fight'.

Tyrconnell urged James to stand firm, and showing more than normal courage, James set out for Drogheda with a force of about 200. He arrived on 6 August, while Schomberg was still at Carrickfergus. The French became agitated. They again advised that it would be madness to confront Schomberg and recommended a return to Dublin. A council of war was held and Sir Richard Nugent was sent back to Dublin to tell Tyrconnell to prepare the main body of the army for an advance northward. Berwick was instructed to conduct a delaying action against Schomberg; to move to Newry, burn it, and destroy as much of the countryside as possible between there and Drogheda.

Schomberg's advance became cautious. When he reached Newry, he found that Berwick had torched and devastated the area. In the days since he left Carrickfergus, the weather broke and the constant rain made it difficult for him to set up night-camps. His men had become depressed and many went down ill. To make matters worse, storms in the Irish Sea held up his supply ships. He felt unable to advance and settled on damp, poorly chosen ground north of Dundalk. No sooner had he dug himself in when the unexpected happened. A clique of French Catholics who had joined his army under false pretences tried to scuttle him. Their leader, du Plessis, made contact with the Jacobites and was not discovered until he was about to leak information. The ringleaders, were detected and executed and about 500 unmasked as Catholics; they were returned to England as prisoners.[2]

In the meantime, James had assembled his army at Dundalk. Von

Rosen did his best to entice Schomberg from his dug out, but the wily old campaigner refused to move. The Irish urged James to storm the entrenchment but he refused. When it came to the point he feared engagement. A number of his officers were enraged. Berwick, in his *Memoirs*, says that Von Rosen was so piqued that he almost threw up his command. Certainly, it is clear that James had a better chance of defeating Schomberg at this time (1 October 1689) than later when the odds against him were greater. In fact, if James had fought and won it is not improbable that William would have thought twice before venturing across the Irish Sea.

Having decided against attack, James withdrew and placed his troops in winter quarters in the Boyne valley and elsewhere. Schomberg having waited to ensure that the enemy had withdrawn, retired back into Ulster and established headquarters at Lisburn. Later it became known that typhus, dysentery and other diseases had ravished his camp and that he lost, incredibly, about 8,000 men due to sickness. Captain John Stevens, an Englishman in the grand priors regiment, described the scene at Schomberg's camp following his withdrawal:

> Besides the infinite number of graves, a vast amount of dead bodies were found unburied and not a few yet breathing, but almost all devoured with lice and vermin.[3]

SIR TADG O'REGAN

Schomberg had failed to impress. A former marshal of France, at the head of 20,000 troops, had done practically nothing, save overcome a weak garrison at Carrickfergus. Thereafter he had remained inactive and lost more men than he would have done had he fought a major battle. The House of Commons demanded an inquiry and William decided, with some reluctance, to come to Ireland himself. It was not until 4 June that he was ready to sail.

In the meantime, additional troops were sent to Schomberg. In January 1690, 7,000 Danes arrived under the Prince of Würtemburg; in May several Dutch and English regiments were landed; money and arms were also sent. The men who survived the epidemic recovered their health and soon Schomberg was strong again. Late in 1689 he took Belturbet; in May 1690, Colonel William Wolseley chased Berwick from Cavan, and the only remaining Jacobite stronghold in Ulster – Charlemont fort on the north-eastern border of Armagh – was put under siege by Schomberg. It was held by one of the most colourful characters of the war, a tough old soldier called Tadg O'Regan, from Ballynecloghy in Co. Cork. He had been soldiering since the days of Cromwell, 40 years before. A sprightly hunchback, he was mildly eccentric and known for perpetually puffing an enormous pipe and spitting on the ground to underline whatever point he was making. Evidently, he was a good soldier, for it took Schomberg over seven months to dislodge him.

During the siege, James sent Colonel Thomas Maxwell and 500 inadequately provisioned men to help O'Regan. Cleverly, Schomberg let them through his lines so that they would speed up the exhaustion of the enemy's provisions. Tadg had no illusions about the ploy. When Schomberg called on him to surrender, he informed the marshal's envoy: 'Tell your master that he is an old knave, and that by St Patrick he shall not have this place'. But it was bravado. On 3 May O'Regan was forced to capitulate. He and his men were allowed to march out to the sound of fife and drum:

> Old Tadg, the governor, was mounted upon an old horse, and he was very lame with the scratches, spavin, ring bones, and other infirmities; but withal so vicious that he would fall a-kicking and squealing if anybody came near him. Tadg himself had a great bundle on his back, a plain red coat, an old weather-beaten wig hanging down full length, a narrow little beaver cocked up, and yellow cravat, but that all to one side, his boots with a thousand wrinkles in them; and though it was a very hot day, yet he had a great muff hanging around him, and to crown it all he was almost tipsy with brandy.[4]

Schomberg was amazed at the number of women and children who emerged, and asked Tadg why he kept so many non-combatants in the garrison. With a grin, the Corkman informed him that the men would not fight without the comfort of their wives and mistresses. 'There is more love to it than policy, then' was Schomberg's reply.

James and Tyrconnell expressed satisfaction when they learned of Tadg's stubborn defence. The king was so taken that he conferred a knighthood on the Corkman and soon appointed him governor of Sligo.

'THE DELIVERER' IN IRELAND
William crossed to Ireland on 14 June with a fleet of 300 transports and six warships. He had 900 horses, 450 bread wagons and, in his purse, £200,000 which was like manna to Schomberg's unpaid troops.

He embarked at Hoylake in Chesire three days earlier on the yacht *Mary* captained by the intrepid Edward Tarlton. Not much can be said, however, for the captain's steering, for the yacht was grounded on a bar.k near the Point of Ayer, off the Isle of Man and remained marooned for several hours. This was a bad omen and the fatalistic William was perturbed, but nevertheless he arrived safely at Carrickfergus two days later. He came ashore in the rear-admiral's barge and reached the Old Quay, under the shadow of the castle, in the early afternoon. The stone step on which he first set his foot on Irish soil can still be seen on the pier, inscribed with the legend: 'William III, 14th June 1690'.

Nearby, his arrival is commemorated on a large blue plaque, and a

William arriving in Carrickfergus

few feet away a life-size statue of him broods over the quay. Strangely, he is in unheroic pose: slightly stooped, with a walking cane in his right hand and wearing a heavily plumed tricorne. Were it not for the inscription he might be taken for a Chelsea Pensioner out for a stroll.

On arrival, William walked onto a red carpet and a guard of honour was waiting to greet him. The town's dignitaries were present in their robes, and William, wearing an orange sash 'of the finest watered silk' stood stiffly as they bowed before him. An aged Quaker had been chosen to give the formal address, but his religious scruples deterred him from doffing his hat or using royal titles. The old man shuffled forward, bareheaded, and said: 'William thou are welcome to thy kingdom'. This quaint greeting delighted the normally gloomy William who brightened up and said: 'You are the best bred gentlemen whom I have met since I have come hither'. An exchange of courtesies followed and William set off for Belfast with his retinue.

Halfway along the shoreside is the little port of Whitehouse where most of the Orange army disembarked. It was here that Schomberg and a number of senior military and civil personnel were waiting to greet William. Some were of noble and even royal blood, including: Prince George of Daamstadt, brother of King Christian V of Denmark, husband of James' young daughter Anne, and therefore, brother-in-law of William; Hans Willem Bentinck, William's childhood friend, shortly to be created Earl of Portland; James Butler, second Duke of Ormonde, commander of the English guards regiments; Charles Montague, first Duke of Manchester; Robert Lumley, Earl of Scarborough, prominent among the Whigs who had invited William to England; and Robert Harley, Earl of Oxford. Other notables included Thomas Coningsby, joint receiver and paymaster general, and Henry Sidney, another Whig who had been party to William's invitation.

When these gentlemen had paid their respects, Schomberg introduced his son, Mienhard, Count Schomberg, a cavalry general who had served in the previous year's campaign in Ulster; next came General Ferdinand Wilhelm, Duke of Würtemburg-Neustadt, commander of the Danish forces; then, Baron Godert von Ginkel of Utrecht, destined to become Earl of Athlone, commander of the Dutch forces; Count Henry Nassau, William's cousin; General Percy Kirk, commander of the English forces, and Governor Gustave Hamilton of Enniskillen, representing the Irish Protestant contingents. Among the high-ranking civic officials were George Clarke, William's secretary of war, Jean Payen de la Fouleresse, the Danish ambassador and Sir Robert Southwell, the Williamite secretary of state for Ireland.[5]

William and Schomberg retired to a mansion at Macedon Point – halfway between Carrickfergus and Belfast – owned by Sir William Franklin, husband of the Dowager Countess of Donegall, and it was observed that there was a coolness between them. This was attributed to William's annoyance at Schomberg's lack of vigour in the previous year. Later, William travelled to Belfast in Schomberg's coach and entered the town by the north gate – near where North Street now crosses Royal Avenue – where a great crowd was present to greet him.

At that time Belfast was a small town. It had only five streets, and these were freshly gravelled each day in preparation for the coming of William. Its principle buildings were Belfast Castle and two churches: the parish church, where St George's now stands on High Street and the Presbyterian meeting house in Rosemary Lane. The population was not more than a thousand, and was wholly Protestant. For days prior to William's coming there were excited flutterings. Every house was hung with bunting and banners were strung across the streets, saying: 'God Save William Our King' and 'Long Live the Protestant King'. Nobody was allowed in the vicinity of the stable reserved for the king's horse.

As William's coach came through the north gate, Rev. Story says that people, at first, could do nothing but stare 'never having seen a king in this part of the world before, but after a while some of them began to huzzah and rest took to it (as hounds to the scent) and followed his coach through several regiments of foot who were drawn up towards his majesty's lodgings'. William was welcomed by the sovereign, Captain Robert Leathes and Rev. George Walker, recently appointed bishop-elect of Derry. An official reception was held in the castle, and after the opening addresses, William commanded that a fast be held throughout the kingdom for the success of the coming campaign. Several royal salutes were fired and, at dusk, great bonfires blazed on the hill-tops.

William appeared relaxed among his most avowedly loving subjects and joked with his new aide-de-camp, Colonel Thomas Bellingham.[6] He wrote a happy letter to Mary, saying that he found the Irish air to his liking – probably a reference to his chronic asthma – and that he was pleased to see that his Irish Protestant subjects were of such fine material.

Next day, 15 June, William attended divine service at the parish church in High Street and listened to the chaplain, Rev. George Royce, preach on the text Hebrews 11:33:

> Go forth then, great prince, in the power and the defence of the Most High … then when you pass through the waters He shall be with you. Then, through God we shall do great acts, for it is He who shall tread down your enemies.

When William read the lesson, some of his listeners marvelled that his Dutch vowel sounds were not too dissimilar to their own. Tradition had it that he pronounced the word 'dog' as 'dug' – an intonation still heard across the channel in Renfrewshire, the ancestral home of many Ulster Protestants. But it was found that in ordinary conversation William's speech was more in line with that of the Gaelic Irish. His use of the word 'after' as in 'I am after eating' was seen as a case in point.[7]

After church, William's officers bought dinner at Rourke's Eating House for three shillings, and the town seemed abuzz, as military reinforcements poured in. The Long Bridge was said to be so damaged by the weight of cannon pulled across it, that seven of its arches collapsed soon afterwards. On 15 June William reviewed a regiment of horse in Belfast Park and later that day was advised by his physician to quit the town, as it was 'not very healthful' in that long, hot summer. But Belfast remained in a flurry and he tarried. The local gentry presented loyal addresses and Rev. Walker introduced an Anglican dignitary who read from a parchment:

> To the king's most excellent majesty, the humble address of the Church of Ireland, now in Ulster: Great Sir – We, your majesty's most loyal subjects, out of the deepest sense of the blessings of this day, and with the most joyful hearts congratulate your majesty's safe landing in this kingdom. As we must always praise God for the wonders which he has wrought by your majesty's hands, we cannot but applaud but admire your majesty's remarkable zeal for the Protestant religion and for the piece of these kingdoms …[8]

A less saccharin address was read by Rev. Patrick Adare, minister of Belfast, 'on behalf of those of the Presbyterian persuasion in the north of Ireland'. This must have pleased William for a few days later he commanded the collector of taxes in Belfast, Christopher Corleton, to pay £1,200 per annum to the clergy of the Presbyterian Church, being assured, he said, 'of their constant labour to unite the hearts of others in zeal and loyalty towards us'. This may be taken as the real commencement of the *Regium Donum* or Royal Bounty, previously granted to dissenting clergymen by Charles II, but irregularly paid, and scrapped altogether by James. The bounty was not only important financially to those who were entitled to receive it, but was a tangible recognition of the status of dissenters under the new dispensation.

THE MARCH TO LISBURN

However pleasant the Belfast interlude may have been, William was anxious to press ahead and announced that he had 'no intention of letting grass grow under his feet'. He left Belfast on 19 June for Loughbrickland in Co. Down where his army had mustered. There are numerous tales of people whom he met as his cavalcade marched south. One holds that he left Belfast by the present Dublin road and that 'William's Park' at the junction of University Road and Lisburn Road is a reminder that he passed close by; it is said also that heavy rain obliged him to take shelter under trees near a house called 'Cranmore' (the big tree) and that its owner, John Eccles, gave him refreshments. The name of the house was later changed to 'Orange Grove' and the cup from which he drank was retained until it disintegrated. In another story, it is said that a Huguenot blacksmith, Rene Bulmer, did him a service, and asked that his reward should be that William embrace him, as French generals often did when conferring an honour. Eyeing Bulmer's attractive wife, William said: *'Mais oui mon vieux je te salueras voluntiers et ta femme aussi'* (But yes, old friend, I greet you gladly and your wife also).

Despite these hold-ups William reached Schomberg's headquarters at Lisburn for lunch, and spent the afternoon inspecting troops at Blaris Moor, not far from Long Kesh/Maze. He stayed the night in Lisburn Castle, and next day sat in the saddle for several hours as he reviewed his army which had now grown to 36,000. It turned out splendidly and comprised 10,000 Scandinavians – Danes, Swedes, Norwegians and Finns; the Dutch and Brandenburg contingents were 7,000 strong and there were 11,000 English and Scots; the Enniskilleners totalled about 1,000 (in four regiments: Wynn's, Tiffin's, Lloyd's and Cunningham's) and two companies from Bandon, of about 100 men.

The review over, the army swung from the parade ground with Schomberg at its head and marched towards Newry, with each man singing 'Lillyburlero' as he went.

THE JACOBITE BUILD-UP

The Jacobites spent the winter months in hibernation. Nothing was done to prepare for the coming struggle. There were few meetings of the high command; the welfare of the troops was neglected and the military administration was deplorable. James spent much of his time in *amours*, and his officers gambled, fought duels and were as flirtatious as the monarch himself. The behaviour of the Dublin court raised eye-brows and was enlivened by the worldly designs of the Duchess of Tyrconnell, who sought to find rich husbands for her flighty daughters.

Among the incidents that disturbed the frivolity was a quarrel bet-ween Henry FitzJames ('the grand prior') and Lord Dungan, one of the best Irish officers. At a party Dungan proposed a toast to 'the confused Lord Melfont and all bad counsellors' and requested FitzJames to drink to it. The young man gruffly refused, declaring that Melfont was his friend, and angrily flung his wine in Dungan's face. The incident would have provoked a duel but for the intervention of Berwick. D'Avaux, who recorded the episode, said that FitzJames was a 'debauched young man, drinking brandy all day, and unable for a long stretch to mount his horse through intoxication'. It was fortunate that Dungan was level headed and did not press the matter, otherwise the king's son may have come to grief.

In the New Year James bestirred himself and sent appeals to France for troops to strengthen his forces. Louis could not provide all that was requested, but between 12 and 14 March a fleet of 41 men-at-war ar-rived in Cork carrying 7,000 trained men of all ranks. The officer sent to command them was, however, a poor choice. This was Antonin-Nompar de Caumont, otherwise, the Comte et Duc de Lauzun. He was no sol-dier, but a courtier and adventurer. His appointment has been seen as one of the greatest French blunders of the war.

Lauzun's career had been amazing. At one time, Louis had become infatuated with one of his mistresses and stole her from him. Lauzun kicked up a storm and the king had him thrown into the Bastille for six months. A few years later, Anne-Marie d'Orleans, Louis' cousin (known as La Grande Mademoiselle, one of the wealthiest heiresses in Europe) astonished the court by announcing that she had proposed to Lauzun. Louis at first consented to the match, but retracted under pressure from the nobles and Lauzun fell from grace. He was again thrown into jail, this time, until he renounced title to lands which the besotted duchesse had fixed on him.

On release, he went to England and curried favour with James. In December 1688 he was commissioned to convey Mary Beatrice and her infant to France. His efficient execution of this service placed James in his debt and even reinstated him in the eyes of Louis. But when James requested his appointment to the Irish command, Louis at first demur-red, and, then – against his better judgement – yielded. D'Avuax spoke out against it, and Louvois was not in favour. Yet this vein, dapper, self-promoting little man, with limited military experience, became com-mander-in-chief of the French forces in Ireland.[9]

His arrival was ignored. There was no one to greet him when he disembarked at Cork and he took offence. He made a formal complaint to James and blame was put on Lord Dover, the recently appointed indentant-general at Cork, who had been inadequately instructed. It took the new commander several days to reach Dublin; his regiments followed and set up camp at the Curragh in Kildare.

Lauzun got down to business. His first task was to assemble the Jacobite army. This was easier said than done as the men were scattered widely and communications between their quarters was poor. The whole of May and much of June was taken up arranging a muster at Dundalk. It was not until 12 June (two days before William arrived at Carrickfergus) that the entire army was assembled. When James arrived in Dundalk from Dublin, William was already marching southward.

A clash was now eminent, and a brief engagement took place at the Moyry Pass – the legendary 'Gap of the North' – just north of Newry where the road runs through a narrowing which could easily be defended. The northern end was held by a Williamite patrol, but on the night of 22 June a troop of Jacobites swept down and drove them off with a loss of about thirty. The victory was hardly gainful, for one of those taken, a Captain Farlow, gave misleading information during cross-questioning. He exaggerated the size of William's army and said that the Prince of Orange planned to flank Drogheda on the west and send a fleet down the coast to cut off a Jacobite retreat on the east. James became anxious, feeling that his army could not cope with such a double threat. He decided to fall back and hold the line of the Boyne, where, as he said, 'he would be in a better position to defend Dublin'.

On 30 June, the Orange army marched in two columns from Ardee to the northern slopes of the Boyne. From Tullyusker Hill outside Drogheda, William surveyed the countryside and made his famous remark: 'Gentlemen, this is a country well worth fighting for'. A troop of dragoons discovered about 200 old scythes in a farmhouse and brought them to him for inspection. William eyed them thoughtfully for a moment or two, and said dryly: 'These are very dangerous weapons', winking knowingly to General Ginkel. His opponents, it was felt, would have to do better than fight with scythes.

The moment of high drama had arrived. It was sensational that two kings related by blood and by marriage should face each other across the waters of an Irish river. The outcome would determine the course of Irish history for generations.

12

THE BOYNE WATER

Here from my hand as from a cup
I pour this poor libation
And ere I drink, I offer up
One fervent aspiration
Let man with man, let kit with kin
Content through fields of slaughter –
Whoever fights, may freedom win
And then, at the Boyne water.
FROM 'THE BOYNE WATER' – AN OLD WILLIAMITE BALLAD

THE GREEN GRASSY SLOPES

The Boyne is not the greatest of Irish rivers, but is surely the most cele-brated. On its banks are the neolithic tombs of Newgrange, Knowth and Dowth, wonders older than Stonehenge and the Pyramids of Egypt. Nearby is the Hill of Tara from where the high kings of Ireland ruled their domains. Christianity itself is said to have come to Ireland through this historic waterway.

The river rises in Co. Kildare and takes a meandering course west and north before entering Co. Meath, through which it flows in a north-easterly direction, passing Trim, Navan and Slane until forming the boundary line with Co. Louth before entering the sea below Drogheda. In the 1690s it was navigable at high tide for nearly ten miles, but at low tide was little more than a stream at certain points between Navan and Slane; from Slane to the village of Oldbridge (now gone) it was fordable by horse at every rood of its length. Past Slane it runs due east for near-ly a mile until, dipping abruptly, it takes a semi-circular sweep for near-ly three miles: the chord of the arc measuring about two miles, and the distance from Oldbridge to Slane – as the crow flies – being about five miles. In the semi-circle lies the focal point of the famous battle.[1]

The contours of the surrounding countryside are singular: on the northern bank for nearly two miles back – and down to the waters edge – the ground is high and firm and holds deep ravines where troops may be hidden and protected from cannon fire; it provides, also, a pano-ramic view of the opposite side. To the south, the terrain is low and sedgy up to the base of the Hill of Donore, beyond which, at the time of the battle, certain pieces of ground were marshy and intersected with ditches. Where the river curls around Oldbridge it is about 150 yards wide, but broadens slightly as it descends towards Drogheda. Behind Donore – and five miles from the river – is the village of Duleek on the river Nanny. Here, all the roads to the south converge and a narrow bridge, provides the only escape route for a retreating army.

Upstream at Rosnaree, between Slane and Oldbridge – but nearer to Slane – there was a ford at which infantry could cross, and at Slane itself, a narrow bridge; there were also numerous crossing points in the vicinity of Oldbridge. The southern bank was therefore approachable on many points and if the river were crossed upstream – at either Slane or Rosnaree – an assailing army could double-back and encroach on the line to Duleek, thereby entrapping an enemy in the Oldbridge half-circle.

The rivers tidal character had significance. When troops in battle cross flowing water they usually do not have unlimited time. If the water rises rapidly during the operation a section of the force may be cut off or stranded and not easily relieved. The water's depth depends on the tides, recent rainfall and the winds. At the time of the battle, it should be noted that the Boyne was fordable at low and spring tides and only slightly less so at neap tides (that is, when the water rises less and falls less). On the date in question – 1 July 1690 – the moon was five days old and the tides were not at their extremes; the neaps were beginning but were low enough to permit crossing at several points before the end of the ebb.[2]

Finally, it should be mentioned that at Drogheda there was a bridge which could be easily defended, and between that point and Oldbridge, a distance of over two miles, there were no crossing points.

On Sunday evening, 29 June, James' army – about 25,000 strong – crossed the river in two columns, one at Drogheda and the other over a ford at Oldbridge. William's army –36,000 strong – arrived next morning. The Jacobites stationed themselves east of the Donore gradient, their right wing extending towards Drogheda and their left stretching upstream. Their first act was to destroy the bridge at Slane and then, throw up entrenchments in front of the old stone houses at Oldbridge. James established his headquarters on elevated ground to the east, with a number of crack cavalry units, including Sarsfield's, protecting him.

There were numerous viewpoints among the Jacobites about engaging, and their reasons for doing so are not entirely clear. Lauzun thought that the river line could not be held and was against engagement. He later wrote that on arrival he reconnoitred upstream and found the river fordable at all points. He recommended that they should fall back on Dublin, burn it, and move westward where James could play cat and mouse with William indefinitely. It was French policy, of course, to drag out the war rather than to conclude it; besides, Lauzun had instructions from Lauvois not to engage in pitch battles. James had, however, his own reasons for making a stand. He wanted to defend Dublin; he felt that if the capital fell, all of Ireland would follow. In his *Memoirs* (written in the conventional royal third person) he acknowledges the weakness of his position, but says that he had no alternative but to risk battle:

> What induced the king to hazard a battle of this inequality was that if he did not, he must loose all without a stroke and be obliged to quit Dublin and Munster and retire behind the Shannon and so be reduced to the Province of Connaught, where having no magazines he could not subsist very long, it being the worst corn in Ireland. Besides, his men were desirous to fight, and being newly raised would have been disheartened to retire behind the enemy and see their country taken without a blow, and in consequence, be apt to disperse giving up all for lost.[3]

Notwithstanding this post-facto *apologia*, Jacobite intentions remain speculative. It was patently imprudent for a poorly trained army, with little ordnance, and inferior numbers to face the might of William across a shallow river. It is even hard to believe that the Jacobites envisioned victory. Belloc has suggested that all they had in mind was a delaying operation – a manoeuvre to stall the Williamite advance and allow time for their army to extricate itself from a tricky situation.[4] As for defending Dublin, while laudable, the proposition seems hyperbolic. Dublin was not militarily important and could not be held indefinitely. Besides, if William was intent on taking it, the stand at the Boyne was unlikely to forestall him; all he had to do was to skirt Slane and move on Dublin from that direction.

Much of this is, of course, conjectural; what actually happened is of greater import. The Jacobites, initially, sought to protect themselves by placing their big guns in three batteries – one, just south of Oldbridge and the others opposite Yellow Island (one of two islands in the river) to the east. The next move came from the Williamites who sent a few troops of horse to Drogheda to test the alertness of the garrison there. Then, the gunners on both sides opened up on each other. Soon, a heavy cloud of smoke and dust hung over the Boyne. An entry in a Danish journal records that William was urged to make a foray across the water on the first day but turned down the suggestion as he felt Mondays to be unlucky.

WILLIAM WOUNDED

William, in fact, spent the first morning seeking information on the fords. He questioned scouts, called for maps and sought reports. In the early afternoon he rode down to the river to scrutinise it for himself. With a few of his staff he stood on the northern bank at Oldbridge making inspections, within enemy musket range. Presently, a group of high-ranking Jacobites on horseback appeared on the other side – Lauzun, Tyrconnell, Berwick, John Parker and Sarsfield. Both parties stared at each other frostily before the Jacobites moved off. Within minutes the Jacobites brought up two field pieces and trained them on William. Nothing happened until he mounted; then a gunner fired and killed a man and two horses about a hundred yards from William. He fired again; this time the ball grazed the river bank and rising upwards hit William on the shoulder, taking away a piece of his leather jerkin and tearing the flesh.[5]

William leant forward heavily and the Jacobites must have thought they had killed him. But the wound was slight and he made little of it, his remark being *T'houbt niet naeder* (it need not have come nearer). A report that he had been killed reached Dublin and even Paris, and gave rise to the lighting of bonfires. The wound, however, was slight and Thomas Coningsby (afterwards a lord justice of Ireland) applied his handkerchief to it. The official report said that the wound was a contusion about as big as a hand and that William lost 'near half a spoonful of blood'. Later, he rode around his camp to allay rumours of his condition.

That evening, William called a council of war in the nearby ruined Mellifont abbey. Schomberg proposed that the army be split into two unequal parts, the smaller of which should assault Oldbridge and tie down the main body of the enemy, while the larger, screened by the hillslopes, should move upstream, cross the river at vantage points, outflank the enemy and double back to cut off a retreat. It was a daring and imaginative plan, but Count Solms, the Dutch leader, disagreed; he favoured a direct attack by the entire army on Oldbridge. William did not favour Schomberg's proposal, perhaps because he was still annoyed by the duke's failure of the previous year. He found Solms' plan 'bold and daring' and more in keeping with his own views. In deciding the matter, he opted for a compromise. Old Schomberg took this as a snub and retired in a huff to his tent. Later, when the order of battle was sent to him, he received it peevishly: 'it was the first which was ever sent to me'.

The compromise included important elements of both proposals and William's own ideas. The duke's son, Count Meinhard Schomberg was to move off at first light, with about a third of the army and cross the river four or five miles upstream and make contact with the enemy at around 9 a.m. Shortly afterwards Old Schomberg, with most of the main body, was to attack through the centre at Oldbridge, and William himself on the left further downstream at Drybridge. These movements were scheduled for between 8 and 9 a.m. when it was calculated that the tide would be at ebb. The computation was, in fact, inaccurate for on the day the ebb was between 9.30 and 10 a.m., but, in the event, the crossings did not begin until later.

After the council of war, William rode by torchlight through his camp, inspecting everything and issuing final orders. He made a striking figure in his plumed hat, flowing wig and long jackboots. The flare of the torches accentuating his Roman nose; his face pale from fatigue, but his eyes bright and penetrating. He seemed like a man whose hour had come.

THE JACOBITE CAMP

The Jacobites also held a council of war. Lieutenant-General Richard Hamilton[6] suggested – indeed begged – that a strong force be sent to defend the broken bridge at Slane which could be overlaid with planks, and another sent to guard the ford at Rosnaree. His views were only partly adopted: no force went to Slane, but 800 dragoons under Sir Neil O'Neill (of Killyleagh, Co. Antrim) was sent to Rosnaree with instructions 'to defend that pass as long as possible, without exposing your men to be cut to pieces'. It was agreed, that if the entrenchments around Oldbridge were breached the defenders should retire to the ditches and hedges which surrounded the old houses, and that if these were overrun, they should retire to Donore; if unable to hold Donore, they should fall back on Duleek and defend the bridge there. Retire and retire again was the dominant Jacobite motif. Little else was considered, which lends credence to the view that they were seeking only a limited engagement. Indeed, James had already sent much of his baggage to Dublin – guarded by guns which would have been needed in a wholescale encounter – and Sir Patrick Trent was dispatched to Waterford to have a ship prepared for his transfer to France.

Petrie has questioned why so few defensive preparations were put in hand: no attempts were made to organise rebouts although their value was well known to the French army of the period.[7] Nothing was done to render the fords difficult or to put obstacles on the riverbed. It is curious that no pre-emptive strike or counter-attack was considered. In these circumstances it is hardly surprising that the Jacobite troops were despondent on the eve of battle.

The French, as we know, were present to represent their own national interest. The Irish sided with James for their meagre wages and in the hope of winning tolerance for their religion. They had an uncomplicated view of the war and tended to believe, gullibly, what their leaders told them. These leaders, drawn almost exclusively from the 'Old English' class had their eyes on a favourable land settlement should the outcome be propitious; further aspirations could wait.

William, it should be remembered, was not only superior in numbers and in the size of his ordnance, but also in the quality of his officers and troops. Many were veterans from other campaigns and some of his high command were among the foremost strategists in Europe. Apart from ordnance, his general fire-power was superior: his infantry had the recently developed flintlock musket which increased the range and speed of their firing, whereas the Jacobites had to make do with the older matchlock type.

A number of different uniforms were worn but none distinguished one side from the other. To recognise each other the Williamites wore green sprigs in their hats; the colour had nothing to do with Irish nationalism (a concept unknown at the time) and was probably adopted because of easy procurement, although green was the traditional colour of the House of Nassau. The Jacobites wore pieces of white paper; white being the symbol of the House of Stuart. The Irish contingents, on both sides fought, as was their custom, in their shirt-sleeves.[8] It is interesting to note that for the most part commands were issued in French. This was because most of the aristocratic commanders were either bilingual or spoke wholly in French.

THE BATTLE BEGINS

Following the settling of plans, the shades of night fell on the Boyne valley and over the sleeping armies. The stars shone down on more than 60,000 souls – brothers in the great human family – who were destined on the morrow to imbue their hands in each other's blood. God and nature had formed them in a common image, but rival factions and warring creeds had set them against each other. Twinkling lights gleamed through the darkness, from the watchtowers at Drogheda, to the peasant cabins along the valley. A dog barked in the distance and the murmur of the river fell faintly on the ear. The only other sounds heard in the Boyne valley that night were the hoarse challengings of the sentries as they paced their rounds and received the patrols.

The night passed. As it blended with dawn, a succession of drum rolls could be heard on Tullyallen. They were answered by a roll from the Hill of Donore. It was not until five o'clock that Count Meinhard Schomberg and his men moved off through the fields towards Slane,

BATTLE OF THE BOYNE 1690

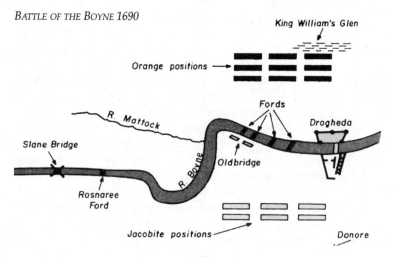

their breaths puffing in the cold morning air.[9] The force was a strong one and included cavalry and dragoon regiments and ten infantry battalions. Its movement could not be detected from James' camp as it was screened by the tumulus of Newgrange, Knowth and Dowth – the burial chambers of ancient Irish warriors – and the men did not come into view until they joined together at Rosnaree at about eight o'clock.

Waiting for them was Sir Neil O'Neill and his dragoons. The clash was immediate and fierce, but O'Neill could not cope with the numbers against him. Yet, he heroically held the ford for half an hour. As his men were swept aside, O'Neill was wounded and rescued only with difficulty. He died a week later at Waterford, while awaiting transfer to France. When William learned of Count Schomberg's breakthrough he sent General James Douglas and further cavalry to support him.

Lauzun and his Frenchmen, lying to the left of Donore, were the first to learn of O'Neill's defeat, and jumped, impetuously, to a false conclusion. He took it that the main Williamite thrust was to be at Rosnaree, rather than, as thought, at Oldbridge and informed James. The bewildered monarch made no objection when Lauzun and his 7,000 men marched off (with all their artillery pieces) to the left, to confront Count Schomberg. James now panicked; he believed that he was about to be encircled and cut off from Duleek – the escape hatch. Without consultation he instructed further sections of the army to follow Lauzun. It was a fatal decision. Sarsfield's and Maxwell's cavalry units had to reposition themselves to follow Lauzun; so too did Cairney's and Waucope's infantry, who minutes before had been stationed between Oldbridge and Drogheda. As they redeployed they could see to the north Douglas' cavalry moving westward; this completed the illusion that the main battle was to be fought upstream. Little did they know that they were marching in the wrong direction. They had, in fact, been sold a dummy by William, and James had responded by weakening his centre.

Count Schomberg had done well to cross the river, but he was scarcely over when he ran into difficulties. Lauzun's men appeared out of the blue and positioned themselves along a hillside in front of him; soon they were joined by Sarsfield's and Maxwell's horse. A major engagement was on the cards until both sides discovered that a large patch of wet, boggy terrain lay between them. To their mutual frustration all they could do was eyeball each other across a morass. They spent several hours galloping up and down, testing the ground and shouting abuse at each other; but it was posturing. The advantage lay, of course, with Count Schomberg. He had succeeding in drawing the best Jacobite units away from the centre and had effectively neutralised them.

This manoeuvring took several hours and it was past noon when James received information from a messenger who galloped up from Oldbridge. The breathless officer reported that William had launched a series of attacks on the downstream fords and that his army was now established on the southern bank in great strength. The Jacobite army was now threatened on two fronts. James' options were running out.

THE FIGHT AT OLDBRIDGE

From early morning William's artillery had been softening up the Jacobite defences around Oldbridge. When he was informed that his right wing had crossed at Rosnaree, he began to put his main body into action. His task was to get enough men across at Oldbridge to establish a bridgehead; those to take the initial plunge would have to be powerful enough to carry the Jacobite defences. Once across they would have to defend the bridgehead and could not advance until supporting troops arrived in sufficient numbers. During these operations they would be without cavalry support and have to stand their ground in the face of Jacobite counter-attack. There were obvious dangers: the Jacobites might choose to fight on a broad front, absorb or suck in the Williamite attack, and then assail from the flanks.

The morning was bright and fresh; the sky was cloudless; the only sound was the roar of cannon and the trudging of feet. The initial assault was planned for shortly after low tide, but was for some reason delayed. Sometime after 10 a.m., the Dutch blue guard – William's favourite regiment – marched down from Tullyallen, under cover of the ravine now known as King William's Glen, their drums beating loudly.[10] At the water's edge the drums went silent and the men waded into the river ten abreast, holding their muskets over their heads. Tightly packed, the guards held back the incoming tide, forming, in effect, a human dam. As their front neared the southern bank a thunderous volley roared against them, but much of it was badly aimed and ineffective.

A lieutenant of grenadiers was the first to emerge. He drew the men up quickly and they pushed their way into the village. The fighting took on a desperate character, but the Dutch prevailed, sweeping aside three Jacobite infantry regiments. They then moved beyond the village and re-formed for a continued advance. As they moved forward, further Williamite forces began to cross the river. Tyrconnell, watching it all from the Hill of Donore, cursed Lauzun and James for weakening the centre. He ordered a cavalry charge and the Dutch, bracing themselves, formed hollow squares and with their bayoneted muskets set up a *chevause de frise* (a piked defence), to meet it.

Although old and ailing, Tyrconnell himself, led the charge with great dash, and it crashed again and again against the enemy. For three quarters of an hour the fighting was so intense that veterans said that they had never seen brisker work. Conspicuous bravery was shown by Berwick and Major General Dominic Sheldon.[11] William, watching from Tullyallen was uneasy. His secretary of war, the Oxford don, Sir George

Clarke, later remembered him mutter: 'my poor guards, my poor guards'. But when he saw them persevere 'he breathed out, as people do after holding their breath'. The vigour of these cavalry charges raises the question of whether the Jacobites could have checked the incursions across the river, had they held the sector in greater strength. The French general Hogutte was of the view that the Williamites could have been foiled, and expressed his disgust at Lauzun for not arranging matters better.[12] The courage and prowess of the Jacobite cavalry drew tributes from even their enemies. The Duke of Würtemburg's comment was: 'the Irish cavalry behaved extremely well, but their foot extremely badly'.[13] Würtemburg could not, however, have been expected to know that the foot consisted of raw levies who had never heard a shot fired in anger; other accounts say that these men put up a better show than could have reasonably been expected.[14]

On seeing his blue guard so heavily pressed, William ordered two Huguenot regiments to give them assistance. As they emerged from the water they were met by Hamilton's infantry and made their way with difficulty. They had scarcely gained the bank when a body of Irish dragoons swung at their flanks and sent them scurrying back into the water. Callimotte, their leader, was wounded in the thigh and died later. As he was carried back across the river, he tried to rally his men by shouting: *'a la gloire, mes enfants, a la gloire'* (on to glory, my children, on to glory).

Old Schomberg, seeing the Huguenots in trouble could not restrain himself. He rushed impetuously into the water and, pointing his sword at the enemy, shouted: *'Allons, messieurs, voite vos perseceutors'* (come on, gentlemen, these are your persecutors). It was a rash venture. In the melee, a lieutenant in Dorrington's Irish regiment, Charles O'Toole, struck the duke in the neck with his sabre. It was not a fatal cut, but in the confusion, a stray shot from Schomberg's own side hit him in the throat. The ball penetrated the windpipe and he died within minutes.

The death of Schomberg maddened the Huguenots, who began firing wildly and roaring: *'Tue! Tue! Tue!'* (Kill! Kill! Kill!). They beat back Hamilton's men and carried Schomberg's body back across the water. It was a tragic end for the old warrior. William, when he was told the news by the duke's aide-de-camp, received it coldly. His displeasure with the dead man apparently still rankled. Yet, it was surprising that Schomberg was not honoured with a military funeral; his body was quietly interred several days later, in St Patrick's cathedral, Dublin. For all his fame he was quickly forgotten. His tomb remained unmarked until several years later, when Johnathan Swift and the chapter of the cathedral placed a plaque on it. This recounts the dean's criticism of Schomberg's relatives for neglecting the grave. A translation of the Latin inscription says:

> Beneath this stone lies the body of Freidrich, Duke of Schomberg, who was
> killed at the Boyne on AD 1690. The dean and chaplain earnestly and re-
> peatedly requested the duke's heirs to undertake the erection of a monu-
> ment to the memory of their father. Long and often they pressed the
> request by letter and through friends. It was of no avail. At long last they
> set up this stone that at least you may know, stranger, where the ashes of
> Schomberg lie buried.
>
> The renown of his valour had greater power among strangers than
> the ties of blood among his kit and kin. AD 1731.[15]

Rev. George Walker of Derry fell shortly after Schomberg. William, also
appeared indifferent to his loss. On learning of his fate, he said, with
irritation: 'what took him there?' An eyewitness said that Walker's body
was stripped of its clothing 'for the Scots-Irish took most of the plunder'. He was buried near where he fell, and sometime later his wife, Isa-
bella, had his body disinterred. It was taken to the church at Castlecauld-
field, Co. Tyrone, where it was reburied near the chancel in 1702.

It was now two hours since the Dutch blue guards had made their
incursion and William decided that the moment had come to make his
own crossing. He had been told of a ford about a mile downstream at
Drybridge, just below Yellow Island, where a flanking movement could
be carried out. Leading the Enniskilling, Danish and Dutch horse, he
plunged into the river, but halfway across his horse became stuck in
deep mud and he was forced to dismount as the animal was dragged
back to the bank.[16] With his right arm in a sling, he carried a sword in
his left hand (in some accounts he is mentioned as carrying a walking
stick) and despite his discomfort, within minutes he was riding at the
head of his cavalry in the direction of the Hill of Donore and threatening to reach it before the now retreating Jacobites. The Jacobite cavalry,
however, were the first to arrive; reaching the summit they wheeled
their horses around and dashed back upon the enemy, driving them
apart in great confusion. William, at this point, was in great danger and
one of the Enniskilleners, not recognising him, was about to shoot him
down, when a colonel shouted out his identity, effectively saving him.
Then, putting himself at the head of the Enniskilleners, he told them:
'Gentlemen, you shall be my guards today. I have heard much of you.
Let me now see something of you'.

The fighting was hot for the control of Donore, where Hamilton's
cavalry dismounted and dug themselves in amongst the ruins of the
old church. William courted danger and was struck by two balls, one
of which carried away the heel of his boot. Finally, he made a fresh
charge at the head of some Dutch cavalry, and after desperate fighting,
the Irish were driven from Donore. Further on, the Enniskilleners were
pressing the retreating Irish, and Hamilton made a cavalry charge which
swept them back; but he pressed them too far and was wounded and

taken prisoner. He was brought before William, who asked him if he thought the Irish were likely to charge again.

'Upon my honour, Sir, I think they will, for they have a good body of horse left'.

'Your honour, Hamilton?' queried William contemptuously. He remembered that his captive had not too long before turned his coat.[17]

THE RETREAT

Earlier, when James learned of the breaching of the fords at Oldbridge, he believed that his army was being trapped in a pincher movement. There was, he felt, only one way ahead and that was to attack Count Schomberg across the morass. Sarsfield was sent to reconnoitre the area dividing the forces, but fate was again cruel to the Jacobites. Sarsfield reported that: 'it was impossible for the horse to charge the enemy by reason of two double ditches with high banks and a little brook that ran along the valley dividing the armies'.[18] The idea had to be dropped, and seeing that the road to Duleek was being threatened from the east, the call for a retreat became imperative. At this time Lauzun became concerned for James' safety. He advised him to quit the field as the road to Duleek was in danger of being cut off. But James appears to have been uncharistically full of fight and was hesitant. He was, however, prevailed upon. Sarsfield and a strong troop of cavalry were assigned to escort him to Dublin.

There was now a great rush for Duleek. On the Jacobite right Berwick and Galmoy covered the fall back of the infantry. On the left, Count Schomberg made a bid to out-distance Lauzun and the French, but had more ground to cover. Lauzun kept shouting to his horse: 'Faster! Faster! Faster!' But on the whole the Jacobite retreat was well managed. At Duleek there was confusion when both infantry and horse arrived simultaneously and collided as they crossed the river Nanny. Captain John Stevens who with the grand priors regiment wrote:

> The horse came on so unexpected and with such speed, some firing their pistols, that we had no time to receive or shun them, but all supposing them to be the enemy (as indeed they were no better to us) took to their heels, no officer being able to stop the men after they were broken.[19]

A measure of discipline was restored when the French General Zurlauban ordered his men to fire on any troops which did not fall into line.[20] For the next hour or so French guns kept the Williamites at bay as the Jacobites made their way to safety. But not all got away. Rev. Story records the fate of those who fell into Williamite hands: 'few or none of them escaped that came into our clutches, for they were shot like hares among the corn …'

The Battle of the Boyne was over, and debate has continued as to its significance. The French dismissed it as a skirmish followed by a re-treat (*e chauffouree suivie d'une deroute*);[21] the Williamites saw its as a glorious victory. Of the two views, the latter is surely the most exaggerated. The Jacobite army, it is true, failed to hold the line of the Boyne, but it was not destroyed. It put up a better fight than, perhaps, could have been reasonably expected. William did not capture a single Jacobite field piece, nor scarcely a standard and, as far as we know, took only a single prisoner, Hamilton. The Jacobites lost about a 1,000 men but 24,000 lived to fight again; the Williamite losses have been variously estimated; 500 is the lowest estimate but in some accounts the figure is greater, and even doubled. Neither side displayed any great generalship. It has to be said, however, that the Williamites failed to capitalise on their advantages. Their plan to catch the enemy in a pincher movement failed when Count Schomberg became immobilised on crossing the Boyne. At many of the downstream fords the Jacobites gave as good as they got until overcome by numbers. It is not untrue to say that it was William's numerical strength that gave him the decided advantage rather than any conspicuous valour on the part of his army.

On the Jacobite side, it must be said that they were beset not only with misfortune and incompetence but with inadequacy of numbers, arms and command. Some wished to fight, others did not, and morale was at rock bottom. James and Lauzun were responsible for weakening the centre and, therefore, for pitting 6,000 raw levies against 15,000 professional soldiers. There was also the failure to properly cover their flanks, and, at the end, the decision that all should fall back simultaneously on Duleek was unwise and, inevitably, caused confusion.

So, who won? Macauley and Whiggish historians have never been in doubt: to them the Boyne was unquestionably a great victory for William. Others – Boulger, Belloc and Petrie – have been less sure, taking the view that the battle was a minor tactical victory for William, but nothing to shout about. Todhunter went so far as to declare the contest a draw.[22] The conventional wisdom then and since has been that William was the undoubted victor. But contemporary celebrations were muted, particularly in London. The gilt was taken off the victory by news of the almost simultaneous defeat of the combined English and Dutch fleets off Beachy Head in Sussex by the French. No such news hamstrung the revels in Austria and Spain. These included the singing of *Te Duems* in Austrian and Spanish cathedrals – a manifestation of thanksgiving that the victorious Irish Protestants found as offensive to their convictions, as the defeated Irish Catholics found it to theirs. Of contemporary Jacobite opinion, we have the views of Sarsfield. On the word of a Williamite bishop, he implied acceptance of defeat when he told an opponent: 'change kings and we will fight you over again'.[23]

13

FALLBACK ON THE SHANNON

Old Limerick is in danger,
And Ireland is not free;
So Sarsfield sends a message
To a fearless rapparee –
Come ride across the Shannon
At the sounding of the drum –
And we'll blow the enemy siege train
To the Land of Kingdom Come

FROM 'THE BALLAD OF "GALLOPING" HOGAN'

THE HINGE OF FATE

The Battle of the Boyne marked a turning point in Irish history. It has been seen as one of a handful of events which decisively changed the country's destiny. If the defeat at Kinsale in 1601 spelled the downfall of the Old Gaelic order, the Boyne marked the doom of the Old English aristocracy. Gone was all hope of the Jacobites using Ireland as a springboard from which James could recover his throne. Gone too was the hope of the old families in having a say in their country's affairs and, particularly, in determining the future of their estates. The Protestants were now in the saddle and their position would remain unchallenged for a hundred years.

But this is known only with hindsight. Had the hinge of fate swung differently at the Boyne the whole complexion of Irish, and even European affairs may have taken a different hue. On the very hour that William drew up his forces on Tullyallen, the combined fleets of England and Holland were almost completely destroyed by Admiral de Tourville at Beachy Head. As he crossed the Boyne, the armies of the League of Augsburg – of which William was the lynchpin – were caught in a double envelopment by the Duc de Luxembourg at Fleurus in Belgium and roundly defeated. While James was hastening to Dublin under Sarsfield's protection, the fleet of Admiral de Seignelay was unmoored and waiting for a favourable wind to destroy the Williamite transports around the Irish coast; the fleet of de Tourville was riding triumphantly around the mouth of the Thames and, it was said that 'there was scarcely 10,000 armed men in all of England for the Dutchman' as the Jacobite cause was being rekindled there.

Certainly had a nominal force been thrown into England at this time, all or most might have been recovered in Ireland. William would have been forced to withdraw his army to 'save the greater stake' and in its absence the Jacobites would, doubtless, have regained control. Or if compelled to remain in Ireland, William may have lost his other two kingdoms, making his hold on the third precarious. His affairs in Holland at this time were also unpromising. The French were predominant everywhere and the Dutch Republic was directly threatened – a matter of greater disquiet to William than even the security of the English crown.

But were the hopes which arose from these circumstances dashed by a single defeat over the waters of an Irish river? It may well have been so. The defeat at the Boyne was a humiliation for Louis XIV and did not endear the Jacobites to him. At this time the French king held many cards and chose to play them to the disadvantage of James. While prepared to drip-feed the Irish war, he was unwilling to provide the Jacobites with enough resources to enable them to stand up effectively to William. This, some historians have said, was one of the greatest mistakes of Louis' reign. Berwick, in his *Memoirs*, did not directly impugn the French king, but attributed the lack of support, at this critical time, to differences within the French cabinet:

> The opportunity was favourable, for Marshal Luxembourg had gained the battle of Fleurus in Flanders; and the Comte de Tourville, who had lately beaten the enemy's fleet, was then at anchor in the Downs, so that the passage to England, being without difficulty or opposition, it was presumed that the king might with ease make himself master of that kingdom. This would likewise have obliged the Prince of Orange to quit Ireland in order to save the greater stake: but M. de Louvois, minister of the war department, who, out of opposition, to M. de Seignelay, minister of the marine department, thwarted all the projects of the king of England, and set himself so strongly to counteract this plan that the most Christian king, overcome by his arguments, refused to consent to it.[1]

WILLIAM IN DUBLIN

Dublin was in turmoil when the result of the Boyne became known. The first news to arrive was that William had been mortally wounded and his army defeated, a tiding which sent Protestants into near hysteria. As one rumour followed another, the streets became crowded and everyone was eagerly newsmongering. Some said that a fleet of French ships had been seen from the Hill of Howth. Others had it that the French had landed in Kent and were proceeding to London; more said that there had been hard fighting at the Boyne, but that the Jacobites had won the day and the Prince of Orange had been put in chains.

Around five in the afternoon the first soldiers arrived. By six, the Catholics knew that all was lost, and the Protestants who had shut themselves away began to emerge. At ten o'clock James arrived protected by Sarsfield and his troop. He rode straight to the castle and on being taken upstairs met Lady Tyrconnell who asked him what he would like for supper. He gave her an account of what he received for breakfast and said he had little stomach for supper. When he told her that his Irish army had run away, she remarked: 'but I see, your majesty has won the race'.[2]

From the dishevelled appearance of the first Jacobites to arrive the citizens expected to see the remnant of a broken army pour into the city. 'We were greatly surprised,' says an anonymous writer, 'when an hour or two after, we heard the whole body of the Irish horse come in, in very good order, with kettle-drums, hautboys and trumpets; and early next morning the French and a great body of the Irish foot. These being rested a little, marched out again to meet the enemy which was supposed to draw near'.

While the army prepared to re-engage the foe, James castigated it. He summoned the lord mayor and council. 'The Irish fled the field', he told them; henceforth he would determine never to lead an Irish army again; 'and now he resolved to shift for himself, as they must do'.[3] Claiming that although he had:

> often been cautioned that when it came to the touch they (the Irish) would never bear the brunt of battle, I could never credit the same till this day, when all preparations made to engage a foreign invader, I found the fatal truth of what I had be precautioned.

This castigation was unjust and took no account of the circumstances under which the Irish troops had fought: they had little equipment, no training and for the most part were raw recruits. But James was gracious enough to acknowledge that 'the army did not desert me here, as it did in England', yet he found this a small consolation:

> … when it came to a trial they basely fled the field and left the spoils to the enemy, nor could they be prevailed upon to rally, though the loss in the defeat was inconsiderable.[4]

After thus reviling the men who fought for him, he uttered words more worthy of a king. He knew, he said, that some of his followers had declared that they would burn Dublin rather than suffer it falling into the hands of the Prince of Orange. Such an act, he thought, would be a disgrace and discredit his cause. The retributions of his enemies would fall on those who had committed such an atrocity. For these reasons he charged his hearers to neither sack or destroy the city.

Next morning, Wednesday 2 July, 'at about four or five' he left Dublin for the last time, crossed the Wicklow hills and did not stop until he was a good distance from the capital. In his own account of his flight, James says that he and an escort rested their horses at Sheldon House, near Arklow, owned by a man named Hackett. Their stay was recalled a century later, in 1771, by Hugh Howard, brother of the first Viscount Wicklow:

An old man, one Richard Johnson, who was the son of a gardener at Sheldon, told me that just after the Battle of the Boyne, being then a young boy, as he was standing one evening in the company of a labouring man of the name of Coughlan in Sheldon Avenue he saw two tall gentlemen, grandly mounted and all covered with dust, ride down Stringers Hill on their way to the ford; but instead of proceeding onwards, they turned up the avenue, whither he followed them, not knowing who they were. When the came to the house ... they alighted and sat down in the porch, where they had some cold meat and a jug of strong beer. While they continued there, which was only for a few minutes, one of them was seized by a violent bleeding of the nose, which stained the post on that side of the porch where the gentlemen sat. When the bleeding was stopped they mounted their horses again and rode down the avenue and across the ford (probably a short cut way to Duncannon fort). He afterwards knew for certain that the person whose nose had bled was King James II, and that the other was a person of distinction ... the porch was afterwards taken down, and the post with the blood on it (which I have seen) long carefully preserved, but has since been burned by the carelessness of servants.[5]

This incident is a reminder that during an earlier period of stress, namely at Salisbury, in the autumn of 1688, James had similarly been afflicted with nasal problems.

From Sheldon House, James pushed on to Duncannon in Waterford estuary. There he found a privateer named, curiously, the *Lauzun* and her captain was ordered to take him to Kinsale, where a squadron of frigates were waiting. Before embarking, he wrote to Tyrconnell, whom he had not seen since the Boyne. He reappointed him lord deputy and sailed for Brest, where he arrived on 20 July, being the first to bring the news of his defeat to his allies.

DUBLIN CHANGES HANDS

Deserted, even defamed by the king for whom they had sacrificed so much, the Jacobite army was left in the lurch. Its senior commanders conferred and Lauzun said that the French contingent must return to France. Favourable terms, he felt, might be negotiated with William, and Tyrconnell agreed. But Sarsfield and the Irish officers said 'no'. All was not lost, they said. They had learned of the French victory at Fleurus, and that de Tourville had beaten the English and Dutch off Beachy Head. Why give up now, when they had suffered little loss at the Boyne, and when the international situation was so favourable? If unity and discipline were maintained, Sarsfield asserted, all might be retrieved; at least the struggle could be prolonged until, perhaps, a fresh French army arrived. It was agreed to fall back on Limerick and orders to this effect were passed on to all the scattered units, who quickly left Dublin and marched south-west.

Most of the civilian administration followed and Dublin, temporarily, was no longer a seat of government. The Protestants who had been in custody were set free and formed mobs which ran about looting the houses that fleeing Catholics had abandoned. Someone had to take charge, and the initiative came from young Robert FitzGerald, a son of the Earl of Kildare, who set about establishing a temporary administration. He acquired the keys of Dublin Castle and made arrangements to control the mobs. Among the first places of pillage was a house owned by Sarsfield, but FitzGerald exercised his authority with 'sword and cane' and prevented much plundering and arson.

Two days later, William established new headquarters at Finglas and rode triumphantly into the city. With much pomp he made his way to St Patrick's cathedral, where the Protestant bishop of Dublin, William King preached on the magnificent deliverance which God and William had wrought on the people. The Protestant magistrates, who had been replaced by Tyrconnell, reappeared in their robes and bowed before the victorious monarch. But William could not be persuaded to stay in Dublin Castle that night; he wanted to be with his troops and so returned to Finglas.

JAMES MEETS LOUIS

On 20 July James landed in Brest in high spirits. Before leaving Kinsale he had been handed a letter from Louis, which gave him news of the French success at Fleurus and which offered to land 30,000 men in England. It was not until later that he learned that Louvois had persuaded Louis to take a different course. But for the moment he had reason to feel content and on the road from Brest remarked again on the perfidy of the Irish at the Boyne.

Within hours of returning to St Germains, James received a visit from Louis. The French king was sympathetic about the events in Ireland, but indicated that he could not continue with his plans of sending troops to England. He made it clear, in fact, that he had changed his mind. James tried to dissuade him and recommended an immediate attack, now that England was denuded of troops. Louis contented himself with saying that nothing could be done until he received reports from his generals in Ireland. Then, he pleaded a headache and returned to Versailles. For weeks afterwards, when James went to Versailles he found that his French cousin was not equal to transacting business.

THE RAPPAREES

The fallback on Limerick was disorganised and the army lived off the countryside during the march. The best account comes from the 'journal' of Captain John Stevens, who, as we have seen, served in the grand priors regiment. This regiment was badly bruised at the Boyne and Stevens says that at one point it was reduced to six musketeers, eight pikemen, four ensigns, one lieutenant and himself – all that was left of 800. At Naas he met up with an ensign with a lame horse, and they both shared the animal until they reached Kilcullen, where they found a bed. Next day, they set out again, but had gone only a few miles when they were 'overtaken by the Duke of Tyrconnell and his family, some of whom wanted the horse, and indeed he had the king's mark; they being too strong for us to cope with (for then might was the greatest rite) they carried him away, leaving us afoot, weary, and without friends or money.'

Two days later the weary men reached Kilkenny:

> All the shops and public houses in the town were shut, and neither meat nor drink was to be had, though many were fainting through want and weariness. Hunger and thirst put me forward to seek relief, where nothing but necessity could have carried me; but the invincible power of want hides all blushes, so hearing of stores at the castle, I resolved to try my fortunes there. I perceived some officers, whom want had carried thither as well as me, but were somewhat more forward. So ill treated were they, first by Brigadier Mackay, and next by the Duke of Tyrconnell, who gave a Lieutenant a thrust on the breast with a cane, that I went away resolved to perish rather than run the hazard of being ill-used.[6]

These hardships were compounded by other misfortunes: as the soldiers swept across the country their boots were broken, their clothes torn and some threw away their equipment to lighten their load. Stevens relates that his regiment was inspected by Brigadier Wauchope outside Limerick. The brigadier became so angry with the men for discarding their weapons that he threatened to shoot a few of them.

During the trek some groups were protected by the rapparees – armed horsemen who supported the cause and lived as outlaws; many had done military service abroad; others were sons of dispossessed Catholic landlords or descendants of Old English stock who had been ousted by the Cromwellians. One of the best contemporary accounts of the rapparees is provided by Rev. Story:

> They were such of the Irish as were not of the army, but country-people, armed in a hostile manner with half-pikes and skeins, and with scythes or muskets. For the past three or four years the priests would not allow an Irishman to Mass unless he brought at least one rapparee along, whose name they say in Irish signifies a half-stick or a half-pike; for thence the men themselves have got their name …
>
> … These men knew the country, nay, all its secret corners; woods and bogs; keeping a constant correspondence with one another and with the Jacobite army, who furnished them with all necessities, especially ammunition. When they heard of any project, their method was to appear as a body … to meet at a pass or a wood at such time of night or day as to their convenience; and although you could not see a man overnight, yet exactly at their hour, you might find three or four hundred, all well-armed and

ready … But if they happened to be discovered, or overpowered, they dispersed, having appointed beforehand another rendezvous, ten or twelve miles away. Our men could not fix a close engagement upon them during winter, so that if they held out another year, the rapparees would have been very prejudicial to our army, as well as by killing our men, stealing our horses and intercepting our provisions … [7]

One of the rapparees who protected the rear of the tattered army was Michael Hogan, known as 'Galloping' Hogan for his extraordinary feats of horsemanship.[8] He was destined shortly to gallop across a page in Irish history. Sarsfield is reputed to have been close to these men and earlier recruited some to the army in Connaught. It is said that he even considered throwing his lot in with them following the Boyne, so disgusted was he with the ineptitude of the Jacobite leadership.

The Defence of Athlone

Limerick was not the sole fall-back point. On the day following the Boyne, Drogheda surrendered and its garrison was allowed to march to Athlone. The town was held by Colonel Richard Grace, a veteran of the Confederate war. A colonel in 1641, he was a colonel still, and in the meantime France, Spain and Ireland were the fields of his adventures. Twice, in youth, he had defended Athlone against Cromwell and now, in his eightieth year, he stood to defend it again. The importance of the town could not be exaggerated, for it was built on the main artery to Connaught, and who ever was in possession of it could command the middle crossing of the Shannon. William did not doubt its importance and sent Colonel James Douglas to reduce it, entrusting him with three regiments of horse, two of dragoons and ten of foot, together with ten field pieces and two mortars.

Athlone stood on both sides of the Shannon. The section to the west was known as 'Irish Town' and that to the east as 'English Town'. The castle, to the west, was its chief fortification. Grace thought the 'English Town' untenable against artillery, so he demolished its suburbs and used the rubble to strengthened the western defences.

Douglas arrived on 17 July and sent a message to Grace to surrender. He got a curt reply. Legend says that Grace drew a pistol and fired over the head of Douglas' envoy saying: 'tell your master *this* is my reply *this* time, and that he will receive something more severe, should I have to repeat the message'. He declared that before he surrender Athlone, he would eat his boots!

Next day, Douglas planted his batteries and opened heavy cannonade against the castle. The response was fast and furious musket fire and he took numerous casualties. After a week he found he had made little impression and that his ammunition had begun to run low. A rumour spread among his men – and was believed – that Sarsfield was coming up from Limerick with 15,000 men to relieve Athlone. The name of Sarsfield was enough to spread fear among the besiegers and they became apprehensive.

Douglas was angry when Grace ran up a red flag, indicating a refusal to capitulate. A further furious bombardment was opened on the castle, but the only reply was shouts of derision and defiance from the walls. Matters then grew worse for Douglas. A plague broke out and he found that a number of his men could hardly stand through illness. He had enough. He raised the siege. It was a wise decision, for it was true that Sarsfield was about to descend upon him, and had left Limerick; besides, he had lost 400 men and did not want to lose more. On the raising of the siege Grace made a triumphant circuit of the walls, amid sustained cheering. Athlone had been saved – for the moment!

When Douglas drew off his men, he intended joining William and his main army which was heading towards Limerick from the southeast. He was fearful of encountering Sarsfield's cavalry who would make short work of his force. So instead of taking a direct route to Limerick, he took the road to Ballymore and Ballyboy, avoiding Banagher, where he learned that Sarsfield awaited him. He passed through Roscrea, proceeded to Thurles which he sacked and burned, and then to Holycross, and, finally, to the village of Cullen where he set up camp on 8 August.

When passing Roscrea he camped on the north side of the Rathnavigue Hill near Dunkerrin and rested a few days. At the Devil's Bit he received a message from William to quicken his march as rapparees were operating all over north Tipperary and that he was in danger of attack. His march passed without incident. Lenihan records that country people brought poultry and other provisions to his camp, all of which he paid for.[9]

THE DECLARATION OF FINGLAS

Before sending Douglas to Athlone, William, from Finglas attempted to entice the Jacobites to lay down their arms. He issued a declaration, drawn up following consultations with leading Dublin Protestants, who were presumed to know the minds of the Jacobites. They were more intent, however, in taking revenge than in an early settlement and urged a hard line.

The declaration promised pardons to the rank and file – labourers, soldiers, tradesmen and such like – if they surrendered and declared allegiance to William and Mary by 1 August. For the rest, who were termed 'the desperate leaders to the rebellion' William was prepared to 'make them sensible of their errors, unless by great and manifest demonstrations, they convinced him that they were deserving of his mercy'. The proclamation was, of course, a crude attempt to drive a wedge between the Jacobite rank and file and their leaders and was seen as such. The Williamite, Bishop Gilbert Burnet's wrote:

> It was hoped that the pardon to the commoners might have separated them from the gentry, and that by this means they would be so forsaken that they would accept such terms as should be offered to them. The king had intended to make the pardon more comprehensible, hoping to bring the war soon to an end, but the English in Ireland opposed this …[10]

The declaration was rejected out of hand. It stiffened the resolve of the Jacobites to carry on the struggle; they were not going to accept a haughty injunction which, apart from the question of allegiance, made no reference to the security of their estates or to their religious freedom. The response took William aback. With an eye to events abroad and wanting desperately to extract himself from the Irish imbroglio, he softened his line. On 1 August a fresh declaration was issued. This time, he assured those of senior rank that their lives would be spared if they submitted, and that if they were destitute they could have subsistence on a scale appropriate to their needs. Again, the offer was spurned. William had not reduced Ireland to obedience.

DEFENDING LIMERICK

All interest now focused on Limerick. It was the third largest city in the country and had a peace-time population of 12,000. Tyrconnell, Berwick, Sarsfield and other prominent Jacobites reached it on 8 July and set about reorganising the army. As a defensive location it was problematic. It was a twin-city with the older part, the 'English Town', built on an island bounded by the Shannon and a small river called the Abbey. On the far side of the Abbey, was the 'Irish Town' linked to the northern half by a stone bridge and more vulnerable as it did not have a water frontage. Both towns were walled, but in many places the mortar had fallen away and the stones were loose. The fortifications were medieval rather than seventeenth-century: there were neither battlements on the walls nor ramparts on which to mount cannon. Vauban, himself, it was said would have had difficulty in fortifying Limerick.

But the Jacobites had a man who was familiar with the great engineers' methods, and who had actually rubbed shoulders with Vauban at Douai, Lille, Maastricht and elsewhere. This was Alexander Rainier, Marquis de Boisselleau; he had participated in nine major sieges and was familiar with the latest techniques of siege warfare. He now assumed responsibility for strengthening Limerick; under his instruction a 'covered way' was built outside the walls, to protect the troops passing from one point to another. St John's Gate – the principle entrance to the city – which opened towards the south-east was strengthened by a redoubt and angular palisades filled with earth. A bastion was erected near Ball's Bridge which connected the two towns, and an earthen fort constructed on King's Island, the guns of which flanked the counter-scarp, and covered the eastern front of the wall as far as the main gate. A tower on the southern angle of this wall held three guns; the redoubt opposite St John's Gate had two guns, and there were two more on the bastion near the bridge and probably two on the fort near King's Island.

Everything was done, however, in haste and some were unsure of the result. Lauzun was unimpressed, and declared, famously, that the walls would collapse if pelted with roasted apples. The defence became more problematic when he announced that he was withdrawing the French contingents to Galway, from where he intended to embark for France; furthermore he took anything under his control – stores, guns and ammunitions – with him.

Tyrconnell, was also sceptical that Limerick could be held. He called a meeting of the staff officers and waved a piece of paper in their faces. It was, he said, a declaration signed by some of the most senior person-nel stating that Limerick could not withstand a siege for longer than three or four days. We do not know who signed this document save Lauzun, some of the French officers and one or two of the Irish commanders. It provoked an uproar. Most of those present spoke angrily against the document and insisted that Limerick could and should be defended.

Among the dissident or diehard faction (as they were called) were Berwick and Simon Luttrell, but most prominent was Sarsfield. It was at this time that he asserted himself as a man with a following. From now until the end of the war he would exercise great influence on Jaco-bite counsels. He rejected Tyrconnell's proposal that a deal be done. The Williamites, he asserted, would keep no deal; besides, the Irish troops were anxious to show that the accusations made against them were false. But Tyrconnell had little fight left; he wished to follow Lauzun to Galway and to France. But he did not propose to hand power to Sars-field, whom he disliked. He appointed de Boisseleau governor, with Ber-wick, Dorrington, Henry Luttrell, Wauchope and Maxwell to be mem-bers of his council. Reluctantly, he also included Sarsfield.

De Boisseleau was not an unreasonable choice for governor, but his military resources were only modest. The cavalry, under Sarsfield, which was posted mostly on the Clare side of the river – with some above the city at Annaghabeg and O'Brien's Bridge – was acknowledged to be of a high standard; some of the dragoon regiments were less so, and the 8,000 infantry were regarded as poor. The total garrison amounted to about 14,000 men, and many were badly armed. MacMahon's regiment had no weapons at all. In contrast, William had 35,000 seasoned and well-disciplined troops, although his numbers had been reduced since the Boyne. Some had been returned to England in the emergency which followed Beachy Head, others were left to garrison Dublin and minor posts which had been taken.

The squabbles at Limerick became known to William. Ignoring the reverse at Athlone, he felt confident that he could take Limerick. His views were confirmed by the ease with which towns in Leinster and Munster fell to him as he marched south. At Wexford the garrison evacuated the town on his approach. Kilkenny and Clonmel were abandoned similarly. The garrison at Duncannon surrendered after a parlay and was granted permission to march to Limerick; Waterford gave up without a fight when its garrison was informed that it could withdraw to Cork.

Plainly, Limerick's salvation (in the absence of French help) could only be found in a diversion or a of some sort. A number of stratagems were hatched. Berwick suggested that he should be allowed to use the cavalry and raid the enemy's lines of communication with a view to cutting them off from Dublin. Tyrconnell – who had not left Limerick – thought this idea too venturesome and it was dropped. Shrewd observers saw the defiance of the diehards as starry-eyed.

WILLIAM AT LIMERICK

On 7 August William's army reached Caherconlish about eight miles south-east of Limerick and set up camp. Next morning, William reconnoitred the city and held a meeting of his high command. Having made dispositions he sent a trumpeter forward to summon the city to surrender. De Boisseleau's answer was communicated through a secretary – he intended to hold Limerick for King James and that he resolved to do so in a manner which would win the respect of the Prince of Orange. William lost no time in putting him to the test. His main body rested on Singland Hill opposite St John's Gate, with his remaining force, well extended, encircled the city round the south and south-west; his right wing being fanned out towards King's Island. Batteries were constructed, bearing on the walls from different points. Field quarters were established in Ireton's fort, an old Cromwellian structure which commanded a view of the entire wall.

The next day began dull and cloudy. A thick mist lay on the Clare hills and fog rose from the river Shannon. As the day progressed the sun broke out and the heat became intense. At eleven o'clock William opened a cannonade. De Boisseleau made a spirited reply, which convinced William that the Jacobites had decided to defend Limerick to the last man. After two days, William had inflicted little damage and decided to direct his mortars against the interior, but he was in a predicament; all he had were light field guns which were inadequate for the task. He knew, however, that eight large cannon would be with him in a matter of days, as his munitions train (or siege train, as it was called) was following behind the main army and had reached Cashel. Within a week he would be able to level the walls.

He did not, however, anticipate the next event. A Huguenot deserter stole into Limerick, mentioned the siege train and pinpointed its location. This was the act of providence which the diehards had hoped for, and Sarsfield saw his opportunity. He renewed Berwick's request in a more modest form, urging that he should take a troop of cavalry and ambush the convoy before it reached Limerick. This time Tyrconnell did not demur and the audacious Sarsfield sprung into action.

SARSFIELD AND 'NED OF THE HILL'

At midnight on 9 August, Sarsfield and a company of horse slipped out of Limerick by the north gate. They made for the main cavalry camp at Clarecastle on the Galway road and increased their numbers; they were augmented further by horse relieved from guarding the Shannon ford at Annaghabeg. Then, 500 strong, he followed the west bank of the Shannon, passed Bridgetown, Ballycorney[11] and on to Killaloe where he turned left and followed the river upstream to Ballyvalley; here, he crossed into Co. Tipperary. Ahead, went a quota of scouts to keep an eye out for enemy cavalry and to monitor the progress of the siege train.[12]

Sarsfield was guided by 'Galloping' Hogan, who was reputed to know every inch of the way, however, this is questioned in the mountain villages of north Tipperary where tradition holds that while Sarsfield was on the Silvermine mountains a message was sent to a local outlaw, Ned Ryan – the famous 'Eamonn an Cnoic' (Ned of the Hill) – who was hiding on the Moher mountains near Rearcross. The story goes that it was Ryan who led Sarsfield, Hogan and the rest to the siege train.

There are numerous tales of Ryan's escapades and it is opportune to say something of him. He is alleged to have been born at Atshanbohy, near Upperchurch (around 1670) to a tenant family who was dispossessed during the Desmond Rebellion. His father was of the Clann O'Riain, chiefs of Kilnalogangarty, and his mother an O'Dwyer of Kilnamanagh. As a young man he studied for the priesthood in France, but on losing his vocation, returned and fell foul of the law. In a fracas with an official he accidentally shot his antagonist and was forced on the run.

For a time he was associated with Ruben Lee, a Cromwellian deserter of Jewish extraction, who lived a similar life. Lee, it seems, struck a bargain with the authorities – to betray Ryan in return for a pardon. But, predictably, the Robin Hood of the Tipperary mountains was too shrewd to fall into this trap, and Lee's scheme came to nothing.

In the end – the story runs – Ryan was betrayed by a relative who took his decapitated head to the authorities to collect a bounty, not knowing that Ned had been pardoned days before. The head, it seems, was placed on a spike at Cashel, and the body released to his sister who buried it at Curraheen, near Hollyford. In the 1960s a descendant erected a monument to the outlaw at Hollyford. Ryan's career is still celebrated at the 'Ned of the Hill' festival, held annually at Upperchurch.[13]

Whatever the truth about Ryan, it is known that movement by Sarsfield's party was by night; there were a number of Protestant estates in the district and their owners were likely to be Williamite sympathisers. Indeed, unbeknown to him, hostile eyes had already spotted Sarsfield. As his 500 horsemen galloped down a laneway near the old cathedral of St Flannan at Killaloe, they were espied by a local Protestant landowner Manus O'Brien and his colleague Mr Bevin.[14]

On the morning of 11 August, O'Brien and Bevin turned up at William's camp and told their story. Initially, they were unheeded, but O'Brien was eventually interviewed by Willem Bentinck, the Duke of Portland, William's life long friend. Portland immediately sent a troop to Killaloe to have the story checked. They returned and confirmed that a number of people had sighted the Jacobites. A report was sent to William, who was conducting the siege. He immediately recognised the danger and instructed that two companies be sent out; one to strengthen the escort on the siege train, the other to locate Sarsfield. Portland passed these instructions to Sir John Lanier, but Lanier was lackadaisical in dealing with them; both troops did not saddle up for several hours.

In the meantime Sarsfield was lying low in the vicinity of Glengar, having made his way through Toor, Knockfine and Rearcross. From Glengar he could see right across the Mulkear valley almost as far as the Galtee mountains. His scouts had no difficulty in tracking down the siege train. It was snaking its way along the low country, stretching for two miles, enveloped in a permanent cloud of dust. As the day wore on it meandered through the village of Cullen, its wagon master, Willem Meesters and his commander, Captain Thomas Poultney, unaware that their every move was being watched; at its front and rear it had a small cavalry escort under Colonel Edward Villiers.

BALLYNEETY
At dusk the siege train turned off the road and wound its way into a meadow, halting near a large conical rock a few hundred yards from Ballyneety Castle. In Co. Limerick, there are two places called Ballyneety, this one is in the parish of Templebraden, twelve miles south-east of the city. The wagoners lit their fires, took supper, and bedded down. Villier's cavalry was camped nearby, their horses champing the grass. Sentries were posted, a password arranged, and in a short time all was quiet. Sarsfield decided to strike. His men, in darkness, stole down from the hills, passed the graveyard at Toem, and then went down by Clonbrick and on to Monard. In this locality, 'Galloping' Hogan met an old woman whom he knew; she had been selling apples in the Williamite

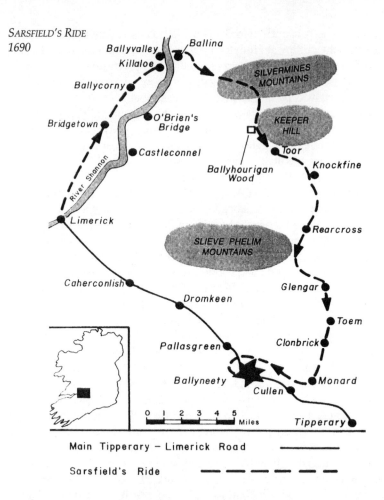

SARSFIELD'S RIDE
1690

Ballyvalley
Ballina
Killaloe
SILVERMINES
MOUNTAINS
Ballycorny
KEEPER
HILL
Bridgetown
O'Brien's
Bridge
Toor
Castleconnel
Ballyhourigan
Wood
Knockfine
River Shannon
Limerick
SLIEVE PHELIM
MOUNTAINS
Rearcross
Caherconlish
Glengar
Dromkeen
Toem
Clonbrick
Pallasgreen
Ballyneety
Monard
Cullen
0 1 2 3 4 5
Miles
Tipperary

Main Tipperary – Limerick Road ———————

Sarsfield's Ride — — — — —

camp and had learned the password. It was Sarsfield.[15]

Around midnight, Sarsfield approached the camp. No attack was expected and it was lightly guarded. As the horsemen stole up a sentry was alerted by the undeadened hooves and challenged: 'Who goes there?'

At this, Sarsfield sprang out, his horse rearing, and answered: 'Sarsfield is the word, and Patrick Sarsfield is the man'.

In a flash the intruders overwhelmed the guards. Standing on their stirrups, they galloped through the camp, cutting down, left and right, the half-awakened troopers. There was bedlam as the Jacobites wheeled their horses again and again. Dozens of Orange soldiers were killed and the rest ran in all directions. In the heat of the fray a number of non-combatants, some of whom were women, fell victims to the onslaught. This was a serious blemish on an otherwise daringly executed operation.[16]

Sarsfield must have been pleased with his booty. The siege train contained six twenty-four-pound cannon; two eighteen-pound cannon; eight brass ordnances of eighteen inches; 800 balls; 120 barrels of powder; 1,600 barrels of match; 500 hand grenades; dozens of pontoon boats and numerous other items. In all there was 153 wagons (drawn by 400 draft horses). Sarsfield instructed that everything be burnt. The guns and mortars were stuffed with powder and their barrels buried in the ground. All the carts, shells, powder and other explosive material was heaped in a circle and a powder trail laid to the end of the meadow. One account says that 'Galloping' Hogan was given the honour of lighting the fuse. The powder trail spluttered and the flame raced towards the huge mound of powder in the middle of the circle. The earth-shaking roar was reputed to be the loudest man made sound ever heard in Ireland. The night sky went red and the sentinels on the walls at Limerick heard the echoing peal; it rolled like thunder over the Cratloe heights and people were awakened on the Clare hills. Then there was quiet for several seconds. Next, came a different – crumbling – sound. The walls of nearby Ballyneety Castle – which two centuries earlier had been burnt by the great Earl of Kildare – were shaken by the explosion, and came crashing down.

Following the operation, Sarsfield and his men returned to base by a different route and so avoided the Williamite force which had sought to intercept them. Lanier was five miles from Ballyneety when he heard the explosion. Realising that he was too late, he diverted to Killaloe in the hope of heading off Sarsfield. He hoped in vain.

When Colonel Albert Cunningham and a troop of Williamites reached Ballyneety at dawn, the burnt grass was still smouldering and pieces of wagon and other debris were scattered all around. The dead bodies when counted, came to 60. The number of women and children among the deceased has always been disputed. Jacobite sources have insisted that they were few, and the Williamites have asserted the opposite.

The destruction of the siege train was a severe blow to William and a shot in the arm to the Jacobites. This was the incident which 'made' Sarsfield; without the drama and daring of this episode he may well be remembered as just another officer in a defeated army. The news travelled quickly. Within a week Amsterdam and Brussels were informed and, in turn, sent reports throughout Europe. The *Gazette de France* used bold type and gave a fulsome account. Only in London was the incident played down. The *London Gazette* told its readers that the loss of the siege train would have a minimal effect on the war.[17]

The hour belonged to Sarsfield. As he recrossed the Shannon at Banagher, Limerick's love affair with him had begun. The news broke to great jubilation, and women and children danced in the streets. The gunners on the old bastion across the river fired a salute and Sarsfield was instantly promoted to the status of a folk hero. Numerous fanciful accounts have been written of his triumphal return to the city, but the evidence indicates otherwise. He rejoined the main body of his cavalry at Loughrea, Co. Galway.

Today at Ballyneety the story of the siege train lives on. The site is a stopping place for the interested and the curious. The moonscape holes cut in the ground by the exploding cannon are still evident. In 1975, the president of Ireland, Cearbhall Ó Dalaigh, unveiled a monument nearby and the Irish tricolour is frequently flown from the conical rock. Local schoolchildren have for long been taught a poem of the deed:

That night by Ballyneety's towers
The English gunners lay
King William's camp in safety lies
But twelve short miles away.

What need for further caution?
What Irish wolf would dare
To prowl around the Orange camp
So near the tiger's lair?

Oh! Sudden flash of blinding light
Oh! Hollow sounding roar!
Down history's page in Irish ears
It echoes evermore.

And Ballyneety's blackened tower
Still marks that famous place
Where Sarsfield and Hogan staked their all
For the freedom of the Grand Old Race![18]

14

THE SIEGE OF LIMERICK

As I pace each still and storeyed street
The pageants of forgotten days arise;
I hear the tumult and the gathering heat
I hear the measured fall of warrior feet
I see the banners in the narrow skies
FROM 'LIMERICK' BY JOHN FRANCIS O'DONNELL (1837–1874)

JACOBITE DISSENSION

The destruction of the siege train filled the Williamites with anger and confusion and William took it with ill temper. In Limerick the besieged were given fresh heart and resolution. The depressing effects of the Boyne were lifted and Sarsfield became the idol of the army.

Tyrconnell and those who sought a deal with William thought that they saw an opening. This, they argued, was a splendid opportunity of securing favourable terms. William was prevented from pressing the siege; the success of Sarsfield's enterprise was a set-back to him and it was probable that he would grant favourable terms for an early submission. On the other hand, if the opportunity was let slip, the Jacobites would have to fight on alone; no help could be expected from the king of France who wanted his troops transferred to Flanders to confront the armies of the League of Augsburg. Then, Limerick, Athlone, Galway and the other towns still held would be taken within weeks and their garrisons forced to surrender unconditionally.

This argument was persuasive, but Sarsfield and the diehards were unmoved. Sarsfield had, in fact, come to suspect Tyrconnell's loyalty, while the latter found Sarsfield irksome. Their antipathy went back to before the Boyne and probably had a 'generational' element to it. Sarsfield was an energetic man in his forties; Tyrconnell was ailing and in his sixties and had become unpopular.

A small clique, among whom Henry Luttrell was the leading light, tried to undermine Tyrconnell's authority. It was rumoured that the lord deputy and Lauzun had conspired to put the Irish and French troops at loggerheads to provide the latter with an excuse to return to France. It was insinuated that Tyrconnell was the true author of the 'peace policy' and that to secure its success he had filled the civil and military administrations with his own people. Whatever the truth of these charges, they spread rapidly and Limerick began to turn against Tyrconnell. Some prominent citizens, including Catholic clergymen, proposed that a fresh administration be established. Sarsfield was not prepared to go so far. Tyrconnell, he said, had been appointed by James, and no man could

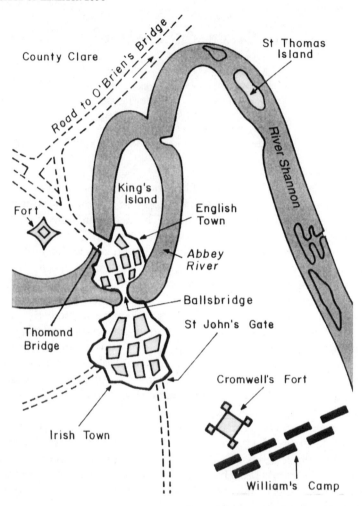

County Clare

Road to O'Brien's Bridge

St Thomas Island

River Shannon

King's Island

Fort

English Town

Abbey River

Ballsbridge

Thomond Bridge

St John's Gate

Cromwell's Fort

Irish Town

William's Camp

seek to depose him without breaching his loyalty. He threw his influence against the proposal and it was dropped.

William was not as constrained by the loss of the siege train as had been thought. Within days another was brought up from Waterford, containing 36 big guns and four mortars, but little ammunition. Tyrconnell transferred to Galway and held a conference which leading officers were obliged to attend. He read a letter from James. It gave permission to those who wished to quit the country to do so; they could embark on ships that were then lying in Galway harbour. To those who wished to remain, leave was given to submit to William and to negotiate the best conditions possible.

Tyrconnell urged that as many as possible should take advantage of James' offer. Lauzun agreed, as he wanted to recruit Irishmen for the French army. Sarsfield would not accept the proposal. The king's letter, he said, was grounded on mis-information, for if James knew the true state of affairs in Ireland, and particularly of the determination of the army, he would never encourage such loyal subjects to abandon their fortifications and submit to the enemies of their country. The matter was hotly debated and most of the officers agreed with Sarsfield.

While they were arguing, news was received that the siege had begun at Limerick and that William had taken the outer defences. Sarsfield decided to return at once; but whether he arrived in the city before the end of the siege is uncertain. Some writers have lost their balance in dealing with him at this time; Lenihan promoted him to the supreme command during the climax of the siege. In fact, it is unlikely that he was there at all. It is more probable that he was with the main body of cavalry somewhere between Annaughbeg and Six-Mile-Bridge.

THE SIEGE

After a week of desultory exchanges the siege began in earnest on 17 August. By this date the area surrounding Irishtown was cut up in 'zig-zag' trenches. After several days of digging, these trenches had advanced as far as a redoubt known as the 'Two Chimneys'. Under darkness William's grenadiers attacked this position with grenades – a new invention being used in Ireland for the first time – and had little difficulty in taking it. A second redoubt was also taken; and three battalions advanced on the 'covered way', but were met with such fierce fire, that they scurried for cover. De Boisseleau followed up this success by ordering a sally, in which one of the redoubts was retaken.

With the arrival of the new siege train, William had 40 pieces of artillery, including a number of twenty-four- and thirty-six-pound cannon capable of firing shells into the city. These guns were set before the walls and in the initial firing the 'covered way' was pierced and numerous shells lobbed inside the walls, setting fire to thatched houses.

After darkness, two Williamite regiments attacked the retaken redoubt, but were driven back by Lord Kilmallock (Sarsfield's brother-in-law) who was sent to defend it. Next day, brisk fire was opened by both sides and William had a narrow escape when a round of shot cut up the ground near him. On 20 August, the Williamites again attacked the redoubt and this time took it. But the struggle for it did not end here: De Boisseleau ordered Purcell and 300 fusiliers and Luttrell with 150 troopers to sally out and recover it. The Williamites were leaked details of this design from 'some friend in the town' and were ready for the Irish when they dashed forth. A body of Williamite horse charged, but Luttrell out-foxed them. He feigned a retreat and drew them to within firing range of the walls. They lost a colonel, a captain and several others.

The main assault was yet to come. William's plan was to push the Irish from the outer defences and then hammer the walls with such force as to open a breach which the infantry could exploit. During the next few days he launched heavy attacks on the outside positions and succeeded in overwhelming the defenders. By 20 August, he moved the cannon closer and began to concentrate his fire on a section of the wall near Cogan's Tower. After a sustained bombardment, this section began to crumble. By 27 August it had a breach about 30 yards wide.

That afternoon, at three o'clock, the Williamite cannon ceased. The storming columns in their flecked uniforms of red, yellow and blue moved down from Singland Heights like clockwork and halted. The fire from the walls paused and an ominous silence hung all around. Both sets of combatants stood motionless. The day was hot and clear. The sun threw a flood of light over the rooftops and the Shannon glided through its banks as if peace had returned and war but a memory.

The moments passed. The only sounds were the cawing of crows and the neighing of horses. The suspense was harrowing. William, then, slowly raised his plumed hat, and the assault began. In a shot, 500 English grenadiers leapt over the palisades, firing and throwing their grenades as they went. They were followed by the Dutch blue guard and the Brandenburg regiment. So quick was their movement that the Irish troops, although waiting for it, were taken by surprise.

The grenadiers reached the breach without hindrance but then were checked by grapeshot. It did not deter them. They pressed on and pushed through a line of Irish infantry drawn up to oppose them. But, to their surprise, de Boisseleau had constructed an entrenchment inside the breach behind which he had placed several pieces of cannon. From these a murderous fire opened. The assailants staggered – shaken by the fatal surprise – but still pushed ahead with the courage of lions. They went no further. A fresh storm of grapeshot thinned their ranks, and the Irish closed in on the flanks and rear with such fury that practically all were slain. The Dutch coming up behind, now leapt forward and the Irish had a problem in holding them. They were continually reinforced from outside, and the Irish found themselves pushed back into the city, where they divided left and right, fighting stubbornly before giving ground.

William now threw forward his Brandenburgers and stormed the breach with other columns. The Irish musket-men were driven from the parapets and civilian onlookers fled from the rooftops. The whole storming force was now within the breach and terrible hand-to-hand fighting ensued. Swords, spears, musket butts and every imaginable weapon was brought into use; fires broke out in several places and the ground was strewn with the dead and wounded. 'It seemed,' said an eyewitness, 'as if the heavens were rent apart, and the smoke which rose from the city reached, in one continuing cloud, the Cratloe hills'.

Victory looked certain for William. Yet, it was at this moment that matters went against him. News of his army's penetration sparked a re-action among the populace. Down every street, lane and alleyway poured the citizens of Limerick – men, women and children. The butcher had his cleaver, the blacksmith his hammer and the harness-maker his blade; each had grabbed the nearest weapon to hand. The women, who had sworn they would prefer to face the mouth of the cannon than the bar-barity of the Williamite soldiery fought like 'liberated furies' and hur-led stones, bricks, bottles and other missiles at their enemies.

De Boisseleau quickly brought up his reserves, and the Irish infan-try began to rally. The firing from the wall was heavy and a storm of canister and chain-shot poured into the Williamites. Soon they wavered and were driven back. The Irish gained ground and moved forward; the enemy was dislodged from position after position; but William still had a grip on the city. Then, there was a sudden pause as both sides gathered strength for the final bout.

At this moment a section of the Jacobite cavalry, this time under Brigadier Mark Talbot, Tyrconnell's son, was ordered to take the enemy in the rear. For long it had been held back. Now its moment had come. Galloping across Ball's Bridge, the 'pavements blazing under the horse's hooves' it swept through the streets and on towards the breach. Two Dan-ish regiments stood in its path. The Irish horsemen charged; cut them down and swept on. Galloping up to the breach they took the stormers from behind, made a pathway through their ranks and rode away with dripping blades.

The whole struggle was suddenly and decisively terminated by a crowning event. It was seven o'clock and the sun was sinking. The battle was raging with unabated fury; near the Black Battery (the ammunition store) the Irish were yielding to the Brandenburgers. Little did they know that the turf beneath them had been mined. Suddenly the earth heaved and yawned; with a great roar, mingled with scores of shrieks, the battery blew and sent the misfortunates flying in the air.

For a moment there was silence; each side seeming to feel the aw-fulness of the annihilation of an entire battalion. Then, a wild shout was heard from the walls, it was the final salvo from the unconquered bat-tlements, a parting salute to the hurriedly retreating enemy.

The assault had failed; Limerick had been saved.

WILLIAM LEAVES IRELAND
William drew off his army; his losses were heavy; an estimate of 1,500 killed and wounded is probably not far out. Some of his commanders urged that the siege be resumed, but most of his ammunition and stores

had been expended, besides, the weather had broken. Autumn was approaching and the ground was heavy. William decided to quit; he sent a drummer to de Boisseleau requesting a truce so that the dead may be buried. The Frenchman said that the Jacobite dead had already been handled, but that he would allow William one hour, from four to five in the afternoon, to withdraw his deceased, provided his forces did not come within twenty paces of the 'covered way'. Furthermore, he told the drummer to inform the Prince of Orange:

> that he was prepared to give him a good reception in any second assault – better still, than at the first.

On Saturday 30 August, three weeks after he had 'sat' before Limerick and three days after the assault, William withdrew to his camp at Caherconlish. Next day his army marched off wearily in the direction of Tipperary. Several of his wagons were loaded with the wounded; the equipage and stores which he was unable to carry, he burnt. When the Jacobites later rode out to Caherconlish the found that up to 1,500 sick and dying men had been left behind. More terribly, they discovered that fire had engulfed a field hospital and burnt about 500 invalids. Whether this was caused by negligence or other reasons it is difficult to say. Numerous atrocities can, however, be placed at the door of the Williamite army as it retired towards Waterford: the district between Tipperary town and Clonmel was laid to waste. The 'Curse of Cromwell' was said to have been repeated as the peasantry were casually butchered and their homes put to the torch. Macpherson in his *History of Great Britain, 1660–1714* comments:

> Excesses of savage barbarity, but on questionable authority, have been escribed to the king himself, on his retreat from Limerick. The disappointment may certainly have raised his resentment. The outrages committed by his troops stained the annals of the time; but whether they proceeded from his orders or want of authority, is hard to decide.[1]

William soon left Ireland. By a warrant dated 2 September 1690, he appointed Henry Sidney, Thomas Coningsby and Sir Charles Porter, lord justices with full civil powers. Baron Solmes was made commander-in-chief of the army but his tenure was brief; he was recalled within a few weeks and the command given to Godart von Reede, or, as he is known, Baron Ginkel. On 4 September, William sailed for Bristol. He was never seen in his Irish kingdom again.

JACOBITE INTRIGUES
The outcome at Limerick took Tyrconnell and Lauzun by surprise. It was a reproach to their judgement and an aspersion on their commitment. It also altered the situation. The cause was given a fresh injection

and the Irish showed that they could not be easily written off. Sarsfield said that if the full story was known in France, the order for the French departure would be countermanded.[2] But neither Lauzun nor Tyrconnell would change their minds about quitting. Tyrconnell handed the reins of power to Berwick, who took the title of acting-viceroy. He was to preside over a military council of twelve, eleven of whom were picked because of their loyalty to himself. The twelfth, was Sarsfield, who was chosen only because his omission would have created an uproar in the ranks.

Tyrconnell and Lauzun sailed from Galway on the second week in September. When they arrived in Brest they found that accounts of Limerick had preceded them and that public opinion in France, which had been anti-Irish after the Boyne, had changed. It was now held that the Irish were not the cowards and poltroons which they had been depicted as; rather they were valiant soldiers who had fought heroically against the odds.

Lauzun was not pleased with this change in the public mind; it portrayed him as a runaway and a cad. Yet he still wished to maintain the story of the cowardly Irish and relied on Tyrconnell to corroborate him. But Tyrconnell – the 'Lying' Dick of old – had a change of heart. He found a way to regain his popularity in Ireland: he would speak only of the heroic Irish and their excellent fighting qualities and represent them to Louis and James as steadfast loyalists. For the moment he kept his resolve quiet; he feigned illness at Brest and suggested that Lauzun proceed him to Versailles. The French adventurer took off, impatient to regale the court with his fabrications.

'Ireland,' Lauzun told Louis, 'was lost'. Its people had no stomach for war and were willing to make peace forthwith. It was, he said, the energy of the lord deputy which had saved Limerick. Without his steadying hand the city would have surrendered; Tyrconnell was the only Irishman who truly wanted to continue the war.[3] Lauzun was lavish in his praise of his friend.

A few days later Tyrconnell arrived at Versailles. In his new frame of mind he did not hesitate to contradict Lauzun. He blamed him for abandoning Limerick and maintained that if the French had remained more might have been achieved. Lauzun was stunned by Tyrconnell's two-facedness and hypocrisy. But 'Lying' Dick had struck again, and he was powerless to curb him. The Frenchman fell into disfavour and would have been slung into the Bastille had not his old mentor, James, interceded. Lauvois rejoiced in Lauzun's fall and induced Louis to vote the Irish money and arms to prolong the struggle. Indeed had Lauvois not died a few months later, it is probable that the Irish would have received greater assistance.

Meanwhile, in Ireland Berwick was aided by his Council of Twelve, but dissension continued to plague the Jacobites. Berwick at twenty was too immature to deal with the older heads around him. Since coming to Ireland he had shown initiative and flare but was now over-shadowed by Sarsfield. His later references show resentment. Ballyneety, he said, 'puffed up Sarsfield and made him think of himself as the greatest general in the world', and although Sarsfield was a man of amazing stature he was 'utterly void of sense'.

Some had come to believe that Tyrconnell had grown indifferent to the Jacobite cause and could not be trusted to present a true picture in France. They felt that a delegation should be sent to make their policy known. Berwick was asked to sanction such a delegation, but declined. Feelings ran high and the threat of a coup was on the cards before he relented. 'Accordingly,' he says in his *Memoirs*, 'I summoned the principal lords, as well as the clergy and laity and all the military officers down to the colonels to attend to me'.[4] From these he selected four to go to France: Dr Creagh, bishop of Cork; Simon and Henry Luttrell and Colonel Nicholas Purcell. His choice was approved by the council and a few days later was ready to sail. But Berwick had a card up his sleeve. He also picked a well-trusted Scotsman, Brigadier Maxwell, to accompany the delegation and covertly instructed him to advise James of the pressure which he had been under, and to request the king not to allow the delegates to return to Ireland, especially those 'two most dangerous incendiaries' Brigadier Henry Luttrell and Colonel Nicholas Purcell.[5]

Things went well until the delegation was halfway to France. Luttrell and Purcell grew suspicious of Maxwell and told him that they believed that he was carrying instructions relating to them. They wanted to throw him overboard, but were restrained by the bishop of Cork. In the event, their mission had little effect on James, but impressed Louis. All four were permitted to return to Ireland, for James was told that should they be molested his son Berwick would suffer. Their demands on the French were not all granted, but some were. They were promised supplies and, importantly, the services of a general of proven capacity to lead the army in Ireland.

Not long afterwards, Tyrconnell returned. He brought money, provisions and arms but no men. He came with a patent from James which made Sarsfield, Earl of Lucan, Viscount of Tully and Baron of Roseberry. Further, he announced that Sarsfield had been raised to the rank of major-general. It was the first tangible recognition that Sarsfield had received since the defeat of Monmouth in 1685.[6]

THE SIEGE AT BIRR

While the delegation was in France, Sarsfield and Berwick took the offensive against the Williamites whose area of control now extended throughout Ulster and east of a line from Enniskillen to Clonmel. They chose Birr as their point of attack. The town supplied garrisons along the mid-Shannon and whoever controlled it was in a position to challenge the crossings at Banagher, Mellick and Portumna.

Early in September 3,000 infantry, 7 battalions of cavalry and 4 field pieces were brought to Banagher, about seven miles from Birr. On the morning of 16 September a party of horsemen appeared on Burkeshill not far from Birr Castle which was garrisoned by Captain John Curry and 100 men. The castle was summoned to surrender, but Curry replied by raising the red flag. Shortly afterwards Berwick and Lord Galway brought up the Jacobite infantry and overpowered the outer defences. Then, the gunners sited their pieces on the green in front of the castle and began firing.[7] The garrison replied with their muskets and actually came off better, killing a number of the besiegers.

The Jacobite guns were too small to have much effect; after two hours of attacking the castle was still intact. Berwick blamed the ineptitude of the gunners but this was unfair. His problems were compounded when he learned that General Percy Kirk held a large Williamite force at Roscrea, twelve miles away. Kirk, on learning of the siege, was bound to come to the castle's relief.

Sarsfield, whose heart was not in the operation, was stationed to the rear of Burkeshill with his cavalry, charged with keeping a look out for Kirk. He came; but on seeing Sarsfield on the elevated ground, retreated, and linked up with a force of 8,000 under General Douglas and Sir John Lanier. The following day when the garrison had taken severe punishment and were on the point of capitulating, the Williamites reappeared. They were too strong for Sarsfield's cavalry and he did not engage them. He advised Berwick to raise the siege and Berwick, seeing the danger, disengaged and fell back about a mile from the town.

For the next few days nothing happened as both sides eyed each other through their telescopes. On the third day, Berwick tired of playacting, and decided to retire completely. The Williamites, however, kept on his tail. When he advanced, they followed; when he halted, they halted.[8] This continued for twenty-four hours, until Sarsfield also wearied. He took the cavalry on a detour and reappeared to hit the Williamites on the flank. A series of skirmishes went on for several hours and then, the sides disconnected. The Jacobites recrossed the Shannon and the Williamites headed for Kilkenny where a muster was held to reinforce the Duke of Marlborough, who was about to land at Cork.

The 'Siege of Birr' was a fiasco. Sarsfield had little hand in it and is not mentioned by Berwick in the account in his *Memoirs*. Had Sarsfield been given to introspection he may have mused that forty-eight years before, his grandfather, Rory O'More, had taken Birr for the Confederates without difficulty.

John Churchill, the Duke of Marlborough, had shown little inclination to take part in the Irish war. Various interpretations have been put on his intervention, not all of them to his credit. Chidsey, one of his biographers, says: 'While James was in the field, My Lord Marlborough preferred to remain at home. He wanted to keep his record technically clear. However, now that James was back in France, there was no reason why Churchill should not indulge himself in a little fighting'.[9]

Marlborough had little liking for William and remained an intriguer throughout his life. As a young man he owed his place at court to his sister, Arabella, one of James' mistresses. The story is told that on a visit to York, James took this drab little maid of honour on a hunting trip. Although he found her an exceptionally good horse, it was too high-spirited and bolted, throwing her off. Riding up behind he found her lying half-stunned on the ground, her clothes in disarray. As he leaned over he was amazed to discover that a girl so plain could have such alluring legs, or as Anthony Hamilton put it: 'that limbs so exquisite could belong to Miss Churchill's face'.[10] James' passion was aroused and in due course Arabella bore him four children (one of whom was Berwick) and retained her influence at court for ten years.

The young Churchill burned with ambition and became a page of honour. His liaison with Charles II's mistress Barbara Villiers did little harm to his prospects, and James entrusted him with many confidential tasks, taking him abroad at the climax of the Exclusion crisis. Later he made him a baron. His wealth increased, and his patron gave him a commission in his own (Duke of York's) regiment. Churchill's future seemed secure when he married a young heiress, Sarah Jennings (a sister-in-law of Tyrconnell's) who was maid of honour to the Princess Anne.

At Sedgemoor, Churchill was second-in-command and James trusted him implicitly, although he was aware that his protégé had no sympathy with his religious policies. James' faith was misplaced; when the crisis came, Churchill helped to snatch away his patron's crown. Now Churchill wanted to deny him Ireland.

William was smarting from the blow at Ballyneety when Marlborough proposed to Queen Mary and her council in London that he be allowed to take a force to Ireland and seize Cork and Kinsale, thus preventing the French from provisioning the Irish through these ports. The council rejected the scheme, believing that it would denude England of troops and leave her vulnerable to invasion. But Mary referred the proposal to William, who against the advice of Solmes and Ginkel, gave his approval. From his camp at Limerick he wrote to Marlborough:

August 14th 1690
I have just received your letter of the 7th. I strongly approve of your plan
to embark with four thousand infantry and marines, which together make
four thousand, nine hundred men to capture Cork and Kinsale. You will
have to take enough munitions with you, and use the ship's guns, for we
can send none from here. But for cavalry I will send you enough and will
take good care that the enemy will not be a burden to you. It is time which
must be saved and you must hasten as quickly as you can ...[11]

Marlborough sailed on 17 September, and a few days later had arrived
at Crosshaven at the entrance to Cork harbour. The city was the second
largest in Ireland and had a population of about 20,000. It was walled and
built on an island in the river Lee; its weakness was that it was overlooked by hills on both sides of the river. The garrison was commanded
Colonel Roger MacElliott (or Macgillicuddy, as the Irish called him); he
was a Kerryman who had fought on the continent, and in 1688 had held
Portsmouth for James. With about 4,500 men, he was undermanned
and in no position to hold out against Marlborough for long.

Cork's walls were high and ran from north to south, in oblong
shape, with gates at both ends leading to bridges over the northern and
southern channels of the Lee. To the south there was a small fort known
as 'The Cat' built on a height called Cat Hill, and another nearer the river
named Elizabeth Fort; on high ground to the north lay Shandon Castle
and Shandon church and insubstantial outworks that MacElliott had
built as a line of defence.

By this time William had returned to England, having left orders to
reinforce Marlborough. Ginkel sent three able commanders, the Duke
of Würtemburg, General Tattau and General Scravenmore, with about
4,000 infantry and 900 horse. Würtemburg's presence caused a problem as he held a higher rank than Marlborough and claimed the right
of command. Contention arose and both men spent some time arguing.
Compromise was reached when Marlborough suggested that they act
on alternate days. Matters were smoothed on the morning of Marlborough's first day; he tactfully chose the word 'Würtemburg' as the password. Würtemburg returned the compliment the next day when he chose
'Marlborough'.

On 24 September Marlborough's men disembarked at Passage
West and marched the eight or nine miles to the city. They drew up near
'The Cat' which was held by Irish dragoons and exchanged light fire.
This did not prevent them from setting up their batteries, nor hinder their
camping nearby that night. In the morning they found that the dragoons
had withdrawn to Elizabeth Fort, and that they could move nearer the
walls.

When Berwick learned of his uncle's landing, he and Sarsfield took
steps to aid Cork and moved troops from Limerick. Berwick marched

to Kilmallock, twenty-one miles away, and made a luke-warm attempt to take the town, but failed; he eventually got as far as Newmarket, Co. Cork, but was then checked. Sarsfield was also unsuccessful. He reached Mallow before encountering Scravenmore's stronger force and was beaten back. The Williamites took great satisfaction in this victory and claimed that they had avenged Ballyneety.

It was now clear that Cork was not to be relieved. Berwick sent MacElliott orders to retreat to Co. Kerry, but MacElliott defiantly ran up the red flag. Meanwhile, Scravenmore and Tattau reached the heights at Shandon and began to attack the castle and demolish the outworks. By evening (25 September) both prongs of the Williamite attack were making things difficult for MacElliott, and he opened a parlay with Scravenmore, but nothing came of it. On 27 September there was a heavy bombardment; the city took severe punishment from beyond both channels; this made MacElliott anxious to resume negotiations. He wrote to Würtemburg requesting terms. The duke was disposed to be generous; he said that if the garrison laid down its arms, it would be permitted to march out.

A note was also sent to Marlborough, but he was less generous; he said that the garrison must surrender unconditionally and be treated as prisoners of war. MacElliott rejected both conditions. As a gesture, he had set free the Protestant bishop of Cork, Edward Wetenhall and 1,300 of his co-religionists. This did not, however, soften Marlborough; next morning – 28 September – the bombardment resumed and an attacking party stormed the walls. The Jacobites made a spirited resistance and the Duke of Grafton – one of Charles II's illegitimate sons – was fatally wounded. A breach was opened on the south wall and Marlborough brought gunships up the channel; these began to lob fire-bombs into the city, which caused great destruction.

The double bombardment was too much for MacElliott. He desperately wanted to resume negotiations and sent the Earl of Tyrone and another officer out to seek fresh terms. This time, Marlborough made a modest concession. His formal terms were the same a before, but he agreed to 'try to obtain clemency for the garrison from King William'. MacElliott was still not prepared to yield. He scoffed at the reply and was about to resume his defence when his munitions officer ran up and informed him that the city's ammunition was practically exhausted; it was found that the munitions store held 'no more than two small barrels of powder, about a hundred balls, but a goodly supply of match'. At this, MacElliott threw in the towel.[12]

Cork was denied the military courtesy which had been given to other garrisons. Its citizens were treated brutally. Its womenfolk were violated; its menfolk were put in pens and, being denied food, had to survive on carrion; more than half died within a fortnight from disease.

Many who survived were killed the following month as they were being marched to a concentration camp at Clonmel. It was said later that Marlborough and his English army were far more barbaric than the Prince of Orange and his continental mercenaries.

As for MacElliott, he came under criticism from his own side for not obeying Berwick's order to evacuate and for rejecting the favourable terms offered by Würtemburg. He was taken to London and thrown into the tower; he remained there until 1697. On release, he went to Paris and joined the Irish brigade.

KINSALE

Marlborough followed up his victory by an assault on Kinsale. The town was not walled and depended for its defence on two forts, one on each side of the harbour. The place was held by the elderly Sir Edward Scott, who decided to abandon it. The garrison and civilian population fled to the forts. Scott had a good reputation but blundered in sending two regiments to Cork when he should have realised that they would have been better deployed at Kinsale.

One fort, known as the old fort (or James' Fort) was perched on a peninsula jutting out from the west shore and had a garrison of 500; the other, the new fort (or Charles Fort) was on the eastern shore and had 1,200 men. Both were well provided with guns and ammunition; the main problem was too few men.

When Marlborough and Würtemburg arrived they decided to make an attempt on the old fort; it was the weaker, but inconveniently located. Tattau was chosen to lead an assault party and set out at night with a company of English and Danish artillery. He attacked at first light and the garrison made good use of its 46 guns in resisting him, but, within a few hours, was overwhelmed.

Two hundred Jacobites were killed and the rest taken prisoner. Marlborough summoned the second fort to surrender but Scott although knowing that help was unlikely, answered that he 'would not consider the proposition for a month'. He was being facetious, but may have thought that Sarsfield would come to his aid. Sarsfield, as we know, did not, and on 14 October the bombardment was so heavy that Scott had little option but to ask for terms. This time Würtemburg took a hard line. He suggested that Kinsale should surrender on similar terms to Cork. But Marlborough allowed the garrison to come out without surrendering their arms and permitted them to march to Limerick. This concession is usually explained by his desire to return early to England to be feted for his success. Later, however, a suspicion was attached to Scott; it was suggested that he was bribed by Marlborough who had promised his friends in London that his stay in Ireland would be brief.[13]

The accusation has not been proven, although it was said that Lady

Scott, who was in the fort, drove out in her carriage in leisurely fashion and that (according to Rev. Story) the place held enough provisions to support 1,000 men for a year. It is hard to believe that Scott was treacherous. He later served with distinction in the Irish brigade and was singled out for special praise in 1692 for his valour at Embrum against Prince Eugene of Savoy.[14]

The loss of Cork and Kinsale were shattering blows for the Jacobites. The ports most suitable for French landings were now denied to them and they were virtually locked up west of the Shannon.

15

THE DEVIL PLAYS THE HARP

Does any man dream that a Gael can fear?
Of a thousand deeds let him learn but one
The Shannon swept onwards broad and clear
Between the leaguers and broad Athlone
FROM 'A BALLAD OF ATHLONE' BY AUBREY DE VERE

THE WINTER WAR

William had scarcely quit Ireland before his lord justices – Porter, Sidney and Conningsby – took up their duties in earnest. They issued a flood of proclamations against 'papists' who lived in areas of Williamite control. One, laid down that Catholics must make good the losses sustained by their Protestant neighbours in the war; another, that they must not gather in numbers greater than ten – a measure aimed, presumably, at Catholic worship as the penalty for its contravention was the transportation of priests; a third, that families having a member in the Jacobite forces must procure the return of 'the misadventurer' or be treated as spies or enemies; a fourth, that families with members killed or taken prisoner in the service of James should remove themselves west of the Shannon.[1]

The Protestant population was also given stern injunctions: one, ordered them to move within Williamite lines of control; another, that rations must be made available to the army. An early result of these decrees was an exodus to both sides of the Shannon. The old, sick and infirm endured the greatest hardships as they undertook the trek to their respective zones. Of the thousands who crossed the river, few ever returned to their homes and, among Catholics, hundreds were driven into the ranks of the rapparees who stepped up their operations.

To counter the rapparees commissions were given to Protestant landowners to raise militias. Ulster Protestants were considered well-fitted for these units which became as a form of 'Protestant rapparees'. Many of these militiamen became members of an organisation established in Enniskillen called the Boyne Society and were known as 'Boynemen'. They were charged with confronting the rapparees and serving the Williamites by maintaining garrisons in the rear and acting as couriers between camps. Frequently their discipline broke down and they plundered indiscriminately, sometimes to the embarrassment of Williamite commanders.[2]

Ginkel controlled most of Munster and Leinster and his writ ran throughout Ulster. An English fleet patrolled the seaboard from Kerry around the meridian to Derry; the Williamite army was extended through the centre of the country, with no unit being more than a day's march from the enemy. Chastened by the reverses at Athlone and Limerick, Ginkel took no chances. He devised a number of strategies to keep the enemy – who had nothing like his numbers – hemmed in tightly in the west. He established bases at Cork, Roscrea, Mullingar and Enniskillen; his battalions at Cork were commanded by Tattau and Scravenmore; at Roscrea by Würtemburg and Count Nassau; at Mullingar, by Lanier, Earls and Brewer, and at Enniskillen by Kirk and Douglas. None of these had less than 10,000 men, and several detachments were posted at intermediate points along this front line. Ginkel himself set up headquarters at Kilkenny so that he could direct operations, north and south, as required.

By October both sides were facing each other across a narrow patch of No-Man's-Land. Towards the end of the year William ordered Ginkel to attack positions in counties Cork and Kerry. The idea was to bring the Jacobites to the negotiating table. Ginkel with greater insight than William, argued that this could be achieved more quickly by granting concessions, but his views were ignored. The attack on Kerry was undertaken in January 1691 by the Danes under Tattau. Many of the local Jacobites had retreated to Ross Castle near Killarney, but Tattau, without heavy guns, was unable to take it and after a short siege was forced to withdraw. Ginkel himself took 4,000 Danes, Dutch and Huguenots to attack Kilmallock, which had been reoccupied by the Jacobites. The garrison learned of his approach and abandoned the town, burning it before leaving.

These were grim days for the Jacobites. After the fall of Cork and Kinsale they had little room for manoeuvre. The Williamite proclamations had filled Connaught with a helpless, beggared population. The numbers pushed up the price of food and lessened the amount available for the troops. The brass coin which James had issued a few years earlier – and in which the army received its pay – depreciated almost daily, particularly in areas of Jacobite control. A list of random items in Connaught, cost four times more than elsewhere:

1 barrel of wheat (in brass coin)	£10
1 barrel of malt	£9
1 pair of men's shoes	£1, 10 shillings
1 quart of ale	2 shillings, 6 pence
1 quart of salt	£1[3]

Added to these difficulties was the reduction of trade with France which until recently had been brisk. Sheer misfortune lead to one disaster following another: a few days following the fall of Kinsale, a French vessel laden with salt and other necessities anchored in the harbour, its captain believing that the town was still in Jacobite hands. His mistakes became apparent only when a Williamite boarding party confiscated his vessel. Another ship, freighted with ammunition and clothing for the Jacobite army, struck a rock in the Shannon estuary and lost its cargo. Within days, an English Jacobite – Captain Troy – deserted to the enemy, seizing a frigate of twelve guns at Galway; he sailed up the west coast until he presented his prize to the Williamites at Carrickfergus. Meanwhile, the military assistance which the French had promised was inexplicably delayed. It was little wonder that many began to question the wisdom of holding out. Some saw the situation as hopeless; many argued for an early accommodation with Ginkel.

Sarsfield Remains Steadfast

Under these pressures Sarsfield did not falter. Both camp and council chamber required his attention and he seemed omnipresent. He worked energetically to bolster the Jacobite defences and keep the enemy at bay. The task was formidable and in the middle of it all he discovered a conspiracy – among his council colleagues – to let the enemy cross the Shannon and hand them Limerick and Galway. Among those involved were MacDonnell, the governor of Galway, Lord Riverston and possibly a colonel named Clifford. Sarsfield furnished Berwick with their names, but the duke refused to move against them as they were friends of Tyrconnell.[4] When Sarsfield mentioned the possibility of a mutiny, Berwick yielded and dismissed Riverston from the secretaryship of the council and relieved MacDonnell of his post. Sarsfield was appointed to replace MacDonnell and given the title of governor of Connaught.

Several accounts of the conspiracy have survived; it is mentioned in a letter from Galway to Louvois dated 28 December 1690 by Abbé Gravel. The abbé says that Sarsfield had good grounds for suspecting MacDonnell who since the fall of Kinsale had been wavering. He writes of Sarsfield's 'wisdom and penetration' and says that he 'made the Duke of Berwick understand the true interests of the king, his father', and that it was a masterstroke on Berwick's part to replace MacDonnell with Sarsfield 'whose fidelity and zeal for the service of the king is well known to him'. The abbé entreats Louvois to help the Irish who 'now under Sarsfield have found a leader in whom they have such confidence that they are ready to follow him wherever he may lead'. He also gives a description of the new fortifications being built at Limerick:

> They will make the city harder of digestion to the Prince of Orange should he attack again. At Galway, Sarsfield is raising several new forts and hornworks and greatly strengthening the place. He is about to visit Sligo and Athlone and will omit nothing against the enemy.[5]

The thwarting of the conspiracy did not end the treachery; dissatisfied members of the council continued to intrigue with the Williamites for a settlement.

During the harsh winter Sarsfield allowed units of the army to join the rapparees so that they could fend for themselves. A number of officers took command of these hardy guerrillas and tried to improve their efficiency. One body moved around Ginkel's army and ravaged deep into Leinster; others hung near Williamite encampments, interrupting their lines of communication, stealing horses and often killing significant numbers. Sarsfield himself occasionally joined these bands.[6] There is a story of him with a unit on the night of 28 November 1690 in Co. Offaly, where, with 'Galloping' Hogan and a man called the 'White Sergeant' they attacked the Williamites at Ballyboy. The place was well-guarded and the rapparees sheltered in nearby woods for two nights before making a swoop. Two companies of Williamites were cut to pieces.

Emboldened, the band went on to attack Philipstown (the present day Daingean) but met with opposition and were driven away. Having been chased for a mile or so, Sarsfield persuaded his comrades to turn about and engage the pursuers. They did, and the chasers became the chased. Two hundred rapparees re-entered Philipstown and galloping through the streets slashed right and left. The result was that up to fifty Williamites were cut down. The Jacobites came away with crimson blades and all the enemy's horses.

SARSFIELD AND TYRCONNELL

Tyrconnell's return from France was in January 1691 and despite the earldom which he brought to Sarsfield their relationship did not improve. Berwick was summoned to France and left a few weeks later, never to return. Tyrconnell resumed his civil and military duties and began to throw his weight around. His reappearance was a disappointment to the diehards; he came with no troops and the money and munitions which he brought were meagre. The former amounted to only 24,000 *Louis d'ors* (as the French coin was then called). He left 10,000 of these in Brest 'to buy meal, etc.' and distributed 4,000 among senior officers, leaving the balance to defray soldiers wages. This sum was soon exhausted; it was doled out at a penny a day and lasted about two months. The soldiers' conditions, in fact, disimproved greatly at this time. They lived on a diet of horseflesh and water; their clothes were scanty; their beds were of straw; those in Galway had to break up old ships for firewood; starvation caused many to defect. If relief did not come quickly their nemesis would be their hunger rather than the Williamites.

Yet Tyrconnell seemed unperturbed. When he arrived in Limerick he was greeted warmly; on moving to Galway, O'Kelly says, he was received with jubilation and:

nothing was seen during his abode there but balls and banquets, bonfires and public rejoicings as if the English were already driven from Ireland, and a glorious peace established in the nation. But what is more remarkable is that Tyrconnell and his friends lived at this rate when the soldiers of the army wanted bread, the common sort of people were starving and whole nation was reduced to the greatest hardships which mortals could suffer.[7]

Sarsfield despised Tyrconnell and tried to keep out of his way. The French commissioner, Fomeron, wrote to Louvois and said that Sarsfield and others had been ordered to attend on the lord deputy but had not yet done so. He added that it was imperative that the senior French general whose services had been promised should be sent without delay lest things 'deteriorate further'.

The *Gazette de France* at this time carried numerous reports of Sarsfield's exploits. Its issue of 30 December 1690 reported 'that Major General Sarsfield with a body of troops advanced to within twelve miles of Dublin and Ginkel had to draw what forces he could from various quarters to meet him'. On 23 February 1691 the paper said: 'the (Williamite) generals who had hoped for success by crossing the Shannon have been very unlucky; they found General Sarsfield at the head of 500 men who disputed their passage; he wore them out by continual skirmishing in which their men suffered heavily'.

This report may have referred to an action which took place in a heavy snowfall; the Williamites attempted to cross the Shannon at Lanesborough and Jamestown, but Sarsfield frustrated them and they were forced, in both instances, to draw back with significant losses. Earlier, he had established headquarters in Athlone and spent most of his time moving up and down the Shannon checking crossing points. In a letter to Mountcashel he claimed that a large area east of the Shannon was in Jacobite control and that the fort at Ballymore was a good point at which to keep the enemy at bay. This was, in fact, a misjudgment as Ballymore fell easily afterwards. He described his own efforts with great confidence and gave little hint of the conditions in which the troops were serving.

THE FALSE MESSIAH

If divided counsels and incipient treason weakened the Jacobites, so did the antics of an adventurer who now enters the drama –a Spanish-born brigadier who played a minor role and added a tragic-comic page to the *dénouement*. The preposterous fellow, O'Donnell, claimed to be a descendent of the great Ulster family which had been exiled during the reign of Elizabeth.

According to prophecy (implicitly believed by the peasantry) the final liberation of Ireland would be achieved by an O'Donnell with a red mark on his cheek and would come about when the Sassanach had been beaten at Limerick. The fellow was called *Bealdearg* (red mouth) and he had such a mark – hence his name – and claimed that the prophecy referred to him. A credulous peasantry marked him out as a Messiah.

After an adventurous trip from Spain O'Donnell arrived in Limerick just before the siege began. He gathered about him a motley crew of 8,000 Ulster Gaels and established a separate camp from the Jacobite army. He declared that James' cause meant nothing to him, as he himself was the king of Ireland and would wage war independently. At Limerick, he did nothing during the siege, but the Williamite defeat boosted his credibility. Shortly afterwards he moved to Connaught. There, safely behind Jacobite lines he subsisted on the countryside, using provisions needed for the army and turning the heads of the peasantry. During this time he corresponded secretly with Ginkel, to arrange satisfactory terms for himself at the appropriate moment. He played his part so ably that he carried on until the end of the struggle, before showing his true colours to his deluded followers. He was a covert enemy and a distraction which the Jacobites could have done without.

THE COMING OF ST RUTH

The proposition that a French general should take command of the Jacobite army was not well-received by Sarsfield or the majority of the troops. Experiences with Von Rosen and Lauzun were disastrous. Some heard the news with anger and most wanted Sarsfield to be given command and felt that if given the tools – more men and munitions – he could stand up to Ginkel.

Sarsfield was irritated at not being appointed. He had been an effective commander during the winter and his exertions alone had prevented the line of the Shannon from being breached. But he had no illusions about his standing in the eyes of James and Tyrconnell; he knew that they disliked him, and that his earldom had been granted as a sop. Disinterested in such gestures, he wanted real authority so that he could repay the Williamites for their crimes. Public sentiment was on his side, he knew that there were elements for success which he, and only he, could call forth. Though he had sworn to serve his king and country in whatever position, however subordinate, he knew well that under a foreign commander the army would have it effectiveness impaired. Such an appointment, he saw, as a blow to the cause.

So frequently are James and Louis linked with the mismanagement of affairs at this period that another blunder by them was scarcely surprising. They insisted on choosing an arrogant and imperious French general, Charles de Chalmot, Marquis de St Ruth, known as 'The Hammer of the Huguenots'. A big, paunchy, ugly-looking man with a menacing demeanour, he had successfully commanded Irish troops in Savoy and this was presumed to qualify him for service in Ireland. Lauzun's stories of the cowardly Irish cut no ice with him; he had got on well with Mountcashel's brigade and extolled their bravery. He was a fighting general and had served under Catinat and acquired some of that great commander's skill as a tactician. It was accepted that he was an immeasurably superior soldier to either Von Rosen or Lauzun.[8]

Adverse gales delayed St Ruth's arrival, but on 7 May a French fleet was spotted off the headlands of Kerry and next day it came riding up the Shannon. The great man came ashore to be greeted by a salute of guns from King John's Castle and a peal of bells from St Mary's cathedral. The arrival caused a stir and hundreds turned out to see the Frenchman and Tyrconnell drive in an open carriage. Throughout the day *Te Deums* were sung in the churches and the afternoon was marked by religious ceremonies.

Though beyond middle age, St Ruth was still a man of vigour. His manner was abrupt and his face unsmiling. He had a certain hauteur towards subordinates and an overweening sense of his own importance: traits which did not impress the Irish. Accompanying him were two senior officers, the Marquis d'Usson and the Chevalier de Tesse, who had considerable military experience. On board also were:

> 146 officers, 150 cadets, 300 English and Scots soldiers, 24 surgeons, 180 masons, 2 bombardiers, 18 cannoniers; 800 horses, 19 pieces of cannon, 12,000 horse shoes, 6,000 bridles and saddles, 16,000 muskets; uniforms, stockings and shoes for 16,000 men; some lead and balls and a large supply of biscuit.[9]

A public reception was held for St Ruth's on his first evening in Ireland; next morning he set to work. After an inspection of quarters in Limerick, he began to re-organise the army. Soon, a problem arose; despite the activities of the rapparees there was a crucial shortage of horses. St Ruth came up with a solution: he issued an order that all gentlemen in the area should repair to Limerick and take cóunsel with him on the state of the nation. Most felt honoured and arrived armed and on horseback. The meeting was held on King's Island and a number of soldiers were present. After a spirited address on the sacrifices all should make, St Ruth invited everyone to dismount and present their horses for military use. Remonstrance was useless, and resistance less so, for the soldiers closed in and took possession of the animals. Most bowed with resignation, indeed, some seemed to relish the trick and others were impressed by St Ruth's no-nonsense attitude.

The Williamites greeted St Ruth's arrival with derision. It was, they said: 'like pouring brandy down the throat of a dying man'. Parker, the Williamite captain, observed: 'St Ruth brought a small amount of money, a great amount of promises, but not so many men'.

St Ruth's late arrival enabled Ginkel to be first off the mark in the new campaigning season. Towards the end of May he began to move large bodies of troops to Mullingar, his intention being to attack Athlone with a single division, while other divisions attempted to breach the Shannon at Ballymore and Mellick. It was decided to begin with Ballymore; the village was situated between Mullingar and Athlone and outside it lay a fort built on a promontory running towards a lake, which surrounded it on three sides.

This fort was isolated except for a pass overlooked by a ruined castle. It had been held by the Williamites until the previous autumn, but the area was too impoverished to support the garrison and it had to be abandoned. The rapparees then took possession and used it as a rendezvous point for the raids on Mullingar. It had strategic importance, but was in poor physical condition. Its garrison now consisted of 800 men, about 60 rapparees, and 400 women and children. It was commanded by Colonel Ulick Burke, who had orders to hold out to the last man.

Ginkel arrived before the fort on 7 June and summoned it to surrender. Burke refused, and Ginkel, not wanting to waste time on the nearby ruined castle, into which Burke had put 15 men – brought up his batteries. But the men in the castle began to make their presence felt with well-aimed fire. Ginkel was forced to storm the ruin before commencing operations on the fort. He was angered by the resistance and, on capturing it, hung the sergeant-in-command in full sight of Burke and his garrison.

Following this, a verbal summons was issued to Burke; he was told that unless he surrendered within two hours he would be hung on capture. Burke questioned the authenticity of the summons. He did not believe that a commander of Ginkel's repute would issue such a barbarous threat and demanded that it be put in writing. It was, and reissued word-for-word over Ginkel's signature, with an addendum that no quarter would be given to the garrison if they did not surrender as prisoners-of-war. It also said that women and children would be spared if evacuated without delay.

Burke was shaken, but tried to parley: he asked that his men be given the honours of war. Rev. Story takes up what happened next:

> Our guns and mortars fell to work, the bombs tearing up the sandy banks, and the Irish running like conies from one hole to another, whilst the guns were battering the works and making a breach. The Irish did what they could with their two guns and small shot; but Lieutenant Colonel Burton,

their engineer, had his hand shot off … and their work went down apace, which made them very uneasy. The siege, however, was very delightful for our whole party who had a view from the adjoining hill.[10]

One wonders whether the reverend gentleman who wrote these lines gave any thought to the helpless women and children who were bombarded by 'our guns'.

The firing continued until noon when the sandstone walls of the fort were almost completely broken down. Burke displayed the flag of truce, but Ginkel, incensed by the obstinacy of the defence, refused to notice and continued bombarding for two hours more. Then, as a storming party were setting out to cross the lake, Burke again hoisted the white flag. Ginkel silenced the guns and lost no time in taking possession of the fort.

The booty was considerable: 430 sheep, 50 cows, a quantity of oatmeal and a few pieces of artillery. The garrison became prisoners-of-war and Ginkel changed his mind about hanging Burke. The women and children were sent behind Jacobite lines and it became known later that the men were taken to Lambay Island, off the Hill of Howth, where all but a few died of disease within months.

Ginkel remained at Ballymore for some days; on 18 June he moved towards Ballybum Pass, where he was joined by Würtemburg and the Count of Nassau. The combined force of 8,000 then marched towards Athlone.

THE BRIDGE OF ATHLONE

Athlone, or as in Gaelic *Áth Luin* – the place of the moon – stands, as we have seen, on both sides of the Shannon in counties Westmeath and Roscommon, with the Irishtown to the west. In 1691 the two towns were of almost equal size and surrounded by a wall of considerable strength, with suburbs extending beyond this area. The Englishtown was almost half a mile in length and its width a little over a furlong (an eighth of a mile); the Irishtown was narrower but extended further north and south of the river. In the middle of the eastern wall was the Dublin Gate, behind which lay the main street, the market place and the bridge.

The bridge was a nine arch structure which connected both towns and was the only means of communication between them. The eastern end abutted onto the riverbank, and on the western end there was a drawbridge of about thirty yards wide, and beyond this, a little to the north, stood the castle, which commanded the whole length of the bridge. If artillery were mounted on the castle it would render the bridge impregnable.

During the previous siege the governor, Colonel Grace, had considered the Englishtown untenable and made his stand in Irishtown. On

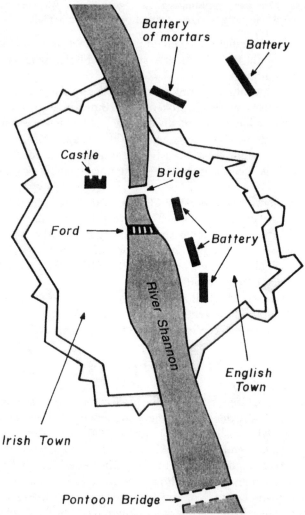

this occasion, the new governor – Colonel Nicholas Fitzgerald – resolved to defend both towns, having been so ordered by St Ruth; the Frenchman had promised to reach him without delay if attacked as his garrison was only 400-strong and could not hope to hold out.

Because of his vulnerability Fitzgerald could not await the arrival of Ginkel; he decided to sally out in an effort to gain time. The resultant skirmishes impeded Ginkel's progress by five or six hours. It was a short respite; by mid-afternoon on 19 June the Dutchman had established himself in front of the walls and begun bombarding. Within an hour the eastern wall began to crumble and a thirty yard gap was opened near the Dublin Gate. Soon, an attacking party, about 400-strong, dashed through in blitzkrieg fashion. The defenders could not stem the tide and fell back across the river and began tearing down the arches of the bridge to prevent pursuit.

Above the din, General Mackay, the Williamite, who recognised the importance of the bridge, was heard to roar: 'Save the bridge!' Fitzgerald, on the other side, likewise roared: 'Break down the bridge!' The place quickly became a killing ground. The defenders broke down two arches and held the enemy at bay.

Next morning, St Ruth arrived at Ballinasloe and learned that Athlone was besieged. He instantly set out with 1,500 horse, leaving the main army to follow. He encamped two miles west of the town and appointed General d'Usson governor instead of Fitzgerald; he then set about defending the town. Heavy cannon was placed on the ramparts overlooking the bridge and breastworks constructed along the river. To overcome the strengthened position it would be necessary for the Williamites to neutralise the castle before moving forward. But the castle was exceptionally sturdy.

Ginkel's gunners set to work, opening the fiercest bombardment ever seen in Ireland. The castle was pounded heavily for days. Twelve thousand balls, 600 bombs and many tons of stone were propelled across the water. The eastern wall was reduced to rubble, the breastworks flattened, and dozens of buildings set alight. In spite of it all, the Jacobites held on.

In the face of such stubborn opposition, Ginkel's options were limited. In desperation he opted for a hazardous frontal assault which meant that he would have to repair the broken bridge. It was a gambler's throw, but his needs were great. Under heavy cover his men advanced to lay planks on the broken arches. A hail of musket fire prevented the Irish from stopping the work, yet it took several hours to lay the timbers.

When the last plank was settled, a single man resolved to frustrate the scheme. He was a sergeant of dragoons in Maxwell's regiment – Custume. He called for ten men to join him in an attempt to topple the planks. Grasping axes and crowbars they dashed onto the bridge and plied at the beams. Their enemies raked the bridge with fire and within seconds all lay dead. When the smoke cleared it was found that they had toppled few of the timbers. Eleven more sprang up and ran onto the bridge. They worked furiously and again a murderous fusillade swept the bridge. When the last timber fell, two men emerged from the dust and smoke and escaped by jumping into the river. Twenty had earned the martyr's crown.[11]

The names of these men are today forgotten. No monument has been raised to their memory and no society or association has ever been found to salute them. History forgets the men who held the bridge of

Athlone, although it remembers the heroes who defended the Pass at Thermopyle. The fate of the heroic Greeks on the plains of Attica was doubtless great, but it hardly surpassed that of the dauntless Irish on the banks of the Shannon. But what history forgets, the poet – often the poignant voice of his people – remembers. One such poet, Brian na Banba, preserved the deed in heroic verse, and although not accurate in every detail, it is yet spirited versification:

Then out leapt Sergeant Custume
And his brave comrades ten
Their hearts athirst with vengeance
With souls of freeborn men ...

With axe and sledge and hammer
They leapt in to the wave
But ere one massive timber cracked
They met a bloody grave.

Ten more brave hearts sprang forward
But soon from iron hail
In deadly shower belched fire and death
Through corselet, jack and mail.

But see! It yields, it totters
With fearful crash they fall
In one rude mass – bridge, guns and horse,
And Brandenburgers all!

Foiled, beaten and defeated
The fierce Ginkel fled
His army broken shattered,
The Shannon choked with dead ...

And God be praised! In Ireland
By every hill and glen
There's many a gallant Custume
To dare the same again![12]

Ginkel summoned a meeting to consider raising the siege. Time was running out and his food and other supplies were low. Mackay was for quitting, Ginkel was unsure, and no decision was taken until three Danes, who had been sentenced to death for some crime, were brought forward and offered a pardon if they undertook to cross the river. With no option, they donned armour and tried to cross at a point downstream. The Williamites were ordered to fire seemingly at them, but in reality over their heads, to give the impression that they were deserters. When the men returned they told Ginkel that the deepest part of the river had scarcely reached their breasts. It was decided to make another attempt to cross.

The attack was planned by Talmash and scheduled for the next morning. It was to be three-pronged – at the bridge, at the newly found low-water points, and over the main expanse by the use of pontoons. Mackay was given command.

At 6 a.m. all was ready, except the pontoons. St Ruth, through his sources, learned of the scheme and threw reinforcements into the town. In the event, the full assault failed to occur; only the bridge was challenged and the attackers were beaten back with ease. Ginkel was on the point of giving up, when three Irish deserters were brought before him. What they said astonished him. St Ruth after the morning's abortive attack, had left Athlone and gone to the rear, believing that the enemy had withdrawn. Further, St Ruth had left the defence of the town to three battalions of raw levies. The Williamite commanders could not believe their ears. They agreed that it would be folly to leave; now was the time to attack again.

The deserter's story was true. Amazingly, St Ruth had concluded that the siege had ended. Earlier, he had boasted that it would be impossible for Ginkel to take the town and that should he try to do so, he deserved to be hung. Further, he said that if Ginkel did take Athlone, he himself deserved to be hung. To celebrate the raising of the siege, he retired to camp and threw a party.

Sarsfield was dumbfounded when he learned what St Ruth had done. He had little doubt but that Ginkel would attack again. He rode in haste to St Ruth's tent to insist that Athlone be reinforced. It was now nearly six o'clock and several messages had arrived from the garrison saying that their look-outs had become worried. But St Ruth remained incredulous.

Curtayne says that 'all indications go to show that a violent quarrel took place between St Ruth and Sarsfield, who was exasperated beyond all endurance'.[13] Sarsfield, it appears, used language unbecoming a subordinate. He told St Ruth that orders would have to be given to save the garrison who were in deadly peril. St Ruth went on scoffing, saying that he would give a thousand *Louis d'ors* to the man who would show that Ginkel was so foolhardy as to attack Athlone again. At the risk of court martial, Sarsfield told him to save his money and to do his duty. Valuable time was lost, but at last the call to arms was sounded. Sarsfield leapt into the saddle and galloped towards Athlone. A mile from the town he was met by a stream of refugees. They told him that the town had fallen. When he came in sight of its western wall, he found that it was already manned by the enemy.

Ginkel's operation had been simple. As the church bells rang the evening angelus, he had sent assault parties over the water. Mackay plunged in first and was almost across before the Jacobites levies realised what was happening. One party made for the bridge and another for the walls. The Jacobites panicked and fled. Too late, St Ruth came up with the main army – the gates were closed against him and the Williamites were in full control. This is how after stubborn resistance of ten days Athlone was lost in half and hour. God, it was said, was on the side of the Williamites and the devil played the harp![14]

16

AUGHRIM'S GREAT DISASTER

The fight goes on, St Ruth prevails,
His troops he animates
And swears he'll drive the heretics
All the way to Dublin's gates
FROM A NINETEENTH-CENTURY ORANGE POEM

ON KILCOMMODON HILL

The loss of Athlone was a crushing blow to the Jacobites. The town fell not through lack of valour or capacity to hold it, but through the folly of their most senior commander. Never had a town been defended more heroically; never had one been lost so unwarrantably. As evening approached the townsfolk had reason to be pleased; an hour or so later, all was defeat and ashes. The Jacobite commander afterwards became as penitent and obsequious as he had earlier been abrupt and intolerant.

There was no time for recriminations. The enemy, flushed with success, was within a few miles of the Jacobite camp and could pounce at any moment. St Ruth undertook to move on; he broke camp and marched to Milton Pass, a small village to the north-west, where he remained until morning. He resumed his march early and went towards the south-west, with his cavalry lingering behind, to protect the rear.

For the Williamites he was now a paper tiger. His deeds were his measure; he knew only too well that at Athlone he had grievously erred. He went through a great mortification and resolved to restore his reputation by the last resort of the fallen hero: the magnificent gesture – which may either bring victory or defeat. He would turn the tables on Ginkel by fighting a pitched battle; should he gain victory the stain would be removed and his honour restored. At worst, he would perish, but this would be preferable to returning to France as a discredited and beaten man.

When Sarsfield learned of St Ruth's resolve he was astonished. To quote O'Kelly, who marched with the army:

> ... Sarsfield and most of the captains gravely represented ... that to hazard a battle against them (the Williamites) with the Irish army ... much discouraged by the loss of Athlone was to endanger the whole kingdom.[1]

But it was impossible to argue against the strong-willed St Ruth. He wanted his set-piece battle whatever the wish of Sarsfield and the commanders.

On 1 July his army reached Ballinasloe on the river Suck, about ten miles south-west of Athlone. He drew up on the west bank and sent orders to Jacobite personnel in other areas to join him. The garrisons on the Upper Shannon, which had been carefully put in place by Sarsfield, were dismantled and the men called in. Jamestown and Lanesborough were abandoned; Shannonbridge, Banagher and Portumna were reduced to nominal strength; Galway was permitted a single regiment and so was Limerick. A requisition for men was sent to Bealdearg O'Donnell, who was holding court somewhere near Tuam – but this did not yield assistance.

Ginkel showed little haste in following St Ruth. He rested at Athlone while awaiting fresh munitions from Dublin; he stationed his army in the ruins of Irishtown, buried his dead, and celebrated the first anniversary of the Boyne with pomp and circumstance. Bonfires were lit on the hilltops all around; toasts drank to William and Mary and there were peals of musketry in the night air. On 2 July, the paymaster general, Robinson, arrived with 'cartloads' of coin and the army received its full arrears of pay, together with promises of reward and booty. In the days following, ammunition and other supplies; even bottles of brandy and other liqueurs began to arrive almost hourly.

Ginkel and the lord justices felt that the time was ripe to offer terms to the Jacobites. The fall of Athlone would, they knew, have produced consternation in their ranks and, perhaps, have made them more prone to settle. After some squabbling with the leaders of Protestant opinion in Dublin, the lord justices issued a proclamation on 7 July, which began with the words: 'Since it hath pleased Almighty God ...' It offered pardons to all soldiers – with recompense for their horses and weapons – who within three weeks surrendered themselves – and to commanders who would deliver up their regiments, and governors who would yield their garrisons. The citizens of Limerick and Galway, in particular, 'who as would be instrumental in relinquishing such places' would be granted pardons and allowed possession of their estates 'where it could be done'.

The proclamation promised also that soldiers, captains, colonels, governors, etc., would be received into their majesties' service and pay, 'as soon as their majesties' affairs would permit' and that a parliament would be called, where endeavours would be made to secure their protection from 'religious persecution'.[2] The document ended by praising the English government and denouncing French tyranny. It was signed by Porter and Coningsby, and ended with: 'God save the King and Queen'.

Simultaneously, Ginkel issued a supplement in his own name. He offered rewards to those who would desert the Jacobite army, renounce James and take service under his standard. To the hard-pressed Jacobite soldier, who most of the time was serving without pay, these inducements were a temptation. But they had little or no effect. The anger spurred by St Ruth's bungling at Athlone had faded and those who deserted were more inclined to join Bealdearg O'Donnell's forces than those of Ginkel. Others, preferring a middle course, opted to join the rapparees.

Prior to the proclamations Ginkel sent one Higgins, a 'converted priest' and a few others to reconnoitre St Ruth's position. On being attacked by Jacobite scouts in the wood of Clonoult they returned to Athlone. Next day, a further party was dispatched under Captain Villiers and that evening orders were issued for the army to march next morning. It left Athlone at dawn but halted after about six miles, while Ginkel awaited news from Villiers. At length, he reported that the Jacobites were in the vicinity of the Suck and had posted guards at the crossing points.

On 9 July, the weather, which had been glorious for a month, broke. There was a sudden downpour, followed by a hurricane. Trees were uprooted, cabins levelled and several horses were struck dead by lightning. No movement was possible and the men sat in their tents wrapped in their greatcoats, cursing the war. Next day, Ginkel broke camp and moved to Kilcashel, six miles further west. From there, he went on the prowl himself. Taking a cavalry escort he rode towards Ballinasloe, only to find that his quarry had moved from the Suck. He crossed the river and rode towards the hills of Donloe; from here he could verify that the enemy was not far ahead.

Jacobite scouts could be seen hovering in the hills of Garbally, and fell back as Ginkel's troop approached. Continuing, he found that the enemy was drawn up on Kilcommodon Hill – a long ridge stretching south-eastwards from the ruined castle and village of Aughrim. It seemed apparent that this was from where St Ruth intended to give battle. Ginkel was taken aback with the location's strength as a defensive position, and spent some time studying it through field-glasses. He ordered that a map be prepared and returned to Kilcashel.

With the eye of a keen strategist St Ruth had selected his position carefully. In front of him lay a red bog through which ran a stream from which Kilcommodon Hill rose to a height of 400 feet. It was impossible for cavalry to cross the bog and difficult even for infantry. On the northern end lay a castle which was approached by a stone causeway, lying between two bogs, one facing the hill, the other reclining to the north. Beyond the hill, to the south, was the Pass of Urrachree, an open, firm piece of ground skirted by hills.

St Ruth's left rested near the castle; his right at Urrachree, and his centre along Kilcommodon Hill, facing Ballinasloe. The sloping ground between the bogland and the hill was nearly half a mile in length and divided by fields, bounded by hedges – through which the Jacobites had cut broad passages to facilitate movement and downhill charges.

St Ruth had taken up his position on 8 July and thus had time to prepare for battle. His army was deployed with care. Its arrangement

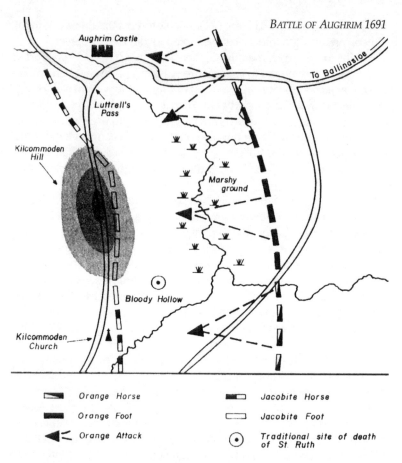

Aughrim Castle

To Ballinasloe

Luttrell's
Pass

Kilcommoden
Hill

Marshy
ground

Bloody Hollow

Kilcommoden
Church

Orange Horse		Jacobite Horse	
Orange Foot		Jacobite Foot	
Orange Attack		Traditional site of death of St. Ruth	

provided for two lines of infantry, supported by two lines of cavalry on either wing. The infantry consisted of 35 battalions, amounting to, perhaps, 14,000 men; in addition, he had 2,500 horse and 3,500 dragoons – making a total of about 20,000 men. Williamite writers have made this number greater, Jacobite writers less, but this figure seems the most accurate.

The Jacobite commanders were men of experience, although not holding the high reputations of their opposite numbers. Colonel Walter Burke and his brother Colonel David Burke were charged with holding the castle and its surroundings. The left wing was under Major Dominic Sheldon, supported by brigadiers Henry Luttrell, Purcell and Palmer. The infantry, in the centre, was under Major General William Dorrington, and he had brigadiers Anthony Hamilton, Gordon O'Neill and Colonel Felix O'Neill in support. The lords Kilmallock, Galway, Clare and Colonel James Talbot commanded on the right. But where was Sarsfield?

There is, in fact, uncertainty as to his position. Contemporary writers have placed him at the left and at the rear. The accepted view has been that he was in command of the cavalry reserve and at the rear of the left wing and told to remain in position until given further orders. Hayes-McCoy disputes this, saying 'that he commanded reserve cavalry is almost certainly inaccurate, since there was no reserve save Galmoy's regiment of horse, which was in the left rear'.[3]

Much of our information is dependent on an account by the Williamite, Captain Robert Parker, of Lord Meath's regiment. From him we learn that Sarsfield was ordered to remain stationary and that this order was obeyed 'very promptly'.[4] How Parker would have known of this is a mystery. In a reference to the cavalry force which augmented the broken Jacobite right wing towards the end of the battle Parker says that Sarsfield was posted not on the right but to the rear of centre. But at that stage Parker probably had difficulty identifying the right from the centre as they had become mixed up.

There is a weak tradition which holds that Sarsfield was not present at the battle at all. This is alluded to by Coddington in his highly rated work, *Battlefields of Ireland* (New York, 1867), but is not endorsed. He gives it in a footnote as follows:

> Some very reliable historians, among whom may be instanced Taylor and O'Driscoll – lean to the opinion that Sarsfield was not at the battle of Aughrim, but only adopt it as a probability. This opinion also gains credence from a tradition still received in that neighbourhood: that owing to an altercation with St Ruth, on the evening proceeding the battle, he withdrew his own immediate command to Redmount Hill, about six miles distant, in a south-easterly direction, whence he returned to the field next day, but too late to restore the battle. That the altercation occurred, and that each general threatened to place the other under arrest is abundantly corroborated; but by the same testimony the presence of Sarsfield is also established. Story names him as second-in-command on the day of battle and the weight of testimony sustains that belief. But what renders it certain, beyond preadventure is this simple fact: that had Sarsfield through neglect and petulance, caused the loss of the battle he would never have appeared in France. There he would have been held accountable by King James; and neither from him nor the French monarch would he have received the consideration which was afterwards accorded to him. On this consideration, if no other, the former opinion is positively rejected.[5]

The last point is a good one. But wherever Sarsfield was posted he does not appear to have played a prominent part in the battle until near the end; we will, therefore, return to him later.

St Ruth's Appeal

St Ruth was ready for battle, but Ginkel was unsure of what to do. The strength of St Ruth's posture made him wary of engagement. His staff had difficulty in producing a map of the ground, but were given one by a local Huguenot family – the Trenches, who owned the Garbally district. A council of war was called and Ginkel listened to various views. The astute Mackay recommended that they advance against the Jacobite right – which was the wing that seemed most likely to be turned – and that, with luck, St Ruth might weaken his centre or left to support that flank. Mackay felt this would open an opportunity in the weakened sector. It was an astute proposal but Ginkel was in two minds about it. Hesitatingly, he agreed to accept it.

At 8 a.m. on 12 July a thick mist lay on the bog and visibility was poor. The Jacobites stood on Kilcommodon Hill, their standards raised and their tents making a vivid background. To the blast of a trumpet and a drum roll St Ruth, dressed in a splendid uniform and bearing 'a snow-white plume in his hat' advanced for an inspection. As he passed each regiment shouts of acclamation rent the air. Then, he mounted a platform and said:

> Gentlemen and soldiers, I suppose that it is not unknown to you what glory I have acquired and how successful I have been in suppressing heresy in France and in propagating the Holy Catholic Faith. I can without vanity boast of being the happy instrument of bringing over thousands of poor, deluded souls from their errors, assisted by members of our holy and unspotted church. It is for this reason that the most puissant king, my master, has chosen me to come hither. I am assured by my spies that the Prince of Orange's heretical army are resolved to give us battle and, as you see before you, are ready to do so. It is now, therefore, that you must recover your honour, your privileges and your father's estates. You are not mercenary soldiers, you do not fight for your pay, but for your lives, your wives, your children, your liberties and your country, and to restore the most pious king to his throne. Stand by it then, my dears, and bear no longer the reproaches of the heretics who brand you as cowards, and you may be sure that King James will love and reward you; all good Catholics will applaud you; I, myself, will commend you; your posterity will bless you; God will make saints of you all and His Holy Mother will lay you in her bosom.[6]

This toxic mixture of God and country was heady stuff. Eighty priests moved through the ranks stressing the importance of the battle for the Catholic faith in Ireland. Macauley says 'the whole camp was in a ferment of religious excitement. In every regiment priests were praying, preaching, shriving, holding up the host and cup, whilst soldiers swore on the sacramental bread not to abandon their colours'.[7] This fervour was fortified by a liberal supply of French brandy provided to each company. The men, thus stimulated, were ready to fight the heretics as never before.

THE BATTLE

Ginkel's army was on the move early that morning. The heavy fog obscured the rising sun as his men tramped across the Suck at Ballinasloe.

The infantry crossed at the town's bridge; the horse and dragoons at various fords – the English and Huguenots above the bridge, the Dutch and Danish below it. The poor visibility slowed down the march, but by eight o'clock the army was within two miles of the enemy and drawn up in order.

The Duke of Würtemburg was second-in-command; the left wing was under Tattau and La Mellioneire, assisted by Count Nassau and the Prince of Hess; it comprised the Dutch, Danish and Huguenot contingents. The cavalry – on the extreme left – was under La Forest, Eppinger and Portland; on the centre right were Mackay and Talmash with the infantry; the right wing cavalry was under Scravenmore and de Ruvigny. About 20,000 men, were spread in two parallel lines, over two miles in length and divided into four divisions, each commanded by brigade and regimental officers.

Matters now began to quicken. By 8.30 a.m. the Williamite right rested on Garbally and its left touched the bank of the Clantusker river. An hour later the right was at Cahir and the left approaching Aughrim. At ten o'clock, the Jacobite scouts and pickets were rushing back to the safety of their lines. By eleven, the mist had melted and the clouds had rolled away. At noon, the armies eyed each other across the bog.

The Williamites came to within a quarter of mile of the morass. As they halted, Ginkel and his staff rode to a hillock directly in front of the Jacobite right at Urrachree – they wanted to make a closer inspection. St Ruth, at this time, stood on the ridge of Kilcommodon, with a full view of the enemy. For some minutes, both generals scrutinised the forces of the other.

The pause was brief. It was gone twelve, and Ginkel began the action at Urrachree. He sent a few Danes forward to drive back the Irish who had advanced to the stream. Instead of driving them back the Danes were put to flight themselves. Help was brought up on either side and what at first seemed a skirmish developed into a small battle. It ended with both parties returning to their original positions. Ginkel was still feeling his way and was in some doubt whether to launch his main attack.

At three o'clock, he held a council of war. Some commanders were in favour of putting off the battle until the following day. Mackay argued against this, saying that the preliminary fighting had thrown the Jacobites into disorder and that St Ruth might withdraw from Kilcommodon Hill, if given the chance. It was noticed that St Ruth was moving troops from left to right and Mackay felt that this provided an opportunity to make a attack on the causeway in front of the castle. Ginkel agreed, and it was decided to put pressure on the Jacobite right in the hope of drawing further numbers away from the castle – after which they could try to force the causeway.

The advance towards the right began at 5 p.m. with the Huguenots and Danes leading the attack. They received as good as their gave; the fighting continued for an hour and a half, during which time their centre and right remained acquiescent and Mackay's plan appeared to be faltering. Ginkel brought his field pieces into action from beyond the bog; but St Ruth's artillery responded effectively. The Williamite centre – up to 3,000 strong – advanced across the bog, up to their waists in mud and water, under cover from the batteries behind them. The Irish infantry who had been holding the hedges fell back from field to field and succeeded, cleverly, in sucking the enemy towards them – in the direction of the summit. As the Williamites established a footing on the lower slope, they were suddenly attacked in a downhill surge by the Irish infantry which drove them back across the bog with heavy losses.

The Williamites were doing badly. They were making progress in one area only; at the castle two of their regiments had penetrated the outer defences. Colonel Burke tried to stop them opening fire as they advanced. Then he was hit with disaster. His ammunition ran low and the men smashed open fresh boxes only to find that the bullets would not fit their muskets. Incredibly the ammunition was of English manufacture and could not be used in their French flintlocks. In desperation they tore the buttons from their coats to use as ball, and even stuffed pebbles into their rifle muzzles. It was a ludicrous situation and would have been serious had the Irish cavalry not come sweeping around the castle and put Ruvigny and the Williamite horse to flight.

It was now sunset and the shadows began to lengthen. From a hillock in front of Kilcommodon Hill St Ruth surveyed the scene. On his right, where the battle commenced, the successive assaults of the enemy had been broken up and repelled. In the centre, he had been completely victorious and Mackay's infantry had fled. On his inner left, the situation was no less satisfactory. There, the infantry columns under the Prince of Hess had been repulsed and sent floundering over the morass. Mackay, however, was now active in this sector and doing all that a clever commander could do to retrieve his force's fortunes.

St Ruth must have felt satisfied; victory seemed within his grasp. Perhaps a great vision opened up before him – a reputation was to be restored and a kingdom regained for its rightful monarch; his own sovereign would be delighted with his triumph and the hated heretics would be destroyed. The general doffed his hat to those around him and shouted with enthusiasm: 'Now, my dears, we will drive them to the gates of Dublin!'

St Ruth Falls

But the Williamite commanders were on their toes. Ginkel rushed here and there urging everyone on – even sharing the danger of the ordinary soldier. St Ruth had been no less active. He had watched every moment of the battle and rode non-stop up and down the field. It has been said that two horses broke under him from fatigue; now, mounting a third, a powerful grey he rode down to the left to congratulate the infantry on the work that they had done. It was here that he saw a troop of William-ites trapped and afraid to attempt a retreat across the bog, but willing to defend their forlorn position. Dismounting, he approached his gun-ners and with his own hands directed one of the large guns.

Remounting, he returned to his staff, who drew his attention to Tal-mash, who, at the head of a cavalry troop, and supported by infantry was approaching the causeway. Inquiring what the enemy meant by this move, he was told that they seemed intent on forcing the causeway to re-lieve the trapped soldiers. 'Then,' he replied, 'we have won the battle'. He could not see how Talmash's men could avoid being cut down and watch-ed him steadily for some minutes through his telescope. In a voice min-gled with admiration and pity he said: 'they are brave, 'tis a pity they have to be destroyed'. He formed a troop to charge and gave orders to call up the cavalry reserve – 'they are beaten but let us beat them with pur-pose'.[8]

These were his last words. They were scarcely uttered when a freak shot from a cannon took off his head. The powerful grey ran wild on the slope with its headless corpse, until caught and led over the sum-mit. The dead man's *aide-de-camp* threw a cloak over the remains and bore it away. Some say the body was later interred at Loughrea church-yard twelve miles away; others maintained that it was buried locally.

THE DEFEAT

The death of St Ruth generated numerous myths. One said that an Irish farmer, Kelly, and his shepherd, Mullen, had pointed out St Ruth to a Williamite gunner. It was claimed that the gunner was unable to raise his cannon to aim at St Ruth until one Trench – of the local Huguenot family – put the heel of his boot under the muzzle. The story goes that Trench, a clergyman, was rewarded by being appointed to the deanery of Raphoe. In the eighteenth century Protestants drank toasts to 'the heel of the dean of Raphoe'.[9]

The Jacobites were nonplussed by the death of their commander. For minutes their left seemed paralysed. This gave the Williamite horse time to dash up the causeway and manoeuvre to the rear. The Jacobite line broke under the impact. De Tesse saw what had happened and charged with two squadrons, but it was too late – the Williamites had turned the Jacobite flank.

Minutes before, Henry Luttrell sat stiffly on his big black horse on the ground beyond the causeway with his dragoons at the ready. It was his job to drive the Williamite horse back. He failed to do so. The charitable explanation is that he was unable to act without cavalry; the less charitable is that he acted treacherously. Ruvigny, leading the William-ite horse, saw Luttrell draw back and pressed his advantage. More and more Williamite cavalry dashed up the causeway. Luttrell retreated fur-ther. So to did Sheldon who was close by with a cavalry troop. Within minutes these two commanders rode off the field. Hayes-McCoy has made the apt comment:

> It was not the first time that the mounted man, the man with a means of doing so, had saved himself and left the man on foot to die. History is full of such treachery, for what was treachery at Crecy where the French knights rode down their own crossbow men was treachery also at Aughrim, where the upper class deserted the lower.[10]

The Jacobite army had been taken on the left wing, the one considered its strongest. The infantry in the centre held out for some time, but when the cavalry quit, its position was hopeless. The Williamites also piled on pressure on the centre, with Ginkel charging in the front and Mackay doing likewise in the flank, the Jacobites were completely overwhelmed.

Now we return to Sarsfield, who was somewhere in the rear – whet-her on the right or left is uncertain – but his first intimation that the tide had turned was when he saw the broken infantry streaming over the hill towards him, with terror on their faces. His experienced eye would have taken in what had happened. It would have been apparent that his cavalry troop, however large, could not retrieve the situation. All he could do was try to conduct an orderly retreat. This, we know, he did. A Williamite report sent to London bears this out. It said:

> Colonel Sarsfield, who commanded the enemy in their retreat, performed miracles and if he were not killed or taken it was no fault of his.[11]

Darkness had now fallen and it was raining lightly. The slaughter of the Jacobite infantry had gone on for an hour. Those who were lucky fled to boggy ground where the enemy cavalry could not easily get at them. The castle had surrendered and Burke was taken prisoner. The defeat was complete. The Jacobites lost in all quarters; eleven standards were taken and all their ammunition, field guns, tents, baggage and other equip-ment. Their dead lay unburied in heaps – 150 here, 200 there, 250 in an adjoining field and so on.

When Rev. Story visited the battlefield three days later he said that the naked bodies of the slain lay scattered for miles along the slopes, re-sembling a gigantic flock of sheep. The death toll was 7,000, the great-est number to fall in an Irish battle. For years afterwards the local peas-antry pointed to a gorge on Kilcommodon Hill where two regiments awaited their doom with sullen determination. It became known as *Gleanna Fola* – the bloody glen. People were afraid to go near the site of the battle for generations to come. It became known as *Áit na Gráinne* – the ugly place.

The defeat represented the destruction of the last vestiges of Catholic power. Colonel O'Kelly in his despairing account said: 'The Irish lost the flower of their army and nation'. Numerous poets wrote poignantly of the defeat. Thomas Moore caught the mood of widespread anguish when he wrote:

> Forget not the field where they perished
> The truest, the last of the brave;
> All gone – and the bright hopes we cherished
> Gone with them and quinched in the grave.
>
> Oh! Could we from death but recover
> Those hearts as they bounded before
> In the face of high heaven to fight over
> The combat for freedom once more.[12]

THE MISSED CHANCE

The defeat was to beget a lively sub-theme in Irish history, the concept of what did 'not' happen and the tale of the missed chance. It was said that had St Ruth lived for a further twenty minutes victory would have gone to the Jacobites. Tied to this thinking was the suggestion of treachery and betrayal. Why did Luttrell and Sheldon leave the field? In Luttrell's case the accusation of treachery seemed proven by his later conduct at Limerick, and his acceptance of a pension from William after the war. To this day the spot where he led the Williamite cavalry off the field is known as 'Luttrell's Pass' or 'The Traitor's Gate'. Years later, near the spot where St Ruth was struck down – known as 'Bloody Hollow' – a bush was grown. Today, one of its successors is marked with a plaque which says:

> The Jacobite General St Ruth died here after a battle with the forces of King William on July 12th 1691.
> His defeat and death spelled the end for the hopes of James II and changed the course of Irish history.

At the bicentenary of the battle in 1891 a committee of local people made arrangements to erect a monument on the site. In that turbulent period in Irish history – the time of the Parnell split – the committee did not escape the pressures of the day and broke up. An incomplete celtic cross of fine granite lay in a stonemason's yard in Ballinasloe for many years.

In more recent times, a local schoolmaster, Martin Joyce, formed a new committee which erected the cross near the ruin of Aughrim castle, where the final stages of the battle were fought. The inscription, in French, reads:

A la memoire du Lieutenant-General Marquis de St Ruth et des morts du
Champs d'Honneur, Aughrim 1691.

And in English: To the memory of Lieutenant-General Marquis of St
Ruth and the dead on the field of honour, Aughrim, 1691.

Underneath is written: Stone presented by Jerry and Leo Beegan,
1960, quarried by their father and grandfather.

GALWAY FALLS

After the defeat at Aughrim the Jacobite army almost disintegrated. The
panic-stricken survivors fled southwards. Some sped over the hills towards Portumna, others in the direction of Scariff and Killaloe. In the
days following, ragged groups of weary men could be seen crossing fields
heading towards Limerick. Among them were small bodies of horse, including Sarsfield and his troop, seeking to guide the unfortunates and
protect their rear.

The Williamites did not give chase. Ginkel stayed on Kilcommodon
Hill burying his dead and inspecting the baggage of the defeated. He
then marched towards Athenry halfway between Aughrim and Galway.

On 15 July, Lord Dillon, the governor of Galway and the Marquis
d'Usson, the military commander, learned of the defeat at Aughrim.
They knew that an attack on Galway was imminent and began making
preparations. They were hamstrung by the attitude of the leading citizens and, generally, public opinion was against resistance. Some people
had done well from the land changes earlier in the century and had their
titles confirmed during Charles II's reign. They represented the 'New
Interest', and were outspoken against the Jacobites. They had responded favourably towards Ginkel's peace proposals and advocated their
acceptance. Their attitudes were later condemned by Colonel O'Kelly,
who castigated them for preferring private gain to 'the interests of their
country and their religion'.

Despite this lack of popular resolve, Dillon and d'Usson were prepared to make a stand. D'Usson wrote to Tyrconnell and Sarsfield in
Limerick, urging that troops be sent to reinforce the garrison; contacts
were opened with Bealdearg O'Donnell and, briefly, there appeared to
be hope that he would assist. But, no assistance came; the town had to
rely on its own resources. It was walled and lay east of the Corrib river
which flows into its famous bay. On three sides it was surrounded by
water and towards the east there was a high ridge which formed the
main approach.

Ginkel arrived on 19 June and summoned it to surrender. Dillon
gave an emphatic 'No', to which he added that Galway would be defended to the last man. Before Ginkel had time to bring up his batteries
he was hit by volleys from the walls and it appeared that resistance
would be stiff. The firing, however, was a waste of ammunition as the
Williamites stayed beyond range.

Rumour reached Ginkel that Dillon expected aid from Bealdearg O'Donnell. He waited until darkness to send Mackay and a detachment across the Corrib about two miles above the town. The idea was to cut off O'Donnell, should he come. At dawn a Jacobite deserter was brought to Ginkel and revealed that the fort which defended the town's approach was depleted of ammunition after the exchanges of the previous day. Ginkel destroyed the fort and closed in on the town's walls. When the attack came, the defenders put up only the slightest resistance. After an hour, much to Ginkel's surprise, the drums beat a parlay and shortly afterwards Lord Dillon sat down to negotiate Articles of Capitulation.

Many Jacobites professed disgust at Galway's failure to fight. D'Usson could do little and later wrote that 'the Irish at Galway contributed more to the ruin of their country than the enemy'. Years later, in his *Memoirs* James laid the blame at the door of Lord Clanricard, whose family had strong commercial interests in Galway. He wrote:

> My Lord Clanricard and others, considering nothing but their security made such haste to surrender the town that they would not wait for the coming of the enemy's cannon.[13]

It was later said that Ginkel played the part of Caesar before the walls of Galway and that there must be a medal somewhere showing him in classical costume, wreathed in laurels and with the words *veni, vidi, vici* carved on the circumference.[14]

Yet Ginkel paid a price. The terms which he agreed were most favourable to Galway and he was criticised in London for being so lenient. Under the Articles (signed on 21 July 1691) the garrison marched out with flying colours, drums beating, their cannon drawn by horses supplied by the Williamites.

The citizens of Galway were later confirmed in the possession of their estates and both clergy and laity were to have 'the private exercise of their religion, without being persecuted under any penal law for the same'. These terms may have been designed to encourage the 'peace party' at Limerick, who were urging Tyrconnell to capitulate.

The remaining pockets of resistance in Connaught were few and soon collapsed. At Sligo, Sir Tadg O'Regan was put under strong pressure by a Williamite force from Donegal, led by Mitchelburn, the governor of Derry. Mitchelburn sent O'Regan a copy of Ginkel's peace proposals, accompanied by a bottle of whisky and a box of snuff. O'Regan held his ground; he did not know how the war was going elsewhere and thought that Sarsfield might come to his aid. He played for time and announced that he would surrender after ten days.

In the meantime, he contacted Bealdearg O'Donnell, who had moved towards Sligo, as Mitchelburn retreated northwards. But O'Donnell, as we know, was no ally of the Jacobites and the time had come for him to insert the knife. He told Ginkel that he would join up with the Williamites if he were given an earldom and a pension. After some haggling this would-be king of Ireland consented to sell his people for £500 a year. A deal was done, and O'Donnell agreed to participate in an attack on Sligo, joining up with the forces of Sir Albert Conyngham. But O'Regan was still not prepared to yield. On a foggy September morning his men made a successful sally and took Conyngham and O'Donnell by surprise. In the skirmish Conyngham was killed, and O'Donnell had a lucky escaped. It was said that if the Jacobites captured him, he would have been hanged immediately.

But it was all no good; new Williamite forces were advancing on Sligo from the south, and Mitchelburn returned from the north. On 14 September O'Regan surrendered on honourable terms: his men were allowed to march out with full honours of war and made their way to Limerick. Whether Tadg departed the town on his famous steed is not known. On this point, as on many others, history is silent.

17

ENDGAME AT LIMERICK

Oh, hurrah! For the men, who when danger is nigh
Are found in the front, looking death in the eye
Hurrah! For the men who keep Limerick's wall
And hurrah! For bold Sarsfield, the bravest of all.

FROM 'THE BALLAD OF LIMERICK' BY THOMAS DAVIS

THE LAST STRONGHOLD

Limerick was now the last refuge for the Jacobites and most of their troops were gathered there by the beginning of August 1691. Their numbers have been variously estimated, but 23,500 is probably not far out. Only half had arms and morale was minimal. Their strategy was to hold out until October when the onset of winter would force Ginkel to abandon the struggle until spring. To achieve this limited objective, help was urgently needed from France. Frantic appeals were sent to Louis and James in the days following Aughrim, but in spite of apparently genuine promises, nothing was received.

To the surprise of many, Tyrconnell, who had been the leader of the peace party, changed his attitude and became an advocate of resistance. He feared that individual officers or groups might try to settle privately with Ginkel. To avert this, he proposed that all officers and men should forthwith renew their oath of allegiance to James. Some thought the proposal silly and said it would only dismay the men and shake their confidence further. A number of heated arguments took place, and Luttrell and Henry Purcell went through the ranks cajoling the men not to cooperate with the suggestion, but most did.

Shortly afterwards, Luttrell was uncovered as a traitor. He had been a friend of Sarsfield's; they had been young soldiers together in Flanders and had campaigned over the years. But since failing to defend the causeway at Aughrim, Luttrell had aroused suspicion. In the end his exposure came easily enough. A messenger from Ginkel arrived in Limerick on 2 August with a communique for Sarsfield. It contained a list of Williamite officers who had been missing since Aughrim and Sarsfield was asked to confirm whether they had been taken prisoner. For some reason Sarsfield grew suspicious of the messenger and asked whether he carried further communiques. The fellow denied that he did. Sarsfield told him that he would be searched and if found lying he would be strung up on a gibbet. At this, the messenger panicked and produced a letter addressed to Luttrell. Sarsfield broke the seal and read it. It was from Lieutenant Colonel Pierre de La Bastride St Sebastian, a Williamite commander known simply as 'Sebastian'. It compromised Luttrell and showed him to be in league with Ginkel.[1]

Whether the revelation was a shock to Sarsfield, we do not know. He did not hesitate, however, to take the letter to Tyrconnell, who took a dim view of it. James refers to the incident in his *Memoirs*:

> My Lord Lucan whose intentions were always right ... was the first to oppose his friends when he found that they went beyond the limits of their duty and allegiance to the king, and it was by this means that Luttrell's secret correspondence was discovered.

Luttrell was arrested and tried by court martial. The French commanders urged that he should be hanged forthwith, but the judges were of divided opinion: some held that the letter was unsolicited and that it would, therefore, be unjust to condemn Luttrell. But Tyrconnell, who presided, noted the angry mood in the army, and went for a compromise. He slung Luttrell into King John's Castle under lock and key, where he remained until the war was over.

TYRCONNELL BOWS OUT

D'Usson, on arrival from Galway, was given command of the Limerick garrison and appointed governor. The army was speedily reorganised and the cavalry sent to quarters in Co. Clare, its task being to defend the passes on the Shannon. Sarsfield established headquarters at Killaloe.

On the evening of 10 August d'Usson hosted a dinner party for his fellow commanders, at which Tyrconnell was the principal guest. The author of the *Jacobite Narrative* says Tyrconnell and the company were very merry but 'that night on preparing to go to bed, he found himself indisposed. The next day his malady increased. Remedies were applied, but to no good effect. On the third day, observing his weakness to be great, he settled his worldly affairs and took charge of his conscience ... His Excellency grew speechless and on Friday, the fourteenth, being the fifth day of his sickness, he expired'.

Suspicion and intrigue was so rife that a rumour spread that Tyrconnell had been poisoned. The finger was pointed, implausibly, at Sarsfield and (perhaps, more implausibly) at the French. These rumours may have had Williamite origins, for O'Kelly writes:

> His death was much lamented by his friends, and not less so by the English who cried him up as an honest man and a lover of peace; they gave that he had been poisoned by Sarsfield and the French commanders.[2]

Whatever their origin, the rumours seem baseless. Tyrconnell's biographer was, perhaps, close to the truth when he wrote:

... that the combined effect of his unceasing toil and anxiety, his excessive bulk and weak heart – and, no doubt, also the over-merry party at d'Usson's – were sufficient to account for the sudden collapse of a man of sixty-one, without recourse to the horrible idea that someone in his own party brought him to an unnatural end.[3]

The lord deputy was buried at night at St Mary's cathedral, 'not with that pomp which his merits exacted,' says the *Jacobite Narrative*, 'but with that decency which the present state of affairs admitted'.[4] It is interesting to note that his widow, Frances, survived him by forty years. After a lengthy period in France, she returned to Ireland and established a nunnery. On 7 March 1731, in her ninety-third year – and long after most of her contemporaries had passed away – she was found dead on the floor of her bedroom.

The day after Tyrconnell's death, Francis Plowden, an Englishman who had arrived from St Germains to take control of Jacobite finances, produced a document written under the great seal of James. It was a commission appointing Sir Richard Nagle, Anthony Fritton and Plowden himself, lord justices in the event of Tyrconnell's death. These appointments were paper ones and unpopular as two of the appointees were Englishmen. D'Usson was confirmed as military commander, but from this point onwards he was ignored. Sarsfield emerged as the key figure and was accepted as such, not only by the Jacobites but by the other side.

There was no let-up in the intriguing. Tyrconnell was scarcely cold when the 'peace party' circulated a device purporting to be his 'Last Will and Testimony'. This uncorroborated document began:

My Dear Fellow Countrymen, if ever you are capable of thought it is now more needed than ever, as you are on the verge of ruin; to wait for French help is a mere chimera ... I do not doubt that some who have more loyalty than sense say: 'let us wait for the king's consent'. I have myself made the same proposal in public, not that I thought it reasonable, but because I knew that Lord Lucan and Luttrell were looking for an opportunity to ruin my reputation with the deluded masses.[5]

This propaganda so unsettled the army that the French – who held the money-bags – were forced to disperse cash to the troops to soothe their anxieties. Some began to desert, and more would have done so if the inducements did not persuade them otherwise.

GINKEL AT LIMERICK
The closing scenes of the drama were now to be enacted. Ginkel waited for a month at Galway before pursuing his quarry. He hoped that the feuding among the Jacobites would induce them to seek terms. He was reluctant to besiege Limerick, being conscious of William's failure before its walls in the previous year. The city's fortifications were stronger

than before and its provisions were greater. Ginkel's best hope was to try to negotiate a surrender or, failing that, to enforce a blockade.

The Williamites crossed the Shannon at Banagher on 12 August and marched slowly via Birr and Nenagh to Limerick. During their march the weather broke and there was a sharp exchange of views between Ginkel and Würtemburg, who favoured an immediate assault on the city, and other commanders who favoured a blockade. By the time they arrived before the walls Ginkel had received direct instructions from William to attack with force.

The Williamites took up positions more to the west and closer to the walls than in the previous year. One reason was that an English fleet, under Admiral Cole, had arrived in the Shannon and Ginkel was anxious to keep in touch with it. Another was that the new positions enabled gunners to direct long-range shells into Englishtown, and to direct fire at the newly-built bastions near St John's Gate.

On 30 August the siege began in earnest, with cannon roaring on both sides. Before morning, the Williamite mortars, which had thundered non-stop all night, had thrown more than 200 bombs into Englishtown. The first shell, it was reported, killed Lady Dillon – the wife of the governor of Galway – and injured several others. But by early September, Ginkel had effected little, and switched his operations from the extreme left to the extreme right, having received information that the section of the Englishtown wall facing the Abbey river was weak. He placed a new battery across the river, north of the present day O'Dwyer's Bridge; this packed a formidable punch, being made up of twenty-four-pound and eighteen-pound guns.[6] Within a few hours it opened a breach in the Englishtown wall where it skirted the present-day Island Road. Ginkel was reluctant to storm this breach, because of a moat in front of the walls and a strong palisade.

He called a council of war and different commanders suggested various strategies. The one with most appeal was that a detachment be sent across the Shannon to the Clare side with the hope of blockading the city and, if lucky, cutting off the cavalry. 'This,' says Rev. Story, 'was melancholy news for the officers and men' – the river was likely to be strongly guarded and the prospects of success were not great. But Ginkel had to make a move quickly lest a French fleet came riding up the Shannon to relieve the city.

On the evening of 15 September a party of Williamites set about constructing a pontoon bridge at Lanahrone, a few hundred yards upstream from the present-day Athlukard Bridge. By the following morning it was completed and a party crossed to secure the opposite bank. The operation would not have succeeded had the Jacobite cavalry been on the alert. That stretch of river had been the responsibility of Brigadier Robert Clifford, but his loyalty had been suspect since the Siege of Athlone, and at this moment much depended on his vigilance. He was positioned favourably at Partine, which afforded him views up and down the river. Yet he failed to challenge the Williamites and fled with his men back towards Thomond Gate.

Colonel O'Kelly later wrote that Sarsfield had been warned of Clifford's unreliability and was urged to take the control of the riverbank himself or to appoint a trustworthy officer. For some reason Sarsfield failed to heed this warning and in O'Kelly's view was culpable. Fumeron was in no doubt that Clifford had been treacherous and later wrote to Paris saying so, and mentioning that he did not even fire a shot to alert other Jacobite units. On his return to the city Clifford was arrested; but the damage was done. Limerick was surrounded and Ginkel was in a position to impose a blockade. The new disposition of the Williamites meant that the Jacobite cavalry was effectively cut off and rendered impotant in Co. Clare.

But a blockade could take several weeks, even months, to be effective against a well-provisioned city. And Ginkel did not have such time at his disposal. Yet now (with a hole opened up in the Englishtown wall and the city encircled) was the time, Ginkel reckoned, to induce the city to capitulate. Accordingly, on 16 September he offered terms to the garrison, with the proviso that if Limerick did not come to its senses within eight days, those who held out would be 'answerable for the blood and destruction they drew upon themselves'.

The 'peace party' in the city said that it would be folly to refuse these terms. Yet Ginkel received no reply. He went into conclave, and decided to exploit the bridgehead to the Clare side. This policy was not without risk, for if he transferred large numbers of troops, the Jacobites might take advantage of the reduction before Irishtown (on the east side) and sally out and destroy the main Williamite positions. It was a risk which Ginkel was prepared to take, but not before he took elaborate precaution against a Jacobite move: he strengthened the field defences facing Irishtown and established a fresh battery near Singland to cover a sally from St John's Gate. Meanwhile, the Jacobites watched anxiously with one question on their lips: where was the promised French relief force?

THE THOMOND BRIDGE MASSACRE

Ginkel's preparations were completed by 22 September. The best part of the army was consigned to the new initiative: most of the cavalry and dragoons, ten regiments of infantry, plus a number of field guns. Mackay and Talmash were to stay behind and continue the bombardment from the original position. By early afternoon the force had crossed the river and swung westward, around the bend of the Shannon, and towards the Jacobite outer defences lying not far from Thomond Gate.

Here they encountered opposition. A Jacobite force of 600 horse, under Colonel Lacy, dashed through the gate in a great sally. The fighting was ferocious and both sides called up reinforcements. After half an hour the Jacobites were forced to retire, by sheer weight of numbers. They fell back upon the outworks, which consisted of two small forts, defended by about 800 men. The guns of King John's Castle blazed to defend these forts, but they were just beyond range and the firing was ineffectual. This was the opportunity which Ginkel needed: as the Jacobite horse retreated, he launched an assault on the forts. Within half an hour the English grenadiers carried the forts, and their defenders fell back towards Thomond Gate, seeking the sanctuary of Englishtown.

Then disaster struck. As they ran towards the gates, with the Williamites on their heels, the French officer in charge of the drawbridge raised it too soon – lest the Williamites should enter the city – thereby trapping a large number of Jacobites on the wrong side. The result was a bloodbath. The Jacobites cried for quarter; some raised their hands or waved their handkerchiefs. But the grenadiers, not disposed to be generous, fell upon them murderously. They did not stay their hand until 600 were either killed or forced over the sides into the gap where the drawbridge had been raised. It was estimated that about 150 lost their lives through drowning.

LIMERICK CAPITULATES

The ineptitude of the officer responsible for the terrible mishap threw the citizens into a fury. They demanded that he be apprehended and handed to them. Had the fellow not been kiled by musket fire, he would have been torn to pieces. The tragedy sparked off the old suspicion of French treachery and set the Irish and the French at loggerheads.

It also reduced morale to its lowest point ever. Many now despaired, including Sarsfield. There was no light in the tunnel – the relief force had failed to arrive; the defenders' ranks had been thinned and further treachery was probably inevitable. Sarsfield called a meeting of the commanders, the senior clergy and a number of prominent citizens. There was only one question before them: should they continue to defend Limerick or capitulate?

The consultations were not protracted: capitulation was agreed upon. The clergy undertook to release from their obligations those who had taken an oath not to surrender without James' permission. Next morning the drums beat a parlay and a white flag was hung out.

The date was 24 September. Limerick had held out for six weeks and endured one of the most infernal bombardments of the war and a terrible massacre. Around noon, Sarsfield and Major General Wauchope rode out to meet Ginkel and were received with courtesy. The Dutchman recognised Sarsfield's title as Earl of Lucan, though it had been conferred after James had fled to France. Sarsfield's main concern seems to have been to obtain an agreement which would permit the Jacobites to evacuate to France. It was a bold demand and, in the eyes of some, seemed an unacceptably high price for Ginkel to pay; the evacuated army would likely continue the struggle from France. But it is a measure of the pressure which Ginkel was under to conclude the war, that he agreed. A temporary ceasefire was negotiated and the question of terms was not discussed until Sarsfield and Wauchope had returned to the city for consultations. Over the next few days a number of meetings took place – often cordially held over good food and wines – at which the military and civil terms of a treaty were hammered out.

Many in the garrison learned of the capitulation with anguish. Some could scarcely believe their ears. Troops ran on the ramparts and broke their swords in anger. The muskets which had so recently kept the enemy at bay were smashed in a frenzy. The rapparees, it is said, cracked the long shafts of their pikes across their knees, crying: 'We need them no longer, Ireland is no more!'

Sarsfield has sometimes been blamed for submitting when he might have held out for weeks, even months, longer. Sir George Clarke found the capitulation inexplicable and wrote:

> It may appear very strange that a numerous garrison, not pressed by any want, should give up a town which nobody was in a condition to take from them at a time when those who lay before it had actually drawn off their cannon and were preparing to walk away and when the garrison did every day expect a squadron of ships to come to their relief, if they needed any.

There is evidence that Ginkel was surprised at the capitulation and may have been preparing to raise the siege. He had sent some of his artillery on board the ships in the harbour – an indication that he had abandoned thoughts of storming the walls. Whatever Ginkel's intentions were, Sarsfield could not read his mind. A consideration of the motives which may have induced Sarsfield to surrender would probably convince most people that he had little alternative: the struggle must have seemed hopeless. The Jacobites had their backs to the wall; their fortifications had received a heavy battering and could not withstand much more. There was no force in the country to attempt their relief, and the French were nowhere to be seen. Since Ginkel's crossing of the Shannon the cavalry had been cut off and anyway were powerless against such large enemy forces. The massacre at Thomond Gate had reduced the ranks and morale had collapsed. The 'peace party' had become more obstreperous and the army was almost 'honeycombed' with treachery. And even if Limerick did hold out for a little longer, what could be hoped for: most observers would say not much.

It was not unreasonable then, that Sarsfield should opt for capitulation. He felt he would receive better terms by capitulating while relatively strong, rather than later, when he might be weak, and forced to surrender unconditionally. That he acted from the best of motives cannot be doubted. Everything we know about him suggests that he would not have submitted, if it could have been avoided.

THE TREATY OF LIMERICK

In the Treaty negotiations, Sarsfield assumed the role of chief Jacobite negotiator. Three lawyers assisted him: Sir Toby Butler, Garret Dillon and John Brown of Westport. The negotiating team also included the bishops of Armagh and Cashel, Dominic Maguire and John Brenan. Ginkel led for the Williamites and before settlement the lord justices, Porter and Conningsby, arrived to participate.

Sarsfield drove a hard bargain. He insisted upon an indemnity for all past actions by the Jacobites and that Catholic landowners be restored to their forfeited estates. He requested, that Catholics be given freedom of worship and put on an equal footing with Protestants. Next, that Jacobite soldiers who wished to transfer their allegiance be given similar status to Williamite soldiers. Ginkel stubbornly refused to accept these terms and said that they were 'contrary to the laws of England and dishonourable to himself'. The negotiations collapsed and it looked as if an agreement could not be reached. Ginkel said that he would resume the siege. Sarsfield, knowing that his position was weak, asked what terms Ginkel had been authorised to grant. The tension broke, and Ginkel said a set of military and civil articles would be drawn up in writing and sent to him for consideration.

They were, and a fresh conference was called. This time the atmosphere was more relaxed and Ginkel laid on a palatable spread for his opposite numbers. But the negotiations remained tough. Sir Toby Butler challenged the title given to the terms. It was: 'Articles granted by Lieutenant-General Ginkel to all persons now in the city of Limerick and in the Irish army that is in the counties of Clare, Kerry, Cork and Mayo and other garrisons in their possession'. Sir George Clarke countered that the terms were only offered to those in a position to give resistance to 'their majesties' forces' – a definition which excluded the civilian populations of these counties. Sarsfield found this unacceptable and objected strongly. Pointing towards Limerick, he declared he 'would rather lay his bones in these old walls than not take care of those who had stuck with us all along'.[7] The negotiations continued, and at length the Williamites conceded, and the terms were extended to include the words 'all those under the protection of the Irish army in the said counties'.

Later that day a full settlement was reached, but both sides agreed to await the arrival of the lord justices before a signing took place. On Saturday 3 October the negotiators put pen to the parchment, reputedly on a large stone near Thomond Bridge.

The treaty was drawn up under two main headings: military and civil articles. The former, twenty-nine in number, were of a short-term nature and concerned the disposition of the Jacobite army following the war. They allowed individual soldiers to elect whether to evacuate to France or, if wising to remain in Ireland, to join the service of William. It should be mentioned that during the succeeding days Ginkel made every effort to induce the Jacobite rank and file to adopt the latter course. Sarsfield, likewise, urged them to go with him to France and promised that within a year they would be back in either England or Ireland as part of a large army committed to pushing the Dutch usurper from the throne.

The Treaty Stone in Limerick

The choice was difficult for the poorly informed, ill-educated individual soldier, faced with exile or the prospect of serving a despised enemy. Sarsfield reinforced his own message by offering the men liberal supplies of French brandy and he arranged for the Catholic clergy to deliver sermons on the desirability of choosing his course. Ginkel undertook to provide shipping for those opting for exile.

The civil articles were thirteen in number and are commonly called 'The Treaty of Limerick'. They affected the country at large; and it is around these that so many disputes have been raised. The drafting of these articles was less than satisfactory. It is a censure on Sarsfield and his fellow negotiators, that in drawing up these – on which so much depended for good or ill – they might have shaped them with more care.

These articles were meant to secure three conditions: religious toleration for the Catholic population; security of life and property for officers and soldiers remaining in Ireland; security for the civilian inhabitants of Limerick and other places held by the Jacobites and areas under their protection.

The execution of the treaty depended on the goodwill and co-operation of the new crown and the Irish parliament. As far as William himself was concerned it must be conceded that he tried to administer it fairly; of the 1,300 persons who formally claimed benefit under its terms all but 16 had their claims allowed. But the all-Protestant Irish parliament took a very different line. It did not ratify the treaty until 1697 and even then only in modified form. The first article which guaranteed that the 'Roman Catholics of this kingdom shall enjoy such privileges in the exercise of their religion, as are consistent with the laws of Ireland, or as they did enjoy in the reign of Charles II' was ignored. Whatever may be said about the looseness of the drafting of this article, there could be no doubt as to its intention. Indeed, the whole series of penal laws, on which the Irish parliament had embarked even prior to 1697, must be said to be contrary to the spirit of the treaty. In these circumstances, it is not surprising that Limerick became known in history as 'The City of the Broken Treaty'.[8]

THE ARMY DECIDES

On the morning of 5 October a singular scene was enacted on the northern bank of the Shannon, beyond the city walls. The Jacobite regiments were to make their choice between exile or joining the service of their conqueror. At each end of a height the royal standards of England and France were placed. It was agreed that the regiments as they marched out – with drums beating and colours flying – should on reaching this spot, wheel to the left or right beneath the flags which they chose to serve. Sarsfield and Ginkel were present to watch the spectacle.

At the head of the Jacobite army marched the foot guards, perhaps the finest infantry regiment in the service, 1,400 strong. All eyes were on them, amidst silence and great suspense. They marched to the spot and, as a body, wheeled towards the colours of France; seven men, it is said, turned to the English side. The next regiment – Lord Iveagh's – marched to the Williamite banner, as did portions of two others. But the bulk of the men filed under the *Fleur de Lis*. Only 1,046 out of nearly 14,000 men, preferred the service of William.

Similar reviews were held over the next few days for the cavalry and troops garrisoned in Kerry and other outlying areas. Two of the cavalry commanders, Henry Luttrell – who had been released from custody on the signing of the treaty – and Colonel John Rice, did all they could to persuade the horse regiments to join the Williamites. Luttrell delivered an impassioned speech to his old regiment which was, in fact, part of a bargain he had struck with Ginkel, under which he was promised a forfeited estate. Rice entered a bond of £10,000, to guarantee his own mens' pay if they turned their coats. But apart from a few losses, Sarsfield's eloquence ensured that the majority opted for France.

One Jacobite leader – albeit, an informal one, had little difficulty in making his choice. This was 'Galloping' Hogan, who refused to accept the treaty and elected to carry on the struggle with a faithful band of rapparees. On 24 September, the day of the capitulation, he and others were active near the village of Cullen, a stone's thrown from Ballyneety. Rev. George Story writes:

Galloping Hogan got upwards of one hundred rapparees together to plunder and rob the settlers and other people that came into his power and was now so bold as to set upon a party of wagons coming towards the camp nigh Cullen and took away with him seventy-one horses.[9]

On the day the treaty was signed Ginkel moved to curb Hogan's raids; two regiments of horse were dispatched to hunt him down, but failed to do so. Tradition has it that he was one of the last to transfer to France and that he ended his career as an officer in the Portuguese army.[10]

THE FLIGHT OF THE WILD GEESE

It now remained for Ginkel was to fulfil the military articles of the treaty by providing transports to take the Jacobites to France. There was a size-able merchant fleet in Cork harbour which he utilised, together with some of Admiral Cole's ships which remained in the Shannon.

As the time for departure drew near, a number of Jacobite soldiers changed their minds and deserted. To stem the tide, Sarsfield detained the volunteers on King's Island; he posted guards on all bridges to the island, but in spite of his efforts, some continued to leave. To prevent further seepage he decided to make haste for Cork and marched his men from Limerick, for the last time, on 16 October.

It was a miserable four day trek and the roads were thronged with wives, children and relatives, many of whom wanted to travel to France. Others came to weaken the men's resolve and encourage them to desert. All along the route there were scenes of inexpressible grief and some weakened. By the time the march reached Cork, the ranks had thinned.

In the meantime, the long awaited French relief expedition arrived in Limerick – a month after Sarsfield had agreed to the city's capitula-tion. It had first assembled at Brest three months earlier, but was unable to sail because of administrative delays. On arrival in the Shannon, it lay off Slattery Island and sent signals to the garrison. On board were enough men and materials to scatter Ginkel's army from the walls. The Dutchman grew fearful lest the Irish would disclaim the treaty and re-new the war.

But Sarsfield was in Cork. When told of the fleet's arrival he is re-ported to have remained silent for a moment, and then despondently said: 'too late, our honour is pledged. Though a 100,000 Frenchmen were to aid us now, we must keep our plighted troth!'[11]

The embarkation took several days to complete. Before it had pre-ceded very far it was found that the number of ships was inadequate. Representations were made to Ginkel, and although further ships were provided, there was still insufficient capacity. Towards the end of the embarkation it was found that not all the women and other relatives who wished to travel could do so. They crowded excitedly onto the water's edge and flung themselves into rowing boats to carry them out to the vessels. Panic arose and there was a dreadful scene which Macauley poignantly describes:

> After the soldiers had embarked, room was found for the families of many. But there still remained at the waterside a great multitude clamouring piteously to be taken on board. As the last boats pulled off there was a rush into the surf. Some women caught hold of the ropes, were dragged out into the depth, clung till their fingers were cut through and perished in the waves. The ships began to move. A wild and terrible wail arose from the shore and excited unwanton passion in hearts steeled by hatred of the Irish race and of the Romish faith. Even the stern Cromwellian ... could not hear unmoved that bitter cry, in which was poured forth all the rage and sorrow of a conquered nation.[12]

Sarsfield sailed on 22 December 1691. He left behind family and friends and what may have been a substantial stake in the country, for Ginkel had been authorised to offer him an estate if he threw in his lot with William. But this was not an option for Sarsfield. He may well have believed his own rhetoric that one day he would return to renew the struggle.

A few months later a royal proclamation announced the end of the war; but all resistance had ceased long before. As early as November 1691 Rev. Story was to write that a man could travel through the whole country in greater safety than in England. The Dutchman had triumphed and the Protestant Ascendancy was born. There was, however, another outcome. The Jacobite defeat destroyed the Old English community as a political force. They had been the original Anglo-Irish and had kept their distinctive identity intact for five centuries, during which time their loyalty had been to England. Since the days of the Reformation they had strained to reconcile their Catholicism with their allegiance to a succession of Protestant monarchs. But the strain had been too much. In the years ahead they would share the same religious disabilities as the Gaelic Irish and in time both would become indistinguishable.

18

The Last of the Brave

From forgotten fields they rally
To the roll of a phantom drum
And march through the land of shadows
Lured by a lively hum.
FROM 'FORGOTTEN FIELDS' BY PATRICK MULLOY

THE JACOBITE ARMY IN FRANCE

When the Jacobite army arrived in France it received a welcoming letter from James:

> Having been informed of the capitulation of Limerick and of the other places which remained to us in our kingdom of Ireland and of the necessity which forced our lord justices and general officers thereunto, we shall not defer to let you know and the rest of the officers who came along with you that we shall never forget this act of loyalty nor fail when in a capacity to give you, above others, particular marks of our favour ...
> James Rex[1]

Shortly afterwards, accompanied by Berwick, he arrived at Brest to inspect the men and announced that by the favour of the king of France they were to have new red coats instead of the grey ones in which they fought at Aughrim and Limerick. He also told them that they would receive the same level of pay as their counterparts in the French army. This did not, in fact, transpire. A few months later an embittered veteran wrote to his son of the manner in which James got his hands on some of the allocation:

> No sooner had we arrived in France than King James made arrangements with Louis XIV by which he had put us on a French footing, reserving for himself the difference for his own upkeep and that of his house. It was with pleasure that we agreed to this arrangement, although made at our expense ...[2]

The first contingents to arrive came to 5,781 men, including 792 officers, 234 servants and 29 private persons; in addition there were 582 women and 266 children. Most were placed in small garrisons around Brittany; the surviving records detail the towns and villages to which they were sent:

Rennes: 1,100	St Brieux: 400
Malstout: 300	Château Landin: 200
Ploermel: 400	Pintrieux: 200

La Trinite: 200	Goungarille: 200
Monmoutier: 300	Redon: 800
Pambast: 400	Vannes: 1,000

Total: 5,500 men and officers[3]

Sarsfield arrived in late December with a further 500 men.

The Jacobite army remained a separate entity for some time, but the French had effective control and began to reorganise it. The infantry was divided into six regiments whose commanding officers were:

The Guards:	William Dorington
The Queen's:	John Wauchope
The Marine:	Henry FitzJames (The grand prior)
Dublin:	Simon Luttrell
Limerick:	Richard Talbot, Jnr
Claremont:	Gordon O'Neill[4]

The cavalry received special attention and two troops of horse guards, of 100 men each, were formed, to act as James' personal bodyguards. These were commanded by Berwick and Sarsfield. It was reported that these troops were as fine as any in the French service and that Louis nominated officers from the *Maison du Roi* to train them in French techniques. The command structures were:[4]

	First Troop	Second Troop
Commander:	Duke of Berwick	Sarsfield, Earl of Lucan
Officers:	Sutherland	Charles O'Brien
	Nugent	Nicholas Cusack
	Trimelestown	John Gaydon
	La Rue	Robert Arthur Cook

The strength of the army after its re-organisation was:[5]

Two troops of horse guards	200
Two regiments of cavalry	744
Two regiments of foot dragoons	1,116
Six regiments of infantry	12,000
Total:	14,060

There were also three so-called independent companies of 201 men, but these were gradually merged with the main body.

Having received control of this considerable force, the question for the French was how to use it. An obvious course would have been to send it to Flanders to join the army of the Duc de Luxembourg and thus enable it to settle old scores with the forces of William. But the French decided to break it up, so that it could serve in garrisons in Savoy, Roustillion and on the Rhine. The diarist Narcissus Luttrell says that Sarsfield was ear-marked to serve in Italy. He never, in fact, went there. Soon he was given a command which involved him in a plan for an invasion of England, which, if realised, may have turned the tables on William.

TROUBLE FOR WILLIAM

The background to this project may be found in the French view of recent events. The struggle in Ireland had served Louis well, for while William was busy at the Boyne and elsewhere the French were enjoying a string of successes on the continent. The Duc de Luxembourg won a great victory at Fleuris; in Italy, Marshal Catinat defeated the Duke of Savoy and of even greater importance was the victory of Admiral Tourville over the combined Dutch and English fleets at Beachy Head. This latter defeat was a great humiliation to the English and for a time left the country open to invasion. But the French failed to exploit their success. Tourville was content to let his sailors burn the town of Teignmouth in Devonshire and to leave it at that. This action could achieve little, but it did call to arms virtually the entire population of the south-eastern coast of England, who stood ready to meet a landing party.

Matters continued to go badly for William in Flanders. So great was the need for his presence that he had scarcely returned from Ireland when he hastened there. It was the first time since the days of Henry VIII that an English king put himself at the head of an army on the continent. Yet, William's appearance made little difference. He was forced to look on while 400,000 Frenchmen surrounded Mons, the strongest fortress in the Netherlands, and in the presence of Louis, make themselves masters of it.

In England, this blow caused great trepidation and revived the hopes of Jacobite conspirators which had been dashed following Tourville's assault on Teignmouth. Leading Tories, like the Lords Clarendon and Dartmouth, opened communications with James, and even Whigs, such as the Earl of Shrewsbury, who felt that they had gained little from William, began to make contact with St Germains. More seriously, perhaps, Marlborough began to play a double game: he sought to ignite a revolt which would drive William from the throne without replacing him with James, by giving the crown to the Princess Anne, whose affections his wife had cultivated.

These were the circumstances in which Louis planned an attack on England, and which gave James a final opportunity of retrieving everything. For two years the exiled court had insisted to French ministers that England was ripe for a restoration. Now, an army of 8,000 Irishmen under Sarsfield, and 10,000 French regulars were assembled around Cherbourg. The whole French fleet, with numerous transports and store ships, were concentrated in the Normandy and Breton ports, waiting to carry the expedition across the channel.

It was not until the middle of April 1692 that Louis' plans became known in Whitehall. Fevered preparations were made on land and sea. As on the approach of the armada in the reign of Elizabeth I, all England was on the alert. Everything turned on the admiral of the fleet, Russell. He, like Marlborough and Shrewsbury, had been in contact with Jacobite agents; William and Mary feared, and James fervently hoped, that he would turn traitor. But it was not to be. Jacobite sources later admitted that Russell plainly told their agent that, as much as he loved James and loathed William's government, if he met the French fleet at sea he would do his best to destroy it, 'even though King James were on board'. Russell kept his word. 'If your officers play you false,' he said to his sailors on the day of battle, 'over board with them, and myself the first'.[6]

On 19 and 20 May, the English and Dutch fleets met Tourville with the main French ships in the Channel off Cape la Hogue. Russell's armada, which carried 40,000 men and 7,000 guns, had 99 ships to 44. Both sides fought hard, and Tourville was decisively beaten. Russell and his admirals, all of whom were on Jacobite lists as pledged adherents to James, followed the beaten French navy to their harbours. The whole apparatus of invasion was destroyed under the eyes of James, whom it was to have borne to England. The Dutchman's throne was made doubly secure by the suppression of a Jacobite conspiracy in England which the invasion was intended to support.

SARSFIELD – MARSHAL OF FRANCE

The victory of the Anglo-Dutch was a bitter pill for James, who became so depressed that he proposed retiring to a monastery. To Sarsfield, it must have been the greatest disappointment in his life. Six months later, Narcissus Luttrell wrote that Sarsfield had been 'clamped up in the Bastille for holding correspondence with the king's enemies'. This was untrue, for in the following month Sarsfield was given high command at the Battle of Steenkirk.

At this famous battle, fought between 24 July and 3 August 1692, William, defending Brussels launched a surprise attack against the Duc de Luxembourg, whose forces were separated from those of another French general. He gained a temporary advantage, but the struggle was inconclusive and there was much butchering on both sides. The English suffered severely and several of the officers who had been prominent in the Irish war– including Mackay, Lanier and Douglas – fell. So too did Mountjoy who had been exchanged for Richard Hamilton. In this battle Sarsfield distinguished himself. He was mentioned in dispatches by Luxembourg to Louis dated 4 August 1692 in which the duc said he showed 'that valour of which he has given such proofs in Ireland,' adding, 'I can assure your majesty that he is a very good and capable officer'.[7]

This battle left France virtually exhausted, and there was an outcry at the carnage. Fénelon, the famous theologian and man of letters, wrote frankly to Louis: 'this country,' he said, 'is a vast hospital'. Sarsfield found that he had several prisoners and wounded men on his hands and wrote to Count Nassau, William's cousin, informing him that they would be well treated and exchanged as soon as possible. Luttrell's diary says Sarsfield arranged for several surgeons in Brussels to look after the wounded. The battle had another outcome for the Irishman. On the Duc de Luxembourg's recommendation he was raised to the rank of lieutenant-general.

Sometime afterwards, Sarsfield received a surprising letter from Ginkel, who was now Earl of Athlone and Baron of Aughrim and serving in Flanders. It was said to be 'obliging' and advised Sarsfield that he was to receive a gift, with King William's compliments, of two horses. History does not relate what lay behind this gesture. It did, however, provide an opportunity for Ginkel to request the return of a number of British transports which had been seized by the French.

One of the proudest moments in Sarsfield's life came in April 1693 when he was made a marshal of France and received his baton. This meant that he had reached the highest rank in the French army and even outranked the Duke of Berwick – to whom he had long been subordinated – and who was then made a lieutenant-general. Sarsfield was not, however, fated to enjoy his new status for long.

BERWICK CAPTURED

The Battle of Landen (or Neerwinden, as it is sometimes called) was fought on 29 July 1693. Once again, it pitted the Duc de Luxembourg against William, who with 70,000 troops was entrenched near the town of Landen in eastern Flanders. General de Noailles attacked Leige which induced William to release 20,000 men to go to the town's aid. But the French outwitted him – they turned back from Leige and counter-marched their 80,000 troops against William's reduced number of 50,000. Instead of retiring behind the river Gheet, which would have afforded protection, William decided to await the attack from his existing position.

He had occupied a few moated villages: Walcowen and Neerlanden, on which his left wing rested. His right was strung out along Neerwinden and Laer; his centre extended from Neerlanden to Neerwinden. In the time available to him, he strongly fortified these villages and built trenches from one to another. He was strong in artillery, having 200 field guns, and was able to hold off attack with strong defensive fire, making it difficult for the French to establish their batteries.

Luxembourg saw Neerwinden as the key and attacked it strongly. Over three or four days it was taken and retaken several times. In the first attack, six French brigades marched abreast in a great assault. The Duke of Berwick, who commanded two brigades, carried the village and drove the enemy to its far end. Heavy fire, however, from open ground on either side led to the brigades crowding the centre, and the whole force, taken at a disadvantage, was counter-attacked and driven out. Berwick was captured and later wrote:

> I found myself completely cut off. Seeing this, I resolved to escape, if possible, by the plain, and having taken out my white cockade, passed for an officer of the enemy. Unfortunately Brigadier Churchill, brother of Lord Churchill, now Duke of Marlborough, my uncle, suspected that I might be there ... made me a prisoner. After mutual salutations he told me that he would conduct me to the Prince of Orange. We galloped a considerable time without meeting with him; at last we found him at a distance from the place of action, in a bottom, where neither friends nor enemies were to be seen.[8]

Berwick was not prepared to acknowledge the man who had deprived his father of three crowns:

> The prince made me a polite compliment, to which I replied with a low bow: after looking steadfastly at me for an instant, he put on his hat, and I mine, then he ordered me to be carried to Lewe.

William, it seems, took umbrage at Berwick's coldness towards him.

The day, however, was going against the allies and as they were driven from their entrenchments, William did all he could with his cavalry to cover their retreat. He had a narrow escape when crossing a bridge on the river Gheet, for amid panic, a number of troops broke, fell from the bridge, and drowned in the waters. He was fortunate in not being crowded over the bridge with them.

SARSFIELD FALLS

It was during the last charge against Neerwinden that Sarsfield fell. At the head of a French cavalry regiment – no Irish horse was involved – he bore down on the enemy and was driving them towards the river, when he was struck by a ball in the chest and fell from his horse. As he lay on the ground he is said to have put his hand on his wound, and realising that it was fatal, gasped: 'Would to God that this were for Ireland.'[9] An eyewitness, Gerald O'Connor, left an account:

> As I was walking over the field a message from Sarsfield reached me, he had been wounded to death in one of our last charges; he sent an aide de camp to call me to his side. The noble form of the hero lay on a pallet in a hut; he feebly lifted his nerveless hand and gave me a letter which he had dictated ... It read: I am dying the most glorious of death; we have seen the backs of the tyrants of our race. May you, Gerald, live to behold other such days; but let Ireland always be uppermost in your thoughts.[10]

Sarsfield was taken from the field and carried to the recently captured town of Huy, twenty miles in the rear where he received attention. But his wound grew worse and he became gripped with fever. He died a few days later. It has long been presumed that he was buried in Huy and this may well be so, but no surviving stone marks his grave.

He met his end characteristically: in the saddle leading a cavalry charge. The carnage that day was dreadful. Old soldiers were aghast at the slaughter and bodies lay piled on each other on the streets of the small villages. Yet some who were present found time to write of Sarsfield. He was said to have been in the thick of the action and 'doing actions worthy of himself' and 'it is not apt to be forgotten how gallant Sarsfield, the Earl of Lucan, behaved at Landen'.[11]

Three years earlier, following his successful operation at Ballyneety, Sarsfield had become the most celebrated Irishman of his time and was held in awe by friend and foe. In death he caught the imagination again and became a romantic hero. To those of the Irish who in later years pondered the 'War of the Three Kings' he was, in the words of Thomas Moore, 'The Last of the Brave'.[12]

THE LAST OF THE SARSFIELDS

He left one son, James Francis Edward. The infant was three months old when his father fell and was brought up by the Duke of Berwick who married his mother, Honora, Lady Lucan, in March 1695. The second Lord Lucan, like his father, became a soldier and celebrated his twenty-first birthday serving with his stepfather at the Siege of Barcelona in 1714, where he was wounded in the final assault. His bravery was conspicuous and he was decorated by the king of Spain with the Collar of the Golden Fleece. He remained in the Spanish service until 1719, when he transferred to France, where he became a colonel in the Irish brigade.

The young man was a firm Jacobite and took a lively interest in Irish affairs. In 1719, with other Irish officers, he had himself smuggled into Ireland where 'he held conferences with divers Papists of distinction with a design to foment a rebellion in favour of the Pretender' and a reward of £1,000 was put on his head. He spent a few weeks as a fugitive in Connaught and received numerous greetings from well-wishers. By that date, however, the Jacobite cause was long dead in Ireland and young Sarsfield returned to France having achieved little. He died without issue a few months later at St Omer.

Sarsfield's mother, the redoubtable former Annie O'More, survived her famous son. Her later life is not recorded but is mentioned briefly in a diary entry for 1694 by a Colonel Drake of Drakeswrath, a Jacobite officer:

From Paris I went to St Germains, where I met with Mrs Sarsfield, mother of Lord Lucan, and two of her daughters, Ladies Kilmallock and Mount Leinster; the elder of whom was my godmother. These ladies, though supported by small pensions, received me with great generosity and treated me with good nature.[13]

Lady Kilmallock's husband, Dominick Sarsfield – a distant relative of Patrick Sarsfield's – briefly succeeded to his brother-in-law's command in the Irish brigade. His side of the family was the progenitor of several Sarsfield families who were to flourish in France and Spain and who, in the eighteenth century, provided a number of senior army officers and one queen, Mary Sarsfield, who married Baron von Neuhoff, King Theodore I of Corsica. This lady was incorrectly identified in *The Jacobite Peerage*, published in London in 1904 as a daughter of Patrick Sarsfield.

Little is known of the courtship by Berwick of Sarsfield's widow, save that provided by a contemporary Irish writer, Eugene Davis, in a long lost work entitled *Irish Footprints on the Continent*. Davis claimed to have visited Lady Lucan at Huy shortly after Sarsfield's death. He wrote:

She was still very young, and even girlish in her manners, despite her widow's weeds, and was remarkably prepossessing in appearance. Her own relatives as well as those of her late husband had completely abandoned her and she was in almost absolute poverty in Huy. Berwick's heart grew full of pity for the desolate widow, and, as pity is a kin to love in such cases, he soon became so enamoured that he offered her his hand, which was graciously accepted.[14]

The match provided Berwick with a son and heir and was successful, although James looked upon it unfavourably as he had hoped that his son would marry into the French aristocracy rather than settle for an impoverished Irish widow. The new Duchess of Berwick did not, however, have long to live. She died two years later, before reaching her twenty-fourth birthday. Her husband was so grief-stricken that he had her heart preserved in a silver box.

Berwick himself went on to become one of the most famous soldiers of the age. During the war of the Spanish succession (1704-1714), which brought Spain and France into conflict with the British, Austrians and the Dutch, he held commands in Spain and the Netherlands. By capturing Nice from Prince Eugene of Savoy in 1706 he earned the title of marshal of France, and the following year decisively defeated the British at the Battle of Almanza, compelling them to evacuate Aragon and helping the Bourbon king, Philip V, to retain his crown. The end came at Philipsburg in Germany in June 1734 when he was struck by a cannon ball during the war of the Polish Succession.

William's war with Louis – known as the war of the league of Aughsburg – dragged on in a dull fashion until the Peace of Ryswick in 1697 when an exhausted France accepted disadvantageous terms. An important provision of the peace treaty was a pledge by Louis to abandon support for the Jacobite cause and to recognise William as king of England. This was not, however, the end of the Jacobites. They continued to intrigue against William and the exiled Stuart court in France (and later in Italy) was often frequented by disgruntled English soldiers and politicians wishing to restore James or his son, James Edward Stuart, the Old Pretender, or one of his grandsons.

After the Peace of Ryswick, William never took to the field again. On 21 February 1702 his favourite horse, *Sorrell*, tripped on a molehill in Richmond Park and threw him, breaking his collar bone. Complications arose and a fortnight later he was dead. He was fifty-two and had reigned for thirteen years and a few days. He lay in state in Kensington Palace for a week; weeks later he was interred, almost furtively, at midnight on 12 April in Westminster Abbey.

During his last years he was unpopular in England and was surly and morose and not easy of access. In several parts of his realm there was rejoicing at his passing. 'No king,' commented a contemporary, 'can be less lamented than this one has been'. The sentiments were different among Irish Protestants whose grief was almost palpable. In Protestant Dublin, William's death was compared to the setting of the sun or to some terrible eclipse passing over the earth. The Anglican archbishop, William King, referred to the extinction of a star, and told his congregation that 'the poetic mind will feel no impropriety in such comparisons, but will see rather a high truth, as standing by the grave of this child of genius it meditates on the loss which we, and the entire world, have sustained'.[15]

James did not outlive William. After the Irish war he was broken in spirit if not in health – he managed to father a daughter, Louise Marie, born in June 1692. He still dreamed of returning to his lost kingdoms but as time wore on the faith for which he had sacrificed everything was all that he had left. He drifted deeper and deeper into religious melancholy and his spiritual devotions became obsessional. He attended mass twice daily and made frequent visits to the monastery of La Trappe; he even scourged himself and took to wearing iron spikes around his thighs.[16]

In March 1701 he had a stroke which left him partly paralysed. On 1 September his condition deteriorated and his son, James Francis Edward, was called to his bedside and requested to make a solemn promise that he would never, even for the throne of England, abandon the Catholic faith. The promise was given. On the afternoon of 5 September James died and was regarded by his supporters as a saint and a martyr.

His body was embalmed and cut up, with various parts distributed around France as holy relics.

THE SCOTTISH REBELLIONS

During the long period of the penal laws which followed the Treaty of Limerick there was no hope for the Jacobite cause in Ireland. Matters, however, were different in Scotland. In the summer of 1715, the Earl of Mar, an embittered former supporter of William raised the highland clans to put 'James III' (as the Pretender was called) on the throne. His army advanced to Perth and wasted much time before challenging the Duke of Argyll's numerically inferior force; the result was the drawn Battle of Sheriffmuir (13 November). At this times hopes of a southern Jacobite rising at Preston melted away. The Old Pretender arrived in Scotland too late to do anything but lead the flight of his supporters to France.

All was not yet over. A final Jacobite rebellion, 'The Forty-Five' took place in 1745 and, although much romanticised, it was the most formidable of the Scottish efforts to restore the Stuarts. The outlook seemed hopeless during the previous year when French invasion plans miscarried and further help could not be expected. The number of highland clans prepared to turn out was smaller than in 1715 and the lowlands were apathetic or hostile. But the personal magnetism of Prince Charles Edward Stuart (the Young Pretender) and the absence of government troops – who were fighting on the continent – produced a daring rising.

When the young prince landed at Barrodale near Arisaig on 25 July, he was initially given a cool reception. Soon, however, his charm won over the MacDonalds of Clanranald, the Camerons of Lochiel and MacDonnells of Glengarry. Between them they had a 1,000 men and at Glenfinnan on 19 August the standard of 'James VIII of Scotland' and 'James III of England' was raised. After a number of small, victorious skirmishes a Jacobite army entered Edinburgh unopposed (aided by the provost, who secretly left the gate open) and Charles Edward declared himself regent of the Three Kingdoms and took up residence at Holyrood House.

On 9 November the army crossed the border to England and on 4 December reached Derby. By this time government troops had been recalled from the continent and were formed into two armies, under the Duke of Cumberland and Marshal Wade. As these forces converged on Derby, Charles Edward reluctantly agreed to a tactical withdrawal to Scotland.

On 17 January, they attacked General Hawley's relieving column at Falkirk and won their second (and final) victory. Charles Edward had hoped that the French would provide reinforcements, but these did not materialise. The Jacobites were forced to make a last stand at Culloden Moor on 17 April. Cumberland, who was King George II's youngest son, had marshalled ten of the government's best regiments and was supported by a contingent of Dutch troops. The Jacobite army – grown to 5,000 – were no match for the regulars who were twice their number and better trained and equipped. About 1,000 Jacobites were killed in battle with many more slaughtered by pursuing dragoons.

Charles Edward escaped, with the assistance of Flora MacDonald, to become 'The Prince in the Heather' of Highland romance. After many adventures in the highlands and islands he got away to France in September 1716.[17]

The Last of the Jacobites

Following 'The Forty-Five' Jacobitism declined as a serious political force in Scotland, but remained as a sentiment. The tale of 'The King over the Water' gained a sentimental appeal, and a whole body of Jacobite ballads were created. The Young Pretender, known to history as 'Bonnie Prince Charlie' spent his remaining days wandering around Europe trying to revive his cause, but became a sad figure whose drunken, debauched behaviour alienated even his friends. On the credit side, he was a humane, generous and warm man who had considerable diplomatic skills, but to whom fate had dealt an unfortunate hand. Few historical figures have been fated to shine so brightly for so brief a period only to be eclipsed thereafter. He died in 1788 a forlorn and broken man.

No greater contrast can be imagined between 'Bonnie Prince Charlie' and his pious brother, Henry, who was to be the last of the Stuarts. Henry was born in Rome in 1725 and was named Duke of York by his father, the Old Pretender, at birth. He was an exceedingly mild person whose religiosity irritated many around him. He was a created a cardinal by Pope Benedict XIV at the age of 21, without first having been ordained a priest. To the Jacobites he became, on the death of his brother, 'King Henry IX' for the last nineteen years of his life.[18]

Henry's Church career was successful. He became bishop of Frascati in Italy and had a substantial income from ecclesiastical preferments. He held sinecures from numerous abbeys and religious institutions in Flanders, Spain and France and had income from Latin America. He used much of his wealth to support needy Jacobites, but took little interest in political affairs. As a prince of the Catholic Church he was forever alienated from Protestants in Ireland and Britain and as a celibate there could be no legitimate issue after his death to maintain the succession.

During the Napoleonic invasion of Italy, Henry lost practically all his property and wealth and after 1800 survived on a pension granted to him by King George III of England.[19] When he died in 1807, the last flicker of Jacobitism went to the grave.[20]

The fate of practically all who left Ireland with Sarsfield is obscure and can be broached only in general terms. Their departure left the country denuded of those best fitted to fight for Catholic rights. Many legends grew up about them, the most poignant being, perhaps, that their souls, after falling in battle, returned to Ireland in the form of migrating geese. Thus, the tag the 'Wild Geese' was given to them and to later military refugees who were forced to make their livings in foreign armies.

Few of these 'Wild Geese' returned to Ireland and their descendants showed a remarkable loyalty to the Stuart cause. After the defeat of the French fleet at La Hogue in 1693 the 8,000 Irish troops who had assembled as part of the would-be expeditionary force were scattered throughout the French army and served in Flanders, Germany, Spain, Italy and elsewhere. On occasion, as in Spain, they had to fight against a dynasty which had always been sympathetic to the Irish cause. Sometimes they found themselves pitted against descendants of soldiers who had fled Ireland after the O'Neill rebellion in 1601 and who had entered the service of the Spanish monarchy.

During the war of the Spanish succession the Irish abroad opposed Marlborough in each of his major battles. At Blenheim in 1704, amid the confusion of a French retreat, they alone retired in perfect order. The famous Marshal Vendôme of France paid tribute to their repeated acts of courage and gallantry. A passionate desire for revenge against the *Sassanach* was doubtless the stimulus which kept fresh the remarkable *élan* of these men.

The Battle of Fontenoy, a major encounter in the war of the Austrian succession, fought on 11 May 1745, was the Irish brigade's crowning glory. The French army contained six regiments of the brigade, those of Dillon, Clare, Bulkeley, Roth, Berwick and Lally – plus a separate cavalry regiment under FitzJames.

The French had opened the campaigning season by besieging Tournai. An allied force of 50,000 under the Duke of Cumberland approached from the east. The French commander, Maurice de Saxe split his 70,000 men, leaving a detachment to carry on the siege while the remainder blocked Cumberland's line of advance between Barry Wood and the river Escaut. On 11 May, after the failure of an attack on the wood, Cumberland ordered a general move forward. His infantry, advancing between Fontenoy village and the wood, came close to breaking the French line, but was checked at the critical moment when the Irish Brigade intervened. They halted the advance by smashing through Cumberland's right wing in heroic fashion. Cumberland lost 7,000 men and fell back. The Irish had saved the day for the French and Tournai surrendered.

Before the Irish intervention at Fontenoy a curious incident occurred when an English guard's officer came face-to-face with a lone Irish soldier – Anthony MacDonough from Co. Clare – in single combat. The Irishman smashed his adversary's sword arm and forced him to the ground. Just then, from behind, came a thousand shouts of 'Remember Limerick' – as the Irish came dashing into battle. According to a French account, they charged the Coldstream guards with fixed bayonets, and a murderous combat ensued until the English broke and fled.

The victory acquired a significance greater than its importance as a feat of arms. For a defeated nation, beaten down by the discriminatory laws which followed the Treaty of Limerick, it showed that a small, poor and badly-treated underdog, when given half a chance, could bite back.[21]

More than forty years later, on the eve of the French revolution, veterans of the brigade could be seen in the Luxembourg Gardens in Paris, reliving – like Uncle Toby in *Tristam Shandy* – their recollections of Fontenoy and other campaigns.[22] Fifty years afterwards, a stirring ballad quickened the pulse of Young Ireland as Thomas Davis commemorated the most important victory won by Irish arms on continental soil:

> On Fontenoy, on Fontenoy, hark to that fierce huzzah
> Revenge! Remember Limerick! Dash down the Sassanach!
> And Fontenoy, famed Fontenoy, had been a Waterloo
> Were not those exiles ready then, fresh, vehement and true.[23]

It was, however, the lines of Emily Lawless (1845–1913) which would endure to modern times. Her poem 'Fontenoy, 1745' poignantly describes the thoughts of a homesick dragoon on the eve of the battle. The poem was once taught to Irish schoolchildren and this may still be so:

> Oh bad the march, the weary march, beneath these alien skies,
> But good the night, the friendly night, that soothes our tired eyes.
> And bad the war, the tedious war, that keeps us sweltering here,
> But good the hour, the friendly hour, that brings the battle near.
>
> That brings us on the battle, that summons to their share
> The homeless troops, the banished men, the exiled sons of Clare.
> Oh little Corca Bascinn,* the wild, the bleak, the fair!
> Oh little stony pastures, whose flowers are sweet, if rare!
>
> Oh rough and rude Atlantic, the thunderous, the wide,
> Whose kiss is like a soldier's kill which will not be denied!
> The whole night long we dream of you, and waking think we're there,
> Vain dream, and foolish waking, we never shall see Clare.
>
> The wind is wild tonight, there's battle in the air;
> The wind is from the west, and it seems to blow from Clare.
> Have you nothing, nothing for us, loud brawler of the night?
> No news to warm our heart-strings, to speed us through the fight?

In this hollow, star-pricked darkness, as in the sun's hot glare,
In sun-tide, moon-tide, star-tide, we thirst, we starve for Clare!
Hark! Yonder through the darkness one distant rat-tat-tat!
The old foe stirs out there, God bless his soul for that!

The old foe musters strongly, he's coming on at last,
And Clare's brigade may claim its own wherever blows fall fast.
Send us, ye western breezes, our full, our rightful share,
For Faith, and Fame, and Honour, and the ruined hearts of Clare.

*'Cora Bascinn' (or Baiscinn) is an appellation once given to a district in north-west
Clare. It has frequently been used by romantic poets to denote Ireland itself. The word
'Cora' translates from Irish as 'district' and 'Baiscinn' is an old Gaelic tribal name for
the district's inhabitants.

GLOSSARY

Artillery: Military firearms too heavy to be carried, including cannon and wheeled guns.

Barrage: a long term military bombardment.

Battery: a) The position at which a gun or guns are placed. b) An artillery battalion.

Battalion: Basic personnel unit in a military system, usually consisting of four or five companies and commanded by a lieutenant colonel.

Bayonet: Short sword attached to the muzzle of a firearm.

Brigade: A formation consisting of a minimum of two companies and commanded by a brigadier.

Chevaux-de-frise: A defensive obstacle created by fixing swords or pikes in close formation, usually to curtail cavalry charges.

Cavalry: A mounted unit deployed for its speed and manoeuvrability.

Company: A sub-unit of a battalion, consisting of about 120 soldiers and usually commanded by a major. Four or five companies make a battalion.

Corps: A formation consisting of two to five divisions commanded by a lieutenant-general.

Division: A formation consisting of two or more brigades.

Evacuation: The removal of civil or military personnel from an area liable to attack.

Fascines: Bundles of branches or brush used to provide a pathway over boggy ground.

Fortification: Military defensive structure, such as a stone castle.

General: A senior military rank, the grades ascending being major-general and lieutenant-general.

Grenade: A small missile containing explosives.

Glacis: The sloping ground in front of a fortified position.

Infantry: Foot-soldiers, the majority troops in any army.

Investment: the containment of a garrison by military force.

Match: Cord used to ignite a fuse for a cannon or mortar.

Marshal: The highest military office, designated in France as a marshal of France. Corresponds with admiral of the fleet in the navy.

Mercenary: Soldiers hired by the army of one king against another.

Mine: Explosive charge at land or sea.

Mortar: Method of projecting a bomb via a high trajectory at a target [usually, a light weight cannon].

Musket: Hand-held firearm, loaded from the end of its barrel.

Platoon: The smallest infantry unit commanded by a lieutenant, containing about thirty to forty soldiers.

Reconnaissance: The gathering of information, usually by small patrols.

Redoubt: A small enclosed defensive trench, often employed in conjunction with other trenches.

Regiment: Military formation equivalent, in part of the British army, to a battalion.

Ravelin: An outwork fortification in a triangular shape, also known as a 'half moon'.

Siege: A prolonged assault on a fortified position, often involving a blockade.

Staff: a group of highly trained military officers, usually specialists in different types of warfare.

CHRONOLOGY

1172   Thomas de Sarsfield arrives in Ireland.

1566   Sir William Sarsfield Mayor of Dublin.

1625   Dominick Sarsfield created Lord Kilmallock.

1641   Uprising in Ulster (Oct) which spreads southwards.
        Old English leaders meet Gaelic leaders on Crofty Hill near Drogheda (Dec).

1642   Patrick Sarsfield Snr expelled from Dublin parliament.

1655   Estimated date of birth of Patrick Sarsfield.

1657   Patrick Sarsfield Snr ordered to quit Tully Castle and given modest estate in
        Connaught.

1660   Charles II restored.

1663   Court of Claims returns Lucan Estate to Sarsfield family (possession to take
        place on the death of Theophelis Jones).

1671   Marriage of William Sarsfield to Lucy Walter.

1672   Patrick Sarsfield serves with Monmouth in Flanders.
        Sarsfield in London as member of life guards.

1678   Popish Plot.

1679   Shaftesbury introduces Exclusion Bill to exclude Duke of York from the suc-
        cession.

1681   Charles II's last parliament at Oxford.

1685   Accession of James II. Monmouth rebellion.

1686   James forms army camp on Hounslow Heath.
        Edward Hales tried under Test Act.
        James tries to restore Roman Catholicism.

1688   Second declaration of indulgence and trial of the seven bishops.
        William invades England (Nov).
        James flees to France (Dec).

1689   Ulster Protestants declare for William.
        Siege of Derry begins.
        Justin MacCarthy reduces Bandon (Mar).
        James lands at Kinsale (Mar).
        Richard Hamilton defeats Protestant force at 'Brake of Dromore' (Mar).
        James at Derry (Apr).
        English and French in naval battle off Bantry Bay (May).
        'Patriot Parliament' meets in Dublin (May).
        'Little Cromwell' defeats Sarsfield at Beleek (May).
        Williamite ships break boom on river Foyle (July).
        Battle of Newtownbutler (July).
        Schomberg arrives at Groomsport (Aug).
        Schomberg's army beset by outbreak of dysentery (Sept).
        James moves his army into winter quarters (Nov).

1690   French fleet arrives at Cork (March) bringing Comte de Lauzun.
        Justin MacCarthy leads Irish brigade to France (Apr).
        Tadg O'Regan surrenders Charlemont to Schomberg (May).
        William arrives at Carrickfergus (June).

James' army crosses Boyne at Oldbridge (29 June).
William's army reaches Boyne and camps at Tullyallen (30 June).
Battle of the Boyne (1 July).
James flees to France (2 July).
William establishes camp at Finglas (9 July).
Williamites fail to take Athlone (17–25 July).
William invests Limerick (9 August).
Sarsfield destroys siege train at Ballyneety (12 Aug).
William's attack on Limerick fails; siege lifted (29 Aug).
William returns to England (5 Sept).
Duke of Marlborough arrives in Cork (21 Sept).
Marlborough takes Kinsale (3 Oct).
Sarsfield and Berwick foil Williamite attempts to cross the Shannon at Lanes-
  borough, Jamestown and Banagher (Nov-Dec).

1691 Tyrconnell returns from France. Sarsfield becomes Earl of Lucan (Jan).
Berwick leaves Ireland (24 Feb).
St Ruth arrives in Limerick (8 May).
Ginkel takes Ballymore (8 June).
Jacobites destroy Bridge of Athlone (18 June).
Athlone falls (30 June).
Ginkel issues peace proclamation (9 July).
Battle of Aughrim (12 July).
Tyrconnell dies at Limerick (14 Aug).
Ginkel besieges Limerick (25 Aug).
Sir Tadg O'Regan surrenders Sligo (14 Sept).
Ginkel crosses the Shannon at Limerick (22 Sept).
Truce agreed at Limerick (24 Sept).
Treaty of Limerick signed (3 Oct).
French fleet arrives in Shannon estuary (30 Oct).
Sarsfield leaves Ireland (22 Dec).

1692 Battle of La Hogue.
Battle of Steenkirk (22 July – 3 Aug)
Sarsfield become marshal of France (Apr)
Sarsfield falls at Battle of Landen (29 July)

1697 Peace of Ryswick ends war.

1701 Death of James (16 Sept).

1702 Death of William (19 Mar).

1715 Rebellion of 'The '15' in Scotland.

1734 Death of Berwick.

1745 Rebellion of 'The '45' in Scotland.
Battle of Fontenoy.

1766 Death of James Edward Stuart, 'The Old Pretender'.

1788 Death of Charles Edward Stuart, 'The Young Pretender'.

1807 Death of Henry, Cardinal of York, 'Henry IX'.

SARSFIELD IN POETRY

From 'The Blacksmith of Limerick'
Now Swarthy Ned and Moran, make up that iron well
'Tis Sarsfield's horse that wants the shoes, to mind not shot and shell!
Ah, sure cried both 'the horse can wait ... Sarsfield's on the wall'.

ANON

From 'The Song of Defeat'
 I call to your mind brave Sarsfield
 And the battle in Limerick street
· *The mine that shattered the wall*
 And battered the breach held good
 And William full in retreat ...

ANON

From 'Patrick Sarsfield'
 Twas the calm hush of night; all silently we sped
 From the city's battered walls, Patrick Sarsfield at our head
 Nor wondered why 'twas so, for we knew his heart was true ...

WILLIAM ROONEY

From 'Sarsfield's Gone Away'
 Oh! Black your heat, Clan Oliver, and colder than the clay!
 Oh high your head, Clan Sassanach, since Sarsfield's gone away!

CHARLES GAVIN DUFFY

From 'Farewell to Sarsfield'
 Good luck, Patrick Sarsfield wherever you may roam
 You crossed the seas to France and left empty camps at home
 Though you left ourselves and poor Ireland overthrown.
 Och! Ochone!

ANON., EIGHTEENTH CENTURY

From 'The Bridge of Athlone'
 St Ruth in his stirrups stood up and cried
 'I have seen no deed like this in France!'
 With a toss of his head Sarsfield replied
 'They had luck the dogs, 'twas a merry chance'.

AUBREY DE VERE

From 'The Battle of Aughrim'
 Sarsfield: I am Lord Lucan, Sarsfield is my name
 And when my sword can reach out I'll guard my fame
 Life I despise now, reck'ning death my friend
 The man's not living who could make me bend
 My neck to bondage.

ROBERT ASHTON

From 'Sarsfield's Defence of Limerick'
 There is a deathless tree on the ancient lines
 Where the old Black Battery stood

216

With leaves still bright as the fame of the fight
That dyed them once in blood.
The heroes are death, but the tree still lives
And still the night wind grieves
Immortal memories wake again
That slept beneath its leaves
And warrior ghosts from the battered walls
Cry forth in Fancy's ear –
Forever curse'd by these foreign dogs,
What demon brought them here?
But we drove them out in olden time
And we'll drive them out again;
Listen to how our fathers fought
When Sarsfield led our men.

THOMAS STANLEY TRACEY

From 'Caithreim Phádraig Sairseal'
He left not a bomb or a copper pontoon
In Baile na Fhaoitigh that he did not disperse
Like the smoke of a candle up into the sky.

DÁIBHÍ Ó BRUADAIR

217

THE SARSFIELD FAMILY TREE

The following is an extract from *Aaron Crossley's Peerage of Ireland* (Dublin 1725):

> *That Thomas Sarsfield was standard-bearer to King Henry II of England in the year of Our Lord 1180. He was the father of Richard Sarsfield, who was captain general under Henry III of England, anno 1230.*
>
> *This Richard had two sons, viz Sarsfield and Henry, and Sarsfield had a son named Sarsfield and Henry had a son named Henry who came to Ireland and lived in Cork for some time, and married the daughter of Fitzgerald, by whom he had the lands from Bealogh Favrye to Kilmallock, six miles in length in the county of Limerick, which fruitful and pleasant estate he and his posterity enjoyed, together with the said Kilmallock for many generations.*
>
> *The genealogy aforesaid from Thomas, the first of all this family of the Sarsfields, to John, who lived in the reign of Henry VI, I had it out of old Irish books now in the custody of Hugh MacCurtain, alias Curtis, one of the chief antiquarians of this kingdom of Ireland, and from several other relations of the family's, to the year 1640; and for the rest I had out of the books of my own office (there being little or nothing in it) and out of several warrantable authors; and also from ancient gentlemen of worth and credit – in witness thereof, nostri saluit feri 1714'.*
>
> *The Most Noble Potent and Honourable Sir Dominick Sarsfield, Viscount Kilmallock, Lord Baron of Barret's Country and primear baronet of Ireland.*

CREATION

'Primear Baronet of Ireland' by Patent, 30 September 1619, 16 Jac 1.

'Lord Baron of Barret's country, Lord Viscount Kilmallock' by Patent dated 8 May 1625.

'Lord Chief Justice of Common Pleas'.

'Attorney General of Munster', 4 September, 42 Eliz. And one of the lords of his majesty's most hon. privy council of Ireland.

FAMILY OF KILMALLOCK

> *Sir Dominick was second son of Edmund, and brother to John; he was created lord baron of Ireland and Viscount Kinsale, by Letters Patent granted at New Market, 13 February, by King John I of England, in the twenty-second year of his reign by reason that the Lord Baron Courcey challenged the said title of Kinsale, but the title of Lord Viscount Kilmallock was continued still by Patent to Sir Dominick, from the time he was created Lord Viscount Kinsale.*
>
> *The original Patent was in my custody in King James II's time.*
>
> *This Henry had a son named John, the father of David, who was the father of Henry, whose son John, was admiral of the fleet of King Henry VI's of England; he married a daughter of – Purcill's, she bore him two sons, Edmund and Roger.*
>
> *This Edmund had two sons, viz. John and Sir Dominick.*
>
> *John had two sons, Patrick and James, Patrick married Hellin daughter to – White, and by her had John, Francis, Geoffrey, Ignatious and Hellin; she was married to Jeffrey Galway.*
>
> *John the eldest, married Catherine, daughter to – Purdon, by her he had Francis, now living; James second son of John and brother of aforesaid, married Hellin Rice, and by her he had Paul, who went to Nantz in France, in Oliver Cromwell's time and married there a French gentlewoman and by her had Sir James Sarsfield, now living in France.*

THE FAMILY OF LUCAN

> *Roger, second son of John, who was thirteen years admiral to King Henry VI as abovesaid was married to a daughter of Christopher Cusack of Kilmallock in the county of Meath and*

had by her John of Sarsfieldstown, in the said county, and by her he had two sons, Patrick and William; Patrick was Mayor of Dublin, anno 1554; he died sans issue.

Sir William, chosen Mayor of Dublin anno 1556 and in the same year Sir Henry Sidney, being lord lieutenant of Ireland and Knight of the Most Holy Garter, in the ninth year of Queen Elizabeth; he being in England and his lady in Drogheda.

John O'Neil came to surprise Drogheda with a strong party, whereupon the Lady Sidney sent to Dublin, and the said Sir William with all speed marched with a select party of horse and foot towards Drogheda, fought and routed John O'Neil and all his adherents and by that means rescued the Lady Sidney from the danger she was likely to undergo; for which service the Lord Sidney, on his return to Ireland, knighted him in Christ Church, Dublin.

This Sir William married Margaret, daughter of Sir Lucas Dillon, and had by her William, Lucas, Robert and Johanna; this William married Anne, daughter of Sir Patrick Barnwell, Knight. Patrick, second son of Sir William married Mabel Fitzgerald, and by her had Peter and many other children.

This Peter married Elinor, daughter of Terlogh O'Dempsey, Lord Viscount Clanmalier and had by her Patrick; he married Anne, daughter of Roger Moor, and by her he had Patrick, created Earl of Lucan by King James II anno 1688. This Patrick was general to King James' army, and married Honora, daughter of the Earl of Clanricard, who bore him one son named Jacobus Franciscus Edwardus.

ARMS

Parted per Pale Ruby and Pearl, a Fleur de Lis of the second and Diamond.

CREST

On a wreath of colours, a Leopard's Face Tropaz. Supporters: supported by two Wolves Sapphire, collared and chained Topaz.

MOTTO

Virtus non veritur (Courage not fear)

Notes

A Tangled Inheritance

1. 'The Irish Army in Scotland 1296' in *The Irish Sword*, Vol. XV, 1961–62.
2. The relationship may have been homosexual, as many of James I's 'relationships' with favourites were. Whether Dominick Sarsfield was of a similar disposition to James, history does not relate.
3. *Life of Sarsfield* by John Todhunter, London 1895, p. 3.
4. For a history of the Sarsfield family see: British Library Add. MSS 39, pp. 267 *ff* 90–202 and British Library Add. MSS 39, p. 270 *opp*. Also see: *Co. Kildare Archaeological Society Journal* IV, July 1903.
5. See entry on Rory O'More in *Oxford Companion to Irish History* edited by S. J. Connolly, Oxford 1998, p. 410. For lineage of O'More see *History of the Ancient Order of Hibernians* by John O'Dea, Indiana 1923, pp. 83–87.
6. *The Luke Wadding Commemorative Volume*, Dublin 1957.
7. O'Dea, p. 313.
8. For an excellent brief account of the Cromwellian Settlement see Part IV, p. 99 of *A History of Ireland* by Robert Dunlop, Oxford 1922.
9. Information on the Lucan land dispute is found in a number of sources: British Library Add MSS 39, 267 *ff*, pp. 90–202. Stowe MSS *f* 451, p. 25; Historical Manuscripts Commission '*Ormonde*'; Historical Manuscripts Commission *Eighth Report*, p. 623.

The Young Cavalier

1. O'Dea, p. 313.
2. There has been a number of books on the life of Lucy Walter. One of the most informative is '*Lucy Walter: Wife or Mistress?*' by Lord George Scott, London 1947.
3. There is scarcely any doubt that the first Earl of Arlington was Mary's father. He was secretary of state under Charles II from 1662–1674 and a member of the famous *Cabal* ministry. He was a corrupt politician who on the one hand supported the king's French policy, but at the same time took bribes from the Dutch. He was well known for the black patch which he wore on his nose to cover a wound incurred during the civil war This may be seen in the famous portrait by Sir Peter Lely, painted in 1665. His career is traced in *Henry Bennet, Earl of Arlington* by V. Barbour, London 1914.
4. British Library, Add MSS 39, pp. 267 *f* 201.
5. The regimental proprietary system came into being when permanent army units began to replace free companies. Most often, the permanent colonel was the proprietor of his regiment and authorised to raise men. Initially, troops were raised for a single campaign and thereafter discharged. As armies became permanent, the standing units were retained and kept up to strength by a constant influx. The system could be profitable for the proprietor as he was paid for the number of men mustered, plus their weapons, equipment and subsistence. Also he could sell his proprietary interest when he retired.
6. The Duc de Luxembourg, François-Henri de Montmorency-Bouteville, 1628–1695, was one of Louis XIV's great commanders in the Dutch war 1672–1678 and in the war of the grand alliance 1689–1697. Although hunchbacked and of slight build he could hold his own among his more robust fellows. Always an enemy of the House of Orange, in the years following 1690 he consistently outmanoeuvred the forces of William III. He achieved notable victories over William at Steenkerke, August 1692 and Neerwinden, July 1693.
7. This was the Dutch war of 1673–78 which arose from the war of devolution 1667–68

– see note 14 to chapter Five.

8. Some sources say that Sarsfield was first recruited to fight the Dutch in 1671 in a regiment raised in Ireland by George Hamilton, a nephew of the first Duke of Ormonde. This regiment served on the Rhine under Turenne and contained numerous figures who became prominent Irish Jacobites. The view that Sarsfield served under Justin MacCarthy in the 'Royal Anglais' is given in *Justin MacCarthy: Lord Mountcashel* by John A. Murphy, Cork 1959, second edition 1999, p. 6. This latter view is supported by the Calendar of State Papers, Domestic, London 1909, pp. 410–12, Cal. S. P 1678 with Add. 1674–79, London 1913, pp. 332–8, 418. Cal. S. P Dom 1680–1, London 1921, p. 179. Also, John Cornelius O'Callaghan in *History of the Irish Brigades in the Service of France*, London 1870 says: 'Sarsfield first served in France as ensign in the regiment of Monmouth', p. 63.

9. *English Army Lists and Commission Registers 1661–1714*, compiled by Charles Dalton. 6 volumes, London 1892.

10. *Stuart England* by J. P. Kenyon, London 1978, p. 212.

11. Murphy, John A., p. 7.

12. *Patrick Sarsfield and the Williamite War* by Piers Wauchope, Dublin 1992, p. 16.

13. *The Irish Catholic Experience* by Patrick Corish, Dublin 1985, p. 121.

14. Narcissus Luttrell, 1657–1732, with Pepys and Evelyn form the trio of diarists on whom we rely for much of the matter-of-fact information on the period. Luttrell was well placed to observe and note what was going on. He was a lawyer who held a number of significant public appointments and served in parliament on two occasions, for Bossiney 1679–80; for Saltash 1690–95. He was a Whig at heart and posthumously had two books published: *Popish Plot Catalogues*, 1956 and *A Brief Historical Relation of the State of Affairs from September 1678 to April 1714'*, 6 volumes, 1875. The latter compilation and what he called *An Abstract ...* (edited by Henry Horwitz in 1972 as *The Parliamentary Diary of Narcissus Luttrell 1691–1693*) are now seen as indispensable source books for the parliamentary and political history of the period. He kept a diary of *private transactions* between November 1722 and January 1725.

15. *Patrick Sarsfield* by Alice Curtayne, Dublin 1934, p. 23.

16. *A History of Ireland in the Eighteenth Century* by W. E. H. Lecky, Vol. I, London 1919, p. 371

17. Information on the Siderfin abduction may be found in Historical Manuscript Commission App. Seventh Report; The Calendar of State Papers – Treasury Books VII; the *London Mercury* June 1682; *Diary of Narcissus Luttrell, 1691–93*.

18. Information on the Lady Herbert abduction is found in the Calendar of State Papers 1683.

THE MERRY MONARCH AND THE POPISH KING

1. For a balanced view on Lord Shaftesbury's character see *The First Earl of Shaftesbury* by K. H. D. Haley, London 1968.

2. *The First Whigs* by J. R. Jones, London 1961 gives a thorough account of the 'Exclusion Crisis'.

3. Details of the Rye House Plot remain cloudy, but it is not disputed that those involved included Monmouth; Arthur Capel, Earl of Essex; Lord William Russell; Thomas Armstrong; Robert Ferguson; Algernon Sidney and Lord William Howard. They all allegedly met at the house of a London wine merchant and discussed various ways of ridding the country of Charles II, or denying the succession to James. The Rye House assassination was but one of the schemes discussed. Essex died in the Tower of London, probably by suicide. Russell, Sidney and Armstrong were executed; the others escaped punishment.

4. The most vivid account of the death of Charles II is in Macauley's *History of England from the Accession of James II*, Folio Society Edition, London 1985. That author could

not resist the temptation of adding an extra touch to the scene: the king indeed apologised for being slow in dying, but it was Macauley who inserted the word 'unconscionable'. It is given here as it has become accepted lore.

5. James fathered twenty-seven children, two less than Henry I who holds the record. Twenty were legitimate: eight by his first marriage, twelve by his second, although five of the latter were stillborn. His favourite mistress was Arabella Churchill, mother of the Duke of Berwick, who bore him four children. Charles II fathered no live legitimate children, although his queen had three stillborn children and one miscarriage. Charles had at least eight officially recognised mistresses, of whom the best known is Nell Gwynne, who bore him two children. He fathered sixteen illegitimate children; the paternity of two of his putative children remains uncertain. William III fathered three children with Mary II, all were stillborn. There has been an unproven assertion that William was homosexual, although it is well known that for a period Barbara Villiers was his mistress.

6. An excellent account of the conversion of James II is given in Meriol Trevor's *The Shadow of a Crown: The Life Story of James II of England and VII of Scotland*, London 1988.

7. Mary Beatrice was born on 5 October 1658, her father being Alfonso IV, Duke of Modena. She was married to James by proxy in September 1673 and did not arrive in England until two months later. Although the Whigs spun the tale that she was a Vatican agent, this was untrue. Her influence on James' political thinking was always negligible. Pope Alexander VII was a particular hate figure to Protestants. During the Peace of Westphelia, 1648 negotiations he urged Catholic princes not to deal with the Protestant heretics.

8. *James II: A Study in Kingship* by John Miller, London 1978, p. 120.

9. A modern view on James II's religious policy is found in *The Stuart Age* by Barry Coward, Harlow 1980. Coward argues convincingly, p. 294, that James was not the villain described by Macauley and other Whig historians.

THE MONMOUTH REBELLION

1. A good account of the duke's exile is found in *James, Duke of Monmouth* by Bryan Bevin, London 1973.

2. An account of Monmouth's relationship with Baroness Wentworth is found in Bishop Gilbert Burnet's *History of My Own Time*, published posthumously in London 1723.

3. Full details of the main Whig rebels are found in Macauley, chapter 5, Vol. I

4. The best account of the people who joined the Monmouth rebellion is found in *Monmouth's Rebels* by P. Earle. London, 1977.

5. Wauchope, p. 30.

6. An excellent account of the Battle of Sedgemoor by a modern military historian is found in *Battles in Britain 1066–1746* by William Seymour, London 1997.

7. A full account of the 'Bloody Assizes' and the fate of the prisoners is given in *Lord Chancellor Jeffreys* by G. W. Keeton, London 1965.

THE TOTTERING CROWN

1. Todhunter, pp. 12–13.

2. *Reluctant Revolutionaries* by W. A. Speck, New York 1988, pp. 62–63.

3. *The History of England* by G. M. Trevelyan, London 1936, p. 557.

4. Wauchope, p. 33.

5. See 'Revocation of Edict of Nantes' by John Laurence Carr in *The Pen and the Sword*, edited by Christopher Hibbert, New York 1974, p. 133. Also see *Europe in the Seventeenth Century* by David Ogg, London 1925, pp. 301–304.

6. *Louis XIV* by Vincent Cronin, London 1964, pp. 256–275.

7. Macauley's account of the trial of the seven bishops and its outcome has not been surpassed, chapter eight.

8. The full text of the document written on 30 June 1688 is shown as an appendix to *The Glorious Revolution of 1688* by Maurice Ashley, London 1966, pp. 201–202.
9. *The Life and Times of James II* by Peter Earle, London 1972, p. 168.
10. An incisive interpretation of William's motives in invading England is found in *James II and English Politics 1678–1688* by Michael Mullett, London 1994.
11. Schomberg has been curiously neglected by historians. As far asI am aware there is no standard biography of him. An account of his military career appeared in the magazine *History Today* in July 1988.
12. *William of Orange: A Dedicated Life, 1650–1702* by Cecil Kilpatrick, Belfast 1998, p. 51.
13. A compelling account of William's career is found in *William and Mary* by Henri and Barbara van Der Zee, London 1973.
14. The French invasion of the Netherlands in 1672 arose from Louis' claim that the Spanish Netherlands was part of his wife's inheritance. He invoked 'The Law of Devolution', a local custom in some provinces of the Netherlands, whereby if a man married twice the succession went to children of the first wife to the exclusion of those of the second. Louis' queen was the daughter of King Philip of Spain by his first marriage.
15. The background to William's interest in England is eruditely traced in *From Counter-Revolution to Glorious Revolution* by Hugh Trevor-Roper, London 1992, pp. 231–349.
16. The Gunpowder Plot occurred in 1605, in the reign of James I, when a band of hot-headed Catholics smuggled barrels of gunpowder into the cellars of parliament intent on blowing it up. Led by Guy Fawkes, they were captured, tried and executed. The plot etched itself upon the collective English memory and 'Burning the Guy' is still a feature of annual bonfire night, 5 November. celebrations.
17. *Battlefields of Ireland* by Robert Coddington, New York 1867, p. 38.
18. A good account of Sarsfield at Wincanton is found in Macauley, pp. 390–391, Vol. II.
19. *1688: Revolution in the Family* by Henri and Barbara van Der Zee, London 1988, pp. 214–215.
20. See *A Detection of the Court and State of England* by Roger Coke, London 1719. Also Wauchope, p. 43.

'BONNIE' DUNDEE – THE SCOTTISH SARSFIELD

1. Viscount Dundee began his military career as a soldier of fortune in France and the Netherlands, and actually served under William in 1676. On returning to Scotland in 1678 he was made captain of dragoons. Although beaten by the Presbyterian insurgents at Drumclog Moss on 1 June 1679 he helped Monmouth to finally suppress them at Bothwell Bridge on 23 June. Never called 'Bonnie' in his own day, the appellation meaning 'handsome', 'beautiful' and 'charming' was given to him by Sir Walter Scott in the mid-nineteenth century. See C. S. Terry's *John Graham of Claverhouse, Viscount Dundee*, London 1905.
2. Macauley, p. 205, Vol. III.
3. *The Lion in the North* by John Prebble, London 1971, p. 271.
4. *The Jacobites* by Frank McLynn, London 1985, p. 12.
5. *The Jacobite Movement* by Sir Charles Petrie, London 1958, p. 91.
6. *A Short History of the English People* by J. R. Green, p. 1496,Vol. IV, London 1894.
7. *Scotland's Story: A New Perspective* by Tom Steel, p. 124, London 1984.
8. From *The Jacobite Relics of Scotland* by James Hogg, 1770–1835. Known as the 'Ettrick Shepherd', Hogg is the best loved of Jacobite poets. He enjoyed a vogue during the ballad revival which accompanied the nineteenth-century Romantic Movement. In more recent times his narrative poems have become popular in Scottish nationalist circles.

THE NEW LORD DEPUTY

1. Sir William Petty, the Cromwellian land surveyor, calculated that there were 800,000

Catholics, 200,000 Dissenters and 100,000 Church of Ireland Episcopalians in Ireland around the beginning of James' reign. Later evidence suggests that these figures are inaccurate but it is not improbable that Catholics constituted up to three-quarters of the population.

2. It was a time of hope and rejoicing for Catholics. Their poets exulted that once again their people could take up arms: *Sin iad Gaeil leir in armaibh/Gunnaí is púdar, puirt is baile acu*: Behold the Gaels in arms / They have guns and powder and possession of the port and the town.

3. *Ireland Under the Stuarts and during the Interregnum* by Richard Bagwell, 1909–1916, Vol. III, p. 59.

4. Sir Charles Petrie devotes an entire chapter of his book, *The Great Tyrconnell*, Cork 1972, to this remarkable incident, pp. 57–78.

5. S. de Beer, ed. *Evelyn's Diary*, Oxford 1955.

6. Text from the official brochure of the Tercentenary Celebrations of the Apprentice Boys of Derry, Londonderry 1988.

7. Quoted in Petrie, p. 157.

8. See John A. Murphy [1999 edition for the Royal Eoghanacht Society], p. 16.

A WINTER OF DISCONTENT

1. *Memoirs of The Marshal Duke of Berwick*. Two volumes, London 1779, Vol. I, p. 129.

2. *The Battle of the Boyne* by Demetrius Charles Boulger, London 1911, p. 25.

3. See *Michel le Tellier et Louvois* by Louis Andre, Paris 1924, also Andre's earlier work *Michel le Tellier et l'organisation de l'armée monarchique*, Paris 1906.

4. This is a slightly edited version of the text. See *Siege City: The story of Derry and Londonderry* by Brian Lacy, Belfast 1990, p. 119.

5. 'The Enniskillen Men' by George Chittick. Revised edition published by the Grand Orange Lodge of Ireland 1994, pp. 11–12.

6. Boulger, p. 42.

7. Mme de Sevigne, Marie de Rabutin-Chantal, 1626–1696, wrote numerous letters, models of the epistolary genre, about day to day life at the court. Her generally low opinion of the Irish was in accord with prevailing views. She was circumspect about King James but her letters show that he was held in low esteem.

8. Vauban's views are found in Boulger, pp. 46–47. See also: *Vauban 1633–1707* by P. Lazard, London 1934.

9. Petrie, p. 160.

10. The passenger listings of eleven ships in James' fleet are extant and are outlined in Boulger, pp. 57–58.

11. The Irish Society otherwise known as 'The Honourable Irish Society' was a joint-stock company established by London Guilds in 1610 to administer the Derry plantation.

12. *Orangeism in Ireland and Throughout the Empire* by R. M. Sibbett, Vol. I, London 1914, pp. 36–37.

13. A brief history of Bandon outlining the loyalty of its Protestant population is found in 'The British-Irish Community in West Cork' by David Brewster, summer 1999 edition of *New Ulster*, the magazine of the Ulster Society.

14. Lord Galmoy was Pierce Butler, third Earl of Galmoy. Of Norman descent the Butlers were represented in the Irish peerage under such titles as Ormonde, Dunboyne, Cahir, Mountgarrett, Ikerrin and Galmoy. Galmoy was a friend of Sarsfield's and left Ireland with him in 1691. He became first lord of the bedchamber to James at St Germains and later distinguished himself in campaigns in Italy, Germany, Spain and Portugal. He died in Paris in 1740.

15. This is an edited version of a quote given in full in *The Making of Modern Ireland 1603–1923* by J. C. Beckett, London 1966, p. 142.

1. *History of Bandon* by George Bennett, London 1876, p. 59.
2. *A Light for the Blind* is the informal name for a manuscript by an unknown Jacobite, edited in 1892 by Sir John Gilbert under the title *A Jacobite Narrative of the War in Ireland 1688–91*. The work, in two volumes, was acquired by Thomas Carte, 1686–1754, the biographer of James, first Duke of Ormonde. Volume I is in the Bodleian Library, Oxford; Volume II, together with a transcript of Volume I, was for years the property of the Plunkett family, The Earls of Fingal, until acquired in 1934 by the National Library of Ireland (MSS 476–7). An explanation of the phrase 'A Light for the Blind' is given in the opening pages: 'The writer regrets that the English people became blind to the merits of James II and hopes that the light of reason will restore their sight'.
3. D'Avaux's letter is quoted by Rev. W. Moran in his *Life of Patrick Sarsfield, Earl of Lucan*, Catholic Truth Society pamphlet 365, undated.
4. The Sir Lawrence Parsons affair and background to events at Birr are found in a contemporary chronicle held in Lord Rosse's collection of manuscripts at Birr Castle, Catalogue ref: A/24.
5. Information on the Burkes is found in various entries in the *Compendium of Irish Biography* by Alfred Webb, Dublin 1878 – see in particular article on William FitzAllen de Burge, pp. 126–7; *A Concise Dictionary of Irish Biography* by John S. Crone, Dublin 1937; *Letters and Memoirs of Ulick Burke, Marquis of Clanricard*, London 1757. Information on Lady Honora, First Lady Lucan and later first Duchess of Berwick, is found in *Berwick*, Vol. 2. See also *The Marshal Duke of Berwick* by Sir Charles Petrie, London 1953, pp. 101–2. A portrait of Honora by Knellner is held in the collection of the Duke of Alba.
6. *War and Politics in Ireland 1649–1730* by J. G. Simms, London 1986, p. 139.
7. D'Avaux's correspondence, in edited form, is found in *Revolutionary Ireland and its Settlement* by R. H. Murray, London 1911.
8. *Ibid.*
9. *A True Account of the Siege of Derry* by Rev. George Walker, 1690; republished in London in 1887 as *Walker's Diary of the Siege of Derry 1688–89*, pp. 60–1.
10. *A Light for the Blind*, 2 above.
11. From 'The Maiden City', an undated poem by Charlotte Elizabeth Tonna, 1790–1846.
12. This account of the sea-battle is drawn, largely, from 'The French Navy at the time of the Williamite War' article by John de Courcey Ireland in *The Old Limerick Journal*, winter 1990 issue.
13. *The Oxford Companion to Law* by David M. Walker, Oxford 1980, pp. 924–5.
14. *The Jacobite Parliament of 1689* by J. G. Simms, pamphlet published by the Dublin Historical Society 1974, p. 5.
15. Quoted in Boulger pp. 95–6.
16. This tale is found in volume III of Macauley, p. 158. A complete listing of members of both houses of the Jacobite Parliament is found in Appendix A to *The Jacobite Parliament of 1689*, see 14 above. No member bearing the surname Daly can be traced.
17. 'Poynings Law', named after Sir Edward Poynings, lord deputy, 1494–5, was enacted by a parliament held in Drogheda in 1494. It required the lord deputy to seek the king's permission to summon an Irish parliament and his approval of proposed legislation. The 'Law' remained on the Irish statute book until the Act of Union (1800).
18. *A History of Ireland* by Edmund Curtis, London 1936, p. 36.
19. Sibbett, p. 21, Vol. I.
20. Remarks by Andrew Hamilton, who participated in the defence of Derry, quoted in *The Siege of Derry* by Patrick MacRory, Oxford 1988, p. 314.
21. Details of the Sligo-Ballyshannon campaign and the war in the north-east generally

are found in: *The Siege of Derry and the Defence of Enniskillen* by John Graham, Dublin 1829; *Derry and Enniskillen in the Year 1689* by Thomas Witherow, Belfast 1876; *History of Sligo: Town and County* by T. O'Rourke, Dublin 1889; *Ballyshannon: Its History and Antiquities* by H. Allingham, Dublin 1879; *The Western Protestant Army* by Oliver C. Gibson, Londonderry 1994; *The Enniskillen Men* by George Chittick, a booklet published by the Grand Orange Lodge of Ireland, Belfast 1994.

22. Wauchope, p. 62.

'DEAR NOTORIOUS'

1. A contemporary account of the Enniskilleners campaign on the Erne basin is found in *A True Relation of the Actions of the Enniskillen Men* by Andrew Hamilton, London 1690.

2. *Berwick*, Vol. I, p. 63.

3. The version of Berwick's letter given here is quoted from 'Co. Donegal in the Jacobite War 1689–91' by J. G. Simms in *The Donegal Annual*, Vol. 7, 1967, pp. 212–214.

4. This account of the Battle of Newtownbutler is based on the version outlined in *Battlefields of Ireland* by Robert Coddington, New York 1867, pp. 90–6.

5. Colonel Charles O'Kelly is one of the most interesting figures of the war. He was born at Screen, Co. Galway, in 1621, the son of a local Catholic lord of the manor and educated at St Omer in the Spanish Netherlands. He returned to Ireland in 1642 to join the royalists against parliament and commanded a troop of horse under the Duke of Ormonde. His family estate was forfeited on Cromwell's victory and he went into exile to serve Charles II. At the restoration the estate was retrieved and O'Kelly became the ninth Lord of Screen Manor. Under James he was a burgess of Athlone and sat in the Jacobite parliament for Roscommon. In 1689, despite being aged sixty-eight he raised a regiment of infantry and was directed by Sarsfield to hold Boyle and, if possible, move on Sligo. At the end of the war he retired to a family residence at Aughrane, or Castle Kelly, as it was known and wrote *Macarie Excidum*. The work is disguised, possibly for reasons of censorship, and purports to be a history of the conquest of Cyprus in classical times derived from a Syrian manuscript. Its full title is given as *Macarie Excidum or the Destruction of Cyprus, containing the last War and the Destruction of that Kingdom, written in Syriac by Philotas Phydocypres Rogullas, PR, and now made into English by Colonel Charles O'Kelly. Anno Domini 1692*. The book is important as it is the only known account of the war written by a member of the Gaelic Catholic aristocracy in contrast to *A Light for the Blind* whose author was a Catholic of Old English background. The book provides information on internal Jacobite dissent but is short on military detail. It confirms also some of the material given in Williamite accounts. In the narrative Cyprus is substituted for Ireland, Cililia for England, Syria for France, Theodore for William, Amasis for James, Lysander for Sarsfield, etc.

6. See 'Sligo in the Jacobite War' by J. G. Simms in *The Irish Sword*, Vol. VII, 1965, pp. 124–135.

7. Quoted in *War and Politics in Ireland 1649–1730* by J. G. Simms London 1986, p. 173.

8. *A True and Impartial History* by Rev. George Story, London 1691, pp. 33–4. Story's book is the most important account of the war from a Williamite viewpoint. The author was a Scot who arrived in Ireland with Schomberg in April 1689 as chaplain to Sir Thomas Gower's regiment of foot. In the preface to the book Story defies the opponents of William to contradict him on any matter of fact and assures them that he has concealed nothing that could be in any way to their advantage. He was a liberal who argued that James would have been one of the greatest princes of Europe notwithstanding his religion if he had not sought to impose his Catholicism on people who rejected it. Present at the first Siege of Limerick, he married Catherine Warter, daughter of Edward Warter of Bilboa, near Doon, Co. Limerick, the home parish of 'Galloping' Hogan. In a petition to William, dated 28 June 1701, Mrs

Story reported that Sarsfield burnt the village of Cullen, near Ballyneety. This accusation against Sarsfield does not appear elsewhere and local tradition is against it. After the war, Story's regiment went to Ulster where it became part of the standing army. In December 1694 he was appointed dean of Connor, and in 1705 he removed to Limerick again where he was installed as dean on 17 April that year. He died in 1721.

9. *Ibid.*

10. See d'Avaux's correspondence in *Revolutionary Ireland and its Settlement* edited by R. H. Murray, London 1911.

11. *Ibid..*

12. Murphy [John A.], pp. 24–5.

13. The incoming French force was under the command of General Lauzun, see chapter 11.

THE DUTCHMAN COMETH

1. Boulger, p. 124.

2. See 'Schomberg at Dundalk, 1689' by J. G. Simms in *The Irish Sword*, X, 1971, pp. 14–25.

3. *The Journal of Captain John Stevens* edited by Rev. R. H. Murray, Oxford 1912, p. 96.

4. Story, pp. 58–9.

5. See 'The Williamite Campaign in Ulster' prepared by Members of the Duke of York, Loyal Orange Lodge, Ballymacarret, Belfast, in *New Ulster*, summer issue 1990, pp. 7–16.

6. See *The Diary of Colonel Thomas Bellingham*, published and edited by Anthony Hewitson, Preston 1908. Colonel Bellingham was appointed *aide-de-camp* to William following the latter's arrival in Ireland on 14 June 1690. He was the son of a cavalry officer who settled in Ireland during the Cromwellian war and was granted an estate, named after him, in Co. Louth. The family represented Co. Louth in the Irish parliament from 1660 to 1755. In a diary entry for 11 July 1691, Bellingham wrote: 'This night about 12 o'clock Sarsfield with a party of horses destroyed our great guns at Cullen and spoiled our boats. Women and children killed by the enemy'.

7. This information is based on a lively oral tradition and was related to me by an Orange folklorist, but any oral tradition – particularly if over 200 years old – must be treated with caution. In my view this information could well be true. It is known from sundry sources that William spoke with a heavy Dutch accent. To this day, Dutch intonations are not dissimilar to those used in certain varieties of English spoken in Ireland.

8. Quoted in Sibbett, Vol. I, p. 110.

9. For details of the Duc de Lauzun's career prior to the 1688–91 war see *Historical Memoirs of Duc de St Simon*, Vol. III. Edited and translated by Lucy Norton, London 1972.

THE BOYNE WATER

1. There is no definitive account of the Battle of the Boyne. The twenty-five eyewitness accounts which are extant, seven Jacobite, eighteen Williamite, contradict one another on important points. These accounts range from letters written on the spot to diaries, journals, narrations and memoirs. A comparative analysis of the material leaves numerous questions unanswered. An analysis of these accounts is found in 'Eyewitnesses to the Boyne' by J. G. Simms in *The Irish Sword*, Vol. VI, 1963. Danish accounts are found in the National Library of Ireland microfilm regs 1026, 3216, 3253. French accounts are held in the Bibliotheque Nationale, Paris, under Ministere de la Guerre Archives Anciennes, Vols. 906–992.

2. See *James the Second* by Hilaire Belloc, London 1928, p. 256.

3. *Memoirs of James II*, edited by J. S. Clarke, London 1816.

4. Belloc, p. 254, also, p. 300.

5. See Todhunter, p. 56.
6. Richard Hamilton was the fifth son of Sir George Hamilton of Donalong, a son of Lord Abercorn. Hamilton was a Catholic and related to Governor Gustave Hamilton of Enniskillen, a Protestant.
7. *The Jacobite Movement* [Petrie], pp. 112–113.
8. For a brief account of the emblems worn see: 'The Williamite Campaign in Ulster and The Battle of the Boyne' article in *New Ulster*, Journal of the Ulster Society, summer 1990 edition, p. 14.
9. The exact nature of the Williamite right wing flank movement has presented historians with the greatest difficulties. The eyewitness accounts are at variance. Some mention General Douglas as the leader rather than Count Schomberg and others refer to a Williamite crossing at Slane. I take Simms' view that it is unlikely that there was a crossing at Slane and that Douglas was the leader of the flanking movement. See 'Eyewitnesses to the Boyne' [Simms]. Critics have suggested that Count Schomberg's move should have begun on the evening before and that the delay was a measure of William's incompetence as a commander, see Petrie's *Jacobite Movement*.
10. Kilpatrick, p. 60.
11. Sheldon was an English Catholic who came to Ireland in the service of Tyrconnell when the latter was appointed viceroy.
12. General Hogutte's views are found in Simms, see 1 above. See also *The Boyne Water* by Peter Beresford-Ellis, Belfast 1976, pp. 80–81.
13. This view is contained in a letter from the Duke of Würtemburg to King Christian V, dated 1 and 5 July 1690. See: Simms and Danagher *The Danish Force in Ireland 1690–1691*, Dublin 1962, pp. 42–43.
14. For adverse comment on the Irish infantry see Macauley, Vol. III, p. 484.
15. *The Monuments of St Patrick's Cathedral, Dublin* by Victor Jackson, Dublin 1987, p. 38.
16. *The Williamite War in Ireland 1688–1691* by Richard Doherty, Dublin 1998, p. 120.
17. *History of Ireland* by E. A. D'Alton, London, undated, Vol. IV, p. 422.
18. Beresford-Ellis, p. 111.
19. *Journal of Captain John Stevens* edited by R. H. Murray, Oxford 1912, p. 121.
20. *The Boyne and Aughrim: The War of Two Kings* by John Kinross, Moreton-in-Marsh, Gloucestershire 1997, p. 49.
21. Boulger, p. 148.
22. Todhunter, p. 71.
23. Burnet, Vol. IV, p. 140.

FALLBACK ON THE SHANNON

1. *Berwick*, Vol. I, pp. 66–68.
2. Lady Tyrconnell was the former Miss Frances Jennings. Her sister, Sarah, was married to John Churchill, Duke of Marlborough.
3. Todhunter, p. 73.
4. Quoted in *Ireland's Fate: The Boyne and After* by R. Shepherd, London 1990, p. 123.
5. This information was given to Sir Charles Petrie by eighth Earl of Wicklow and is quoted from his book *Berwick*, pp. 72–73.
6. Steven's journal in manuscript form is entitled *A Journal of my Travels since the Revolution, containing a Brief Account of the War in Ireland impartially related and what I was an Eyewitness to and deliver upon my Own Knowledge distinguished from what I received from Others*. It is preserved in the British Library, London, Add Ms 36292. The passage quoted here is from p. 85 *et seq*. Stevens was a scholar who disliked soldiering. He provides one of the two extant accounts of the 'the battle of the breach' during the first Siege of Limerick, 1690 but curiously does not mention Sarsfield's destruction of the siege train in August.
7. See Story, p. 142. Also *Temple Bar* magazine, Vol. 92, No. 366, May 1899, Article: 'Pat-

rick Sarsfield: A Jacobite Rapparee' by Frederick Dixon.

8. *The Wandering Irish in Europe* by Matthew J. Culligan and Peter Cherici, London 2000, p. 150.

9. *Limerick: Its History and Antiquities* by Maurice Lenihan, Dublin 1866, p. 216.

10. Burnet, Vol. IV, p. 99.

11. Lenihan, p. 261 in his romantic account says that Sarsfield's party stopped at Bally-corney Bridge where a Protestant family named Cecil resided and abducted a young man of the family.

12. At Labadhy Bridge, near Boher, Lenihan says: 'Sarsfield discovered … a number of men at his left, whose presence excited him. He ordered the horse to halt, apprehensive that he was being betrayed by Hogan. But the delusion was dispelled in an instant; the men whose presence caused such alarm were a body of rapparees who had a den or hiding place here …' p. 232.

13. For information on 'Ned of the Hill' I am indebted to Martin O'Dwyer, Curator of Cashel Folk Village, Cashel, Co. Tipperary, whose work *A Biographical Dictionary of Co. Tipperary*, Cashel 1999 contains the best account of the outlaw's career.

14. There is a tradition that Sarsfield's party rode through Law's Fields at the back of the town of Killaloe. The more popular account mentions the laneway near the cathedral, where today a roadsign bears the legend: 'Sarsfield's Ride'.

15. Lenihan, p. 232 does not mention the apple women but says that one of Sarsfield's troopers, whose horse was lamed, met the wife of a Williamite soldier who provided the password. This account is uncorroborated; I find the apple woman story more feasible. Hogan, who is believed to have come from the nearby parish of Doon would likely have known such a woman. This tradition is still held in the villages of Oola and Pallasgreen which are close to Ballyneety.

16. Sarsfield was criticised in Williamite accounts for the 'excessive barbarity' of the attack. Captain Robert Parker, a Williamite officer, however, exonerates Sarsfield. In his *Memoirs* he says: 'This was certainly a well-conducted affair and much to Sarsfield's honour had there not been so much cruelty in the execution of it; for they put man, woman and child to the sword, though there was the least opposition made. However, we cannot suppose that so gallant a man as Sarsfield certainly was, could be guilty of giving such orders; it is rather to be presumed that at such a juncture it was not in his power to retrain the natural barbarity of his men'. See: *Old Limerick Journal*, winter 1990 edition, p. 205.

17. The *London Gazette* was the newspaper of the British court and was first issued in 1665 as the *Oxford Gazette* when the outbreak of the plague forced Charles II to move the court from London to Oxford. It consisted of a single sheet, of about A4 size, printed on both sites in double columns. The news of Ballyneety is given on Issue No. 2582, which covers the period 11–14 August 1690. The paper's policy was to present William's Irish campaign in a favourable light and to minimise the effect of reverses on public opinion.

18. A slightly different and fuller version of this poem is found in *The Quest for Galloping Hogan* by Matthew Culligan Hogan, New York 1979, pp. 65, 66, 67.

The Siege of Limerick

1. *History of England, 1660–1714* by James MacPherson, London 1775, Vol. I, p. 664.

2. *Macariae Excidium*, pp. 67–8.

3. D'Alton, Vol. IV, pp. 433–4.

4. *Berwick*, pp. 361–2.

5. *Macariae Excidium*, pp. 396–397.

6. *Ibid.*, pp. 407–8, 410–2.

7. Birr Castle is today most interesting. In its demesne is found a spectacular array of rare and exotic plants as well as a giant telescope dating from 1845, once one of the largest in the world. A new telescope and observatory has recently been in-

stalled and the demesne is to be the home of Ireland's proposed science museum.
8. Coddington, p. 200.
9. *Marlborough: Portrait of a Conqueror* by D. B. Chidsey, London, undated, pp. 140–1.
10. Quoted in *The Great Marlborough and his Duchess* by Virginia Cowles, London 1983, p. 15.
11. Quoted in *Marlborough: His Life and Times* by Sir W. S. Churchill, London 1933, Vol. I, pp. 326–7.
12. For an authoritative account of the 'Siege of Cork' see 'Cork, Marlborough's Siege, 1690' by J. G. Simms in *The Irish Sword*, 1969, Vol. IX, pp. 113–123.
13. Coddington, p. 204.
14. General Catinat's praise for Sir Edward Scott is found in Boulger, p. 331.

THE DEVIL PLAYS THE HARP
1. Coddington, p. 206.
2. J. T. Gilbert in his *History of Dublin*, Dublin 1859 says that the Boyne society was formed in Dublin 'in the first half of the last century', Vol. III, p. 45. Sibbett attributes its founding to the 'Island Town', i.e. Enniskillen, Vol. I, p. 185. This accords with Williamite/Orange tradition. As the Boyne Society evolved into a secret brotherhood information on it is scanty. For the general background see the my *Orangeism: The Making of a Tradition*, Dublin 1999, pp. 100–7.
3. These prices are drawn from Coddington, p. 211.
4. *Macariae Excidium*, pp. 70–1.
5. Portions of the abbé's letter are quoted in Todhunter, pp. 123–4.
6. For Sarsfield's involvement with the rapparees see O'Dea, Vol. I, p. 339.
7. *Macariae Excidium*, p. 77.
8. Boulger, p. 225. Also for biographical details of St Ruth see Webb, p. 462.
9. *Ireland's Fate: the Boyne and After* by Robert Shepherd, London 1990, p. 152.
10. As quoted in Todhunter, p. 134.
11. For an account of the breaking of the bridge see *The Story of Ireland* by A. M. Sullivan, Dublin 1898, pp. 444–453.
12. I have been able to uncover information on this poet who was of the romantic nationalist school of the mid nineteenth century. The well-known poem 'The Boys who Broke the Van', about the Manchester Martyrs, is also attributed to Brian na Banba.
13. Curtayne, p. 132.
14. This saying is taken from the essay 'The Devil and the Irish' by Arthur Gerald Geoghegan, 1809–1889. See also the poem 'After Aughrim' by the same author who was a frequent contributor to *The Dublin Penny Journal*, *Dublin University Magazine* and *The Irish Monthly* in the mid-nineteenth century.

AUGHRIM'S GREAT DISASTER
1. *Macariae Excidium*, p. 87.
2. These quotations from the Proclamations are taken from Coddington, p. 226.
3. *Irish Battles: A Military History of Ireland* by G. A. Hayes-McCoy, Belfast 1990, p. 250, see also, pp. 268–269.
4. For Parker's account of the battle see *Memoirs of Military Transactions … from 1683–1718* by Robert Parker, London 1747.
5. Coddington, pp. 287–288.
6. This is an edited version of the speech which is found in Story. Its authenticity has been doubted. Some historians have thought it blatant Williamite propaganda. Others have found it unduly pompous and lacking in credibility. The main doubt to its authenticity is that St Ruth, as far as we know, did not speak English. Against this, it should be noted that Story in his preface challenged opponents of William to contradict him on any matter of fact.
7. Macauley, Vol. IV, p. 69.

8. These remarks of St Ruth are found in Coddington, p. 317.

9. Shepherd, p. 158.

10. G. A. Hayes-McCoy, p. 167.

11. Curtayne, p. 148.

12. A full version of this poem is found in A. M. Sullivan, pp. 463–464.

13. Todhunter, p. 173.

14. Quoted in *Jacobite Ireland* by J. G. Simms, Dublin 1969, p. 239.

ENDGAME AT LIMERICK

1. Boulger, p. 248.

2. *Macariae Excidium*, p. 97.

3. *Little Jennings and Fighting Dick Talbot* by P. W. Sergeant, Vol. II, London 1913, p. 252.

4. See *A Jacobite Narrative of the War in Ireland 1688–91* edited by J. T. Gilbert.

5. Wauchope, p. 250.

6. *The Sieges and Treaty of Limerick* by Frank Noonan, Dublin 1991, p. 20.

7. Quoted in *Jacobite Ireland* by J. G. Simms, p. 252.

8. A detailed analysis of the treaty negotiations and the disputes which arose in regard to the signed instrument is found in 'The Treaty of Limerick' by J. G. Simms, Dublin Historical Association pamphlet, Dundalk 1966.

9. Wauchope, p. 275.

10. For the various traditions about 'Galloping' Hogan see Culligan-Hogan.

11. Sullivan, p. 470.

12. Macauley, Vol. IV, p. 86.

THE LAST OF THE BRAVE

1. Boulger, p. 289.

2. Shepherd, p. 188.

3. Boulger, p. 284.

4. *Ibid.*, p. 284.

5. *Ibid.*, pp. 291–292.

6. *A History of the English Speaking Peoples* by Winston S. Churchill, London 1957, p. 13, Vol. III.

7. Todhunter, p. 199.

8. *Berwick*, Vol. I, pp. 113–114.

9. The last words of Sarsfield cannot be authenticated and are derived from the *Berwick* who was present at the Battle of Landen. The words are sometimes considered to be a concoction from the romantic period of Irish nationalism in the mid-nineteenth century, but this is incorrect.

10. *Memoirs of Gerald O'Connor* by William O'Connor Morris, London 1903.

11. Quoted in O'Callaghan, p. 175.

12. The phrase comes from the second line of Moore's poem 'Lament for Aughrim'.

13. Todhunter,p. 202.

14. *Ibid.*, p. 203.

15. A more complete account of the death of William is provided in my *Orangeism*, pp. 90–1.

16. *The Stewart Dynasty* by Stewart Ross, Nairn, Scotland 1993, p. 281.

17. This account of the Jacobite Rebellions is drawn from *The Parragon Micropedia of Scottish History*, general editor Dr J. Mackay, Bath 1999, p. 244–258. For a more detailed background see works of Scottish historian John Prebble: *Culloden*, 1961, *The Highland Clearances*, 1963 and *Glencoe*, 1966, all published in London.

18. See *The Cardinal King* by Brian Fothergill, London 1958, pp. 20–1.

19. *The Jacobites* by Frank McLynn, London 1985, pp. 205–6.

20. The present Stuart heir if he wished to press his claim is the Duke of Bavaria. Organisations such as the Royal Stuart Society still keep alive a token Jacobitism.

21. *The Irish Empire* by Patrick Bishop, London 1999, pp. 51–5.
22. *A History of Modern Ireland* by Giovanni Costigan, New York 1969, pp. 108–9.
23. In 1907 a Celtic cross was erected in Fontenoy to the memory of the Irish brigade by the subscriptions of Irish people resident in New York, London and Dublin. The inscription reads: 'To the soldiers of the Irish brigade who on the field of Fontenoy avenged the violation of the Treaty of Limerick'. It also mentions that the war cry of the Irish soldiers as they hurled themselves on the English was 'Remember Limerick'. There is also a tablet to the Irish brigade on the wall of a churchyard about a quarter of a mile from the memorial cross which reads:

> *In memory of the heroic soldiers who changed defeat into victory at Fontenoy, 11 May 1745. God Save Ireland.*
> *A la memoire des heroiques soldats Irlandais qui changérent une defaite en victoire a Fontenoy le 11 Mai 1745. Dieu sauve l'Irlande.*

BIBLIOGRAPHY

This bibliography includes details of author, title and year of publication. It does not follow the convention of supplying place and publisher, since neither is necessary for locating books in libraries and bookshops.

Acton, Lord, *Lectures on Modern History*, 1906
Adamson, Ian, *The Ulster People*, 1991
– *William and the Boyne*, 1995
Allingham, A., *Ballyshannon: Its History and Antiquities*, 1879
Anderson, M. S., *The War of the Austrian Succession*, 1995
Anderson, Perry, *Lineages of the Absolute State*, 1974
Andre, Louis, *Michel le Tellier et l'organisation de l'armée monarchique*, 1906
– Louis, *Michel le Tellier et Louvois*, 1924
Ashley, Maurice, *Louis XIV and the Greatness of France*, 1965
– *The Glorious Revolution of 1688*, 1966
Bagwell, Richard, *Ireland Under the Stuarts*, 1916
Barbour, V., *Henry Bennet, Earl of Arlington*, 1914
Bardon, Jonathan, *A History of Ulster*, 1992
Barnett, Correlli, *Marlborough*, 1994
Bartlett, T. and Jefferies, K., *A Military History of Ireland*, 1996
Baxter, Steven, *William III and the Defence of European Liberty*, 1966
Beckett, J. C., *The Making of Modern Ireland 1603–1923*, 1966
Beddard, R. A., *The Revolution of 1688*, 1991
Belloc, Hilaire, *James the Second*, 1928
Bennett, George, *History of Bandon*, 1876
Beresford-Ellis, Peter, *The Boyne Water*, 1976
Berwick, Marshal Duke of, *Memoirs of …*, 1779
Bevin, Brian, *James, Duke of Monmouth*, 1973
Bishop, Patrick, *The Irish Empire*, 1999
Black, Jeremy, *Culloden and the '45'*, 1990
– *European Warfare 1660–1815*, 1994
Boule, John, *The English Experience*, 1971
Boulger, D. C., *The Battle of the Boyne*, 1911
Bowen, D., *History and the Shaping of Irish Protestantism*, 1995
Bowen, Marjorie, *Brave Employments*, 1931
Bredin, Brig. A. E. C., *The History of the Irish Soldier*, 1987
Burke, Ulick, *Letters and Memoirs of Ulick Burke, Marquis of Clanricard*, 1757
Burnet, Gilbert, *History of My Own Time*, 1723
Caldicott, C. E. J., *et al*, *The Huguenots in Ireland*, 1997
Chacksfield, K. M., *The Glorious Revolution of 1688*, 1988
Chandler, D., *Marlborough as Military Commander*, 1989
Chartrand, R., *Louis XIV's Army*, 1988
Chidsey, D. B., *Marlborough: Portrait of a Conqueror*, undated
Churchill, Winston S., *A History of the English Speaking Peoples*, 1957
Clarke, J. S., *Memoirs of James II*, 1816
Clarke, Howard B., *Irish Cities*, 1995
Coddington, Robert, *Battlefields of Ireland*, 1867
Coke, Roger, *A Detection of the Court and State of England*, 1719
Corish, Patrick, *The Irish Catholic Experience*, 1985
Costigan, Giovanni, *A History of Modern Ireland*, 1969

Cowan, Ian B., *The Scottish Covenanters 1660–1688*, 1976
Coward, Barry, *The Stuart Age*, 1980
Cowles, Virginia, *The Great Marlborough and his Duchess*, 1983
Croker, T. C., *Narratives Illustrative of the Contests in Ireland 1641 and 1690*, 1841
Crone, John S., *A Concise Dictionary of Irish Biography*, 1937
Cronin, Vincent, *Louis XIV*, 1964
Culligan, Matthew J. & P. Cherici, *The Wandering Irish in Europe*, 2000
Culligan-Hogan, Matthew, *The Quest for Galloping Hogan*, 1979
Curtayne, Alice, *Patrick Sarsfield*, 1934
Curtis, Edmund, *A History of Ireland*, 1936
D'Alton, E. A., *History of Ireland*, undated
D'Alton, J., *King James Army Lists 1689*, 1860
Dalton, Charles, *English Army Lists and Commission Registers 1651–1643*, 1892
David, J., *Limerick and its Sieges*, 1894
Davis, T., *The Patriot Parliament of 1689*, 1893
de Beer, S., *Evelyn's Diary*, 1955
de Paor, L., *The Peoples of Ireland*, 1986
Doherty, J. E. & Hickey, D. J., *A Chronology of Irish History since 1500*, 1989
Doherty, Richard, *The Williamite War in Ireland*, 1998
Drake, P., *The Memoirs of Captain Peter Drake*, 1755
Duff, R. H., *The Culloden Papers*, 1815
Earle, P., *Monmouth's Rebels*, 1977
 – *The Life and Times of James II*, 1972
Ettinger, A. A., *James Edward Oglethorpe*, 1936
Fellows, N., *Charles II and James II*, 1995
Figgis, J. N., *The Divine Right of Kings*, 1914
Fitzgerald, Brian, *The Anglo-Irish*, 1952
Ford, Alan, *The Protestant Reformation in Ireland 1590–1641*, 1987
Foster, R. F., *Modern Ireland*, 1988
 –*The Oxford History of Ireland*, 1989
Fothergill, Brian, *The Cardinal King*, 1958
Frazer, Antonia, *Cromwell: Our Chief of Men*, 1973
Garrett, Jane, *The Triumph of Providence*, 1980
Geyl, Pieter, *The Revolt in the Netherlands*, 1932
Gibson, O. C., *The Western Protestant Army in Ireland 1688–1690*, 1989
Gilbert, Sir John, *A Jacobite Narrative of the War in Ireland 1688–91*, 1892
 – *History of Dublin*, 1859
Goubert, Pierre, *Louis XIV and 20 Million Frenchmen*, 1972
Graham, John, *The Siege of Derry and the Defence of Enniskillen*, 1829
Green, J. R., *A Short History of the English People*, 1894
Hackett, General Sir J., *The Profession of Arms*, 1983
Haddick-Flynn, Kevin, *Orangeism: The Making of a Tradition*, 1999
 – *A Short History of Orangeism*, 2002
Haley, K. H. D., *The First Earl of Shaftesbury*, 1968
Hamilton, Andrew, *A True Relation of the Actions of the Enniskillen Men*, 1690
Hamilton, Lord E., *The Irish Rebellion of 1641*, 1920
Harris, Tim, *Politics Under the Late Stuarts*, 1993
Hassall, A., *Mazarin*, 1896
Hatton, Reginald, *Europe in the Age of Louis XIV*, 1979
Hayes-McCoy, G. A., *Irish Battles: A Military History of Ireland*, 1990
Hewitson, Anthony, *The Diary of Colonel Thomas Bellingham*, 1908
Hibbert, Christopher, *The Pen and the Sword*, 1974
Hogg, James, *The Jacobite Relics of Scotland*, 1819
Holmes, Geoffrey, *Britain After the Glorious Revolution*, 1969

Holmes, Richard, *Oxford Companion to Military History*, 2001
Hopkins, P., *Glencoe and the End of the Highland War*, 1986
Horwitz, Henry, *The Parliamentary Diary of Narcissus Luttrell 1691–1693*, 1972
Irish, J. P., *The Scottish Jacobite Movement*, 1952
Israel, Jonathan, *The Anglo-Dutch Movement*, 1991
Jackson, Victor, *The Monuments of St Patrick's cathedral, Dublin*, 1987
James, F. G., *Ireland in the Empire 1688–1670*, 1973
Jarvis, R. C., *The Jacobite Risings of 1715 and 1745*, 1954
Jones, J. R., *The First Whigs*, 1961
– *The Revolution of 1688 in England*, 1972
Kane, Col R., *Campaigns of King William III*, 1735
Keegan, J., *A History of Warfare*, 1993
Keeton, G. W., *Lord Chancellor Jeffreys*, 1965
Kenyon, J. P., *Revolutionary Principals*, 1977
– *Stuart England*, 1978
Kilpatrick, Cecil, *William of Orange: A Dedicated Life*, 1998
King, William, *The State of the Protestants of Ireland Under the Late King James Government*,
    1691
Kinross, John, *The Boyne and Aughrim*, 1997
Kishlansky, Mark, *A Monarchy Transformed*, 1996
Krieger, L., *Kings and Philosophers 1689–1789*, 1970
Lacy, Brian, *Siege City: The Story of Derry and Londonderry*, 1990
Lang, Andrew, *Prince Charles Edward Stuart*, 1903
Latimer, T. W., *A History of Irish Presbyterianism*, 1893
Lazard, P., *Vauban 1633–1707*, 1934
Lecky, W. E. H., *A History of Ireland in the Eighteenth Century*, 1919
Lenihan, Maurice, *Limerick: Its History and Antiquities*, 1866
Lenman, Bruce, *The Jacobite Risings in Britain 1689–1746*, 1980
Linklater, Eric, *The Prince in the Heather*, 1965
Litton, Helen, *Cromwell*, 2000
Luttrell, Narcissus, *A Brief Historical Relation of the State of Affairs*, 1875
– *Popish Plot Catalogues*, 1956
Lynn, John A., *The Wars of Louis XIV*, 1999
Macauley, T. B., *History of England from the Accession of James II*, Folio Society Edition,
    London 1985
MacBride, Ian, *The Siege of Derry in Ulster Protestant Mythology*, 1997
MacCormick, *A Further Impartial Account of the Actions of the Enniskillen Men*, 1690
MacCurtain, Margaret, *Tudor and Stuart Ireland*, 1922
Mackay, J., *The Parragon Micropedia of Scottish History*, 1999
MacManus, Seamus, *The Story of the Irish Race*, 1921
MacPherson, James, *History of England 1660–1714*, 1775
MacRory, Patrick, *The Siege of Derry*, 1988
Maxwell, C., *A History of Trinity College, Dublin 1591–1892*, 1946
McLynn, Frank, *The Jacobites*, 1985
Merriman, John, *A History of Modern Europe*, 1996
Miller, Derek, *Still Under Siege*, 1989
Miller, J., *James II: A Study in Kingship*, 1978
– *The Life and Times of William and Mary*, 1974
Mitford, Nancy, *The Sun King*, 1966
Moody, T. W., *A New History of Ireland*, Vol. IV, 1986
Mullett, M., *James II and English Politics 1678–1688*, 1994
Murphy, John A., *Justin MacCarthy: Lord Mountcashel*, 1959
Murray, R. H., *Revolutionary Ireland and its Settlement*, 1911
– *The Journal of Captain John Stevens*, 1912

Norton, Lucy, *Historical Memories of Duc de St Simon*, 1972

O'Brien, Barry, *Studies in Irish History* Vol. II., 1903

O'Callaghan, John Cornelius, *History of the Irish Brigades in the Service of France*, 1870

O'Connor, Matthew, *Military History of the Irish Nation*, 1845

O'Connor Morris, William, *Memoirs of Gerald O'Connor*, London 1903

O'Dea, John, *History of Ancient Order of Hibernians*, 1923

O'Dwyer, Martin, *A Biographical Dictionary of Co. Tipperary*, 1999

O'Kelly, Col Charles, *Macariae Excidium*, 1692

O'Rourke, T., *History of Sligo: Town and County*, 1889

Ogg, David, *England in the Reign of James II and William III*, 1955

Parker, David, *The Making of French Absolutism*, 1983

Parker, Geoffrey, *The Army of Flanders and the Spanish Road*, 1972

Parker, R., *Memoirs of Military Transactions … from 1683–1718*, 1747

Petrie, Sir Charles, *The Great Tyrconnell*, 1972

–*The Jacobite Movement*, 1958

– *The Marshal Duke of Berwick*, 1953

Petty, William, *The Political Anatomy of Ireland*, 1691

Pinkham, L., *William III and the Respectable Revolution*, 1954

Prebble, John, *Culloden*, 1961

– *Glencoe*, 1966

– *The Highland Clearances*, 1963

– *The Lion in the North*, 1971

Richardson, Joanna, *Louis XIV*, 1973

Robb, Nessa A., *William of Orange – A Personal Portrait*, 1966

Ross, Stewart, *The Stewart Dynasty*, 1993

Rowse, A. L., *The Early Churchills*, 1956

Ruvigny, Marquis, *The Jacobite Peerage, Baronotage, Knightsage and Grants of Honour*, 1904

Scott, Lord George, *Lucy Walter: Wife or Mistress?*, 1947

Sergeant, P. W., *Little Jennings and Fighting Dick Talbot*, 1913

Seymour, William, *Battles in Britain 1066–1746*, 1997

– *Great Sieges in History*, 1991

Shepherd, Robert, *Ireland's Fate: The Boyne and After*, 1990

Shield, A., *Henry Stuart, Cardinal of York*, 1908

Sibbett, R. M., *Orangeism in Ireland and Throughout the Empire*, 1914

Simms, J. G. & Danagher K., *The Danish Force in Ireland 1690–1691*, 1962

Simms, J. G., *Jacobite Ireland*, 1969

– *War and Politics in Ireland 1649–1730*, 1986

Speck, W. A., *Reluctant Revolutionaries*, 1988

Steel, Tom, *Scotland's Story: A New Perspective*, 1984

Story, Rev. George, *A True and Impartial History*, 1691

Sullivan, A. M., *The Story of Ireland*, 1898

Tayler, A. & H., *A Jacobite Exile*, 1937

Tayler, Henrietta, *The Jacobite Court at Rome in 1719*, 1938

Temple, John, *History of the Irish Rebellion*, 1644

Terry, C. S., *John Graham of Claverhouse, Viscount Dundee*, 1905

Todhunter, John, *Life of Sarsfield*, 1895

Trevelyan, G. M., *The English Revolution 1688–89*, 1938

Trevelyan, G. M., *The History of England*, 1936

Trevor, Meriol, *The Shadow of a Crown*, 1988

Trevor-Roper, Hugh, *From Counter-Revolution to Glorious Revolution*, 1992

Van Der Zee, Henri & Barbara, *William and Mary*, 1973

– *Revolution in the Family*, 1988

Von Ranke, L., *History of England*, 1875

Walker, David, *Oxford Companion to Law*, 1980

Walker, Rev. George, *Walker's Diary of the Siege of Derry*, 1887
Wall, Maureen, *The Penal Laws*, 1961
Watson, J. Steven, *The Reign of George III*, 1960
Wauchope, Piers, *Patrick Sarsfield and the Williamite War*, 1992
Webb, Alfred, *Compendium of Irish Biography*, 1878
Wedgewood, C. V., *The King's Peace*, 1955
– *The King's War*, 1958
– *The Trial of Charles I*, 1964
–*William the Silent*, 1944
Western, J. R., *Monarchy and Revolution*, 1972
Wilde, Sir William, *The Beauties of the Boyne and the Blackwater*, 1849
Wilkinson, Richard, *Years of Turmoil: Britain 1603–1714*, 1999
Witherow, Thomas, *Derry and Enniskillen in the Year 1689*, 1876
Wolf, John B., *Louis XIV*, 1968
Woods, Maurice, *A History of the Tory Party in the seventeenth and eighteenth Centuries*, 1924
Wrightson, Keith, *English Society 1550–1760*, 1982
Wroughton, John, *The Stuart Age 1603–1714*, 1997

ARTICLES FROM *THE IRISH SWORD* – JOURNAL OF THE MILITARY HISTORY SOCIETY OF IRELAND

Barry, J. C. 'The Groans of Ireland' II, No. 6, p. 130
Cox, L. 'A Diary of the Siege of Athlone' IV, No. 15, p. 88
– 'Death of St Ruth at Aughrim' III, No. 15, p. 66
– 'The Williamite War in Westmeath' III, No. 37, pp. 308–17
Doherty, R. 'Robert Lundy' XVIII, No. 31, pp. 232–4
English, N. W. 'The Dog of Aughrim' VIII, No. 31, pp. 141–2
Ferguson, K. 'The Organisation of William's Army in Ireland 1689–1692' XV, No. 60, pp. 62–79
Garland, J. L. 'Galmoy's Horse' I, No. 3, p. 228
Le Ferve, P. 'The Battle of Bantry Bay, 1 May 1689' XVIII, No. 70, pp. 1–16
Mangan, H. 'Sarsfield's Defence of the Shannon 1690–91' I, No. 1, pp. 24–32
Melvin, P. 'Irish Troop Movements and James II's Army in 1688' X, No. 39, pp. 82–105
Murtagh, H. 'Galway and the Jacobite War' X, No. 46, pp. 1–14
Murtagh, D. 'Colonel Richard Grace' I, No. 3, pp. 173–80
O'Carroll, D. 'An Indifferent Good Post: The Battle of the Boyne' XVIII, No. 70, pp. 49–56
Simms, J. G. 'A Letter to Sarsfield' II, No. 6, p. 109
– 'The Invasion of Kerry' XIV, No. 55, p. 171
– 'The Garrison of Carrickfergus, 1689' VI, No. 23, p. 118
– 'Cork, Marlborough's Siege, 1690' IX, No. 35, pp. 113–23
– 'Dominick Sarsfield, Lord Kilmallock' II, No. 7, pp. 205–10
– 'Eyewitnesses to the Boyne' VI, No. 22, pp. 16–27
– 'St Ruth's Career' VI, No. 24, p. 213
– 'Schomberg at Dundalk' X, pp. 14–25, 1971
– 'Sligo in the Jacobite War' VII, No. 27, pp. 124–35
– 'The Surrender of Limerick' II, No. 5, pp. 23–32
– 'The Siege of Derry' VI, No. 25, pp. 221–233

BOOKLETS, MAGAZINES AND PAMPHLETS

Chittick, George, *The Enniskillen Men*, Belfast, 1994
Donegal Annual, Vol. 17, 1967
History Ireland, winter, 2000

History Today, July, 1988
Irish Historical Studies, March, 1938
Irish Historical Studies, March, 1951
Moran, Rev. W., *Life of Patrick Sarsfield, Earl of Lucan,* undated
New Ulster, summer, 1990
Noonan, F., *The Sieges and Treaty of Limerick,* Dublin, 1991
Old Limerick Journal, winter, 1990
Simms, J. G., *The Treaty of Limerick,* Dundalk, 1966

PAPERS AND OTHER SOURCES

Calendar of State Papers, 1680
Gazette de France, September, 1690
London Gazette, September, 1690
The London Mercury, August, 1682
The Orange Standard, February, 2000

INDEX

Foyle, 70, 86, 90, 214

France, 7, 11, 13, 21, 24, 25, 30, 31, 40, 49, 52,
55, 56, 60, 67-69, 73, 75, 91, 105, 106, 109,
115, 121, 123, 132, 135, 138, 140, 143, 145,
151, 152, 154, 160, 162, 163, 173, 177, 178,
187, 189, 193, 195-197, 199, 202, 203, 205-
210, 213-216, 218

Franklin, Sir William, 112

Frascati, 209

Fritton, Anthony, 189

Fumeron, 191

Galmoy, Lord *(Pierce Butler)*, 11, 78, 80, 95,
98, 101, 127, 153, 177

Galway, 12, 18, 85, 98, 138, 140, 144-146, 151,
161, 162, 174, 184, 185, 188-190

Galway, Lord, 105, 176

Garbally, 175, 178, 179

Gardon, John, 200

Garvagh, 69

Gazette de France, 143, 163

George II, 208

George III, 209

George of Denmark, Prince, 51

George V, 93

Ginkel, see *De Ginkel*

Glencoe, 59

Godfrey, Lord, 42, 51

Godfrey, Sir Edmundbury, 25, 42, 51

Gore, Colonel Francis, 99, 102

Gore, Sir William, 98

Goungarille, 199

Grace, Colonel Richard, 135, 136, 167

Grafton Duke of, 51, 156

Gravel, Abbé, 161

Gravesend, 67

Gray, Mary, 48

Green Ribbon Club, 32

Grey, Lord, 27, 28, 34, 39, 41-43

Greyhound, 90

Groomsport, 107, 214

Gunpowder Plot, 51

Gwyn, Frank, 31

Hague, The, 22, 38, 50, 64, 76

Hales, Godden V., 45

Hales, Sir Edward, 45, 46, 214

Halifex, Lord, 25, 54

Hamilton, Anthony, 100, 101, 154, 176

Hamilton, Gustave, 11, 65, 72, 73, 75, 76, 96,
98, 99, 101, 112

Hamilton, Richard, 11, 76-79, 86-90, 121,
125-128, 202, 214

Harley, Robert, Earl of Oxford, 111

Haverford west, 22

Hayes-McCoy, G. A., 177, 182

Henrietta, 67

Henry II, 15, 218

Henry III, 218

Henry IX, 209, 215

Henry VI, 218

Henry VIII, 201

Herbert, Admiral Arthur, 47, 49, 91, 92

Herbert, Lady, 30

High Barnett, 26

Hillsborough, 65, 76, 78, 79, 98

History of Great Britain, 1660–1714, 150

Hogan, 'Galloping' Michael, 129, 135, 140,
141, 143, 144, 162, 196, 197

Hogue, La, 202, 210, 215

Hoguette, General, 125

Holland, 11, 12, 33, 34, 38, 129

Hollyford, 141

Holycross, 136

Hopkins, Dr Ezekial, 70, 71

Houndslow Heath, 46

House of Commons, 18, 26, 32, 33, 45, 47-
50, 53, 54, 93, 94, 109

House of Lords, 33, 45, 54

Howard, Hugh, 131

Hoylake, 110

Huddleston, Fr, 35

Huguenots, 13, 46, 47, 49, 103, 114, 125, 140,
160, 164, 178-181

Hungary, 38, 39

Hutchinson, David, 18, 19

Huy, 205, 206

Hyde, Anne, 36, 50, 61

Inverness, 57

Irish Footprints on the Continent, 206

Irish Society, 76

Isle of Man, 110

Isle of Wright, 49

Iveagh, Lord, 196

James II, 8, 11, 25, 32, 33, 35, 36, 37, 45, 46,
47, 48, 50, 51, 52, 53, 55, 56, 57, 61, 62, 63,
64, 66, 67, 68, 69, 74, 75, 76, 82, 83, 84, 87,
88, 92, 93, 105, 107, 108, 109, 110, 114, 115,
116, 118, 121, 123, 124, 127, 128, 129, 130,
131, 132, 133, 139, 145, 146, 147, 154, 164,
193, 196, 199, 201, 202, 206

Jacobite Narrative, 188, 189, 206

Jacobite Peerage, 206

Jeffreys, Lord George, 43, 51, 53

Jenkins, Sir Llewllyn, 28

Jennings, Sarah, 154

Jones, Sir Theophilis, 18-20, 22, 23, 214

Joyce, Martin, 183

Keames, 64

Keating, John, 76

Kennedy, Alderman Horace, 70

Vendôme, Marshal, 210
Vere, Aubrey de, 159, 216
Versailles, 30, 67, 68, 75, 133, 151
Vienna, 38
Villiers, Barbara, 154
Villiers, Colonel Edward, 141
Villiers, Captain, 175

Wadding, Luke, 17, 18
Wade, Marshal, 208
Wade, Nathaniel, 39
Walcowen, 203
Walker, Rev. George, 64, 89, 90, 112, 113, 126
Wallace, 15
Walter, Lucy, 12, 22, 32, 214
Walter, Mary, 13, 22
Warton, Thomas, 63
Waterford, 78, 121, 123, 132, 139, 146, 150
Wauchope, Brigadier, 123, 134, 138, 192, 193, 200
Wentworth, Baroness, 39
Westminster, 37, 167, 207
Westonzoyland, 42

Wetenhall, Edward, 156
White, Rebecca, 29
Whitehall, 26, 34, 52, 53, 54, 56, 57, 66, 202
Wicklow, 16, 131
Wild Geese, 12, 106, 197, 210
Wilhelm, General (*Würtenburg*), 109, 112, 125, 155-157, 160, 167, 179, 190
William II, 11
William III, 7, 38, 48, 49, 50, 51, 52, 53, 54, 55, 57, 59, 60, 66, 68, 72, 76, 77, 107, 109, 110, 111, 112, 113, 114, 116, 118, 119, 120, 121, 123, 124, 125, 126, 127, 128, 130, 133, 135, 136, 137, 138, 141, 145, 146, 147, 149, 195, 198, 201, 202, 203, 204, 206, 207, 208
Williamson, Sir Joseph, 26
Wincanton, 51
Windsor, 29
Wolseley, Colonel William, 101, 109
Worchester, 35
Würtenburg, see *Wilhelm*

York, 154

MORE INTERESTING BOOKS

A SHORT HISTORY OF ORANGEISM
Kevin Haddick-Flynn

Tracing the development of the Orange tradition from its beginnings during the Williamite War (1688–91) to the present day this book comprehensively covers all the main events and personalities. It provides information on such little known organisations as the Royal Black Preceptory and the Royal Arch Purple Order, as well as the institutions like the Apprentice Boys of Derry.

Military campaigns and rebellions are set against a background of intrigue and infighting, and anti-Catholic rhetoric is matched with anti-Orange polemic. This compelling book narrates the history of a quasi-Masonic organisation and looks at its rituals and traditions.

THE GREAT IRISH FAMINE
Edited by Cathal Póirtéir

This is the most wide-ranging series of essays ever published on the Great Irish Famine and will prove of lasting interest to the general reader. Leading historians, economists, geographers – from Ireland, Britain and the United States – have assembled the most up-to-date research from a wide spectrum of disciplines, including medicine, folklore and literature, to give the fullest account yet of the background and consequences of the Famine.

THE COURSE OF IRISH HISTORY
Edited by T. W. Moody and F. X. Martin

A revised and enlarged version of this classic book provides a rapid short survey, with geographical introduction, of the whole course of Ireland's history. Based on a series of television programmes, it is designed to be both popular and authoritative, concise but comprehensive, highly selective but balanced and fair-minded, critical but constructive and sympathetic. A distinctive feature is its wealth of illustrations.